Boccaccio's Dante and the Shaping Force of Satire

Boccaccio's Dante and the Shaping Force of Satire

Robert Hollander

Ann Arbor

THE UNIVERSITY OF MICHIGAN PRESS

2000   1999   1998   1997   4   3   2   1

*A CIP catalog record for this book is
available from the British Library*

Library of Congress Cataloging-in-Publication Data

Hollander, Robert, 1933–
    Boccaccio's Dante and the shaping force of satire / Robert
Hollander.
        p.   cm.
    Includes index.
    ISBN 0-472-10767-4 (alk. paper)
    1. Boccaccio, Giovanni, 1313–1375.   Decamerone.   2. Dante
Alighieri, 1265–1321.   Divina commedia.   3. Dante Alighieri,
1265–1321—Influence.   I. Title.
PQ4287.H65   1997
853'.1—dc21   96-51312
                                                             CIP

for Ron Berman, who twenty years ago suggested
that I write this book,
and Michael Bernstein, who later seconded the motion

Acknowledgments

These studies were originally published in the following periodicals and book, the editors of which have graciously granted permission for their republication here.

"Boccaccio's Dante." *Italica* 63 (1986): 278–89.
"Boccaccio's Dante: Imitative Distance (*Decameron* I, 1, and VI, 10)." *Studi sul Boccaccio* 13 (1981–82): 169–98.
"*Decameron:* The Sun Rises in Dante." *Studi sul Boccaccio* 14 (1983–84): 241–55.
"*Utilità* in the *Decameron.*" *Studi sul Boccaccio* 15 (1985–86): 215–33.
"The Proem of the *Decameron:* Boccaccio between Ovid and Dante." In *Miscellanea di Studi Danteschi in memoria di Silvio Pasquazi,* ed. A. Paolella, V. Placella, and G. Turco, 423–40. Naples: Federico & Ardia, 1993.
"Day Ten of the *Decameron:* The Myth of Order," *Studi sul Boccaccio* 23 (1995): 113–70.
(The last of these was written in collaboration with Courtney Cahill.)

Translations within are my own except where otherwise indicated.

Contents

Introduction

The essays gathered in this book were produced during the past fifteen
years. Most of them are rooted in questions that arose in the early 1980s,
first in a course on the *Decameron* that I taught with Pietro Frassica in the
spring semester of 1981 at Princeton. How significant is the textual presence of Dante's *Commedia* at certain moments in Boccaccio's *Decameron*?
And how deep does this Dantean current run through Boccaccio's greatest
work? It is fair to say that before the studies that Attilio Bettinzoli and I
published independently in the volumes of *Studi sul Boccaccio* for 1981–82
and 1983–84, there was little recognition of the surprisingly large debt of
Boccaccio to Dante hidden in the pages of the *Decameron*. That debt is
now beginning to receive the attention it deserves. It had simply been a
mainly unexamined commonplace among many of his commentators that
the "young" Boccaccio either did not know well or did not understand
sufficiently the texts of Dante. In an important study published seventeen
years ago, Carlo Delcorno demonstrated, once and for all, that Boccaccio's
Elegia di madonna Fiammetta (ca. 1344) is filled with obvious borrowings
from Dante, particularly from the *Commedia*.[1] If this is the case (and no
one has come forward with arguments that would cast Delcorno's findings
into doubt), those of us who believe that we frequently look on citations of

---

Some of these opening remarks are adapted from my forthcoming contribution to James
McGregor's volume *Approaches to Teaching Boccaccio's "Decameron"* concerning Boccaccio
in the series overseen by the Modern Language Association.

1. See "Note sui dantismi nell'*Elegia di madonna Fiammetta*," *Studi sul Boccaccio* 11
(1979): 251–94. And now see Delcorno's edition of the *Elegia* (Milan: Mondadori, 1994), 3, for
the probable date of the work: as late as 1348, but almost surely 1344. For ample demonstration of the Dantean background and sources of Boccaccio's first major attempt at vernacular fiction in verse see *Diana's Hunt/Caccia di Diana,* ed. and trans. A. K. Cassell and V.
Kirkham (Philadelphia: University of Pennsylvania Press, 1991), 12–13, and the notes to the
text, passim.

Dante as we read through the *Decameron* are in possession of a major fact, the certainty that Boccaccio was closely familiar with Dante's texts by 1350. That may now be taken as a given, as even cursory knowledge of such works as the *Caccia di Diana, Amorosa visione,* or *Comedia delle ninfe fiorentine* should have made plain, even without Delcorno's convincing labor.

The overall similarities between the *Decameron* and its major vernacular precursor are too obvious to have gone undetected. They have come to be understood as commonplaces, requiring little in the way of supporting evidence or ingenious demonstration. The hundred cantos of Dante's "divine" *Commedia* are echoed in the hundred *novelle* of Boccaccio's engagingly human comedy. Both texts seem to celebrate their "Italianness," that is, their use of the vernacular in work that is obviously meant to be considered significant; yet most think of Dante's language, as did Boccaccio and most of Dante's readers, as being noble, lofty, even austere, while Boccaccio's seems typically to be streetwise, low-mimetic, and playful.[2] Thus each of these similarities is intrinsically conjoined with a distancing difference. In such a view Boccaccio is conceived to have had Dante very much in mind, but only as a general idea or as a rather distant model. His purpose is held to be so far from Dante's that no one seems prepared to argue the proposition that he not only is Dante's greatest champion[3] but is deeply involved in thinking about Dante's *magnum opus* as he creates his own. In such a view Boccaccio may emulate Dante in general terms, but he is not thinking of the poetry of the *Commedia* as an extended challenge to his own extended effort in prose. In short, in this view the *Commedia* is for Boccaccio a monument, a potential model, but not a pressing literary presence.

While I in no way desire to insist that the two works are not greatly different in many respects, I hope that there will be no confusion about the strength of my disagreement with the view that Dante served only as a distant model for Boccaccio. The *Decameron* is thick with reminiscences of the *Commedia,* the text that Boccaccio believed the greatest "modern" work and the only one that had achieved a status similar to that reserved

---

2. In fact, Boccaccio, as has been noted fairly widely, was puzzled, for various reasons, that Dante called his work a "comedy," and he thought of Dante's style as being composed in the elevated style, not the low style of comedy. The point is made most recently by Carlo Delcorno, "Ironia/parodia," in *Lessico critico decameroniano,* ed. Renzo Bragantini and Pier Massimo Forni (Turin: Bollati Boringhieri, 1995), 173.

3. See *Filocolo* 5.97.6; *Amorosa Visione* 5.70–6.24.

for the greatest writers of antiquity. He can hardly make a move without thinking of how Dante had moved before him. The *Decameron,* we now realize, is dotted with not dozens but hundreds of citations of the *Commedia.*[4] The only surprising thing is that it has taken us so long to acknowledge so obvious a phenomenon.[5] The reason for this delay in perceiving what all must now admit to being only evident is fairly obvious. Since, in the traditional view of Boccaccio's relationship to Dante, Boccaccio was not writing a text that really had anything in common with Dante's *Commedia,* there was no reason to believe he was frequently thinking of that text. A countering view claims that Boccaccio was so totally involved in thinking of Dante's poem that, no matter how different his purposes might have been, he could not fail to cite Dante's text, which for him contained a sort of *lingua franca,* words that he heard again on the slightest pretext. For him to write in the Italian vernacular was, perforce, often to rewrite Dante. This view is currently becoming dominant. Nothing written by Boccaccio, from his earliest work of any length *(Caccia di Diana)* through the *Decameron,*[6] reflects the textual presence of any author so frequently as it does Dante.[7] This is no less and no more than a fact. What follows is speculation.

If the *Decameron* is so filled with *dantismi,* why has their presence been so imperceptible to so many students of the work? The answer is, one might argue, simple. The tone of the *Decameron* is "wrong." That is, when Boccaccio considers Dante as promoter of a vision of the afterworld or as

4. See Attilio Bettinzoli's two important studies of Dantean borrowings, "Per una definizione delle presenze dantesche nel *Decameron,*" parts 1, "I registri 'ideologici,' lirici, drammatici," and 2, "Ironizzazione e espressivismo antifrastico-deformatorio," *Studi sul Boccaccio* 13 (1981–82): 267–326; 14 (1983–84): 209–40.

5. It is important to be aware that such sources as Vittore Branca's notes to his various editions of the *Decameron* frequently give notice of Dantean sources or, at least, analogues. What recent work has added is twofold: a greater number of these and, more importantly, a more focused concentration on the phenomenon, which Branca never dealt with frontally. I do not wish to find fault with the man who is arguably the greatest student of Boccaccio we have ever had but only to point to the status of the argument until the 1980s. Before that time, "Boccaccio's Dante" was simply not a major subject in the study of Certaldo's most famous son.

6. And for the *dantismi* strewn thick in the pages of the later *Corbaccio* see Hollander, *Boccaccio's Last Fiction: Il "Corbaccio"* (Philadelphia: University of Pennsylvania Press, 1988), Appendix I: "Texts in the *Corbaccio* Reflecting Passages in Dante," 59–71.

7. My concentration on Boccaccio's debt to Dante should not obscure the fact that I am keenly aware that he is not a one-author reader. We are also beginning to pay more attention to his heavy debt to French writers, among others. The importance of the *fabliau* and the *lai,* for instance, is restated most recently and forcefully by Delcorno, "Ironia/parodia" (see n. 2), 175–77.

arbitrator of the moral behavior of humankind, Dante will always come out the loser. "That is beautiful, Dante," Boccaccio would seem to be saying, "but you cannot expect us to believe it, can you?" Thus, at the strategic level, Boccaccio's references to Dante are frequently generic (a bourgeois gentleman who thinks he is in Purgatory [III.viii], a lady in the pine forest outside Ravenna who behaves like a denizen of *Inferno* 13 [V.viii], a friar who claims he has visited other worlds [VI.x]) and gently, but firmly, derisory. Perhaps these two issues trouble Boccaccio most: Dante's granting himself visionary knowledge of the world to come and his unyielding belief that humankind can learn how to live in just political and religious communities. Boccaccio, man of the world, may admire Dante for his optimism yet knows in his all-too-human heart that these are impossible dreams. And so his fictive world is filled with much of Dante's, but these lovely bits and pieces tend to be deracinated from their contextual habitat. In the *Decameron* we hear nothing true of the world to come, only lies about it (often purveyed by friars); and we see little positive about the human family, which spends most, if not all, of its time seeking its own pleasures (sex, money, getting the best of another human being) or the avoidance of pain or blame. There is not much room for anything Dantean but words.

There will be occasion in the following essays for consideration of some of the numerous and arresting Boccaccian citations of Dante. Now we might begin at the beginning, the *Decameron*'s subtitle, *Prencipe Galeotto*, an obvious reference to the verse "Galeotto fu 'l libro e chi lo scrisse" [a Gallehault was the book and the one who wrote it] (*Inferno* 5.137), in which Francesca da Rimini blames a book for kindling passion in her and in her kinsman. No one will claim that this is not a reference to that text. Some will insist on rather implausible ideas about the reference, for instance, the notion that it has no negative sexual resonance or the idea that, if it does, it was only added by Boccaccio late in his life (thus necessitating credence in the notion that the old fellow had to make his way around northern Italy, sneaking into people's houses, to add the subtitle to the many circulated copies of the work).[8] While there are many instances of Boccaccio's appropriating a phrase from Dante without necessarily being aware that this is what he is doing, there are some remarkable moments in which we can see him playfully and meaningfully pillaging his poet for a passage that

---

8. For my earlier view that those who have argued for a morally positive valence in Boccaccio's subtitle have made claims that are unsupportable see the chapter "The Book as *Galeotto*" in *Boccaccio's Two Venuses* (New York: Columbia University Press, 1977), esp. 102–6.

enters his work with its full Dantean context.[9] Since the first three studies of this book are devoted to this subject, for now let me conclude by saying that our work on this aspect of Boccaccio's keen awareness of Dante's text has only begun. There are few aspects of the *Decameron* that are as intriguing and as understudied.

If we continue, as I wager we shall, to discover still more evidence of Boccaccio's debt to Dante among the *novelle* of the *Decameron,* what will it tell us of the shaping force of so great a precursor on the prose masterwork? Such a question calls for only a speculative response, since we are at the beginning of an investigation that will take years and, most likely, will never reach a term at which someone will proclaim it finished. If the *Commedia* plays a role that frequently furnishes both models and antimodels for the *Decameron,* we are nonetheless more likely to find a radical disjunction between the effects of the two works than even a large similarity. The form of the *Decameron,* which has only once been examined in ways that seem essentially convincing to this reader,[10] may or may not conform to a harmonious, Dantean model. The consideration of the Tenth Day that I wrote in collaboration with Courtney Cahill, with which this collection of essays concludes, sees Boccaccio as avoiding the temptation of a Dantean "comic" resolution, yielding, instead, to the exponents of a satirical vision of Roman men and women, Ovid and Horace. In a shorthand that may be guilty of oversimplifying, I argue that Boccaccio's fiction captures a Dantean literary world in a "Roman" reality and thus transforms that Dantean world, in which we are allowed to know the good guys from the bad and the universe that contains them in its harmonizing arc above us, into an uneven and disharmonious, quotidian "real world," in which nothing can be finally embraced with certitude, except a sort of human solidarity

---

9. For some recent considerations of specific textual confrontations see, among others, Franco Fido, "Dante personaggio mancato del *Decameron,*" in *Boccaccio: Secoli di vita,* ed. M. Cottino-Jones and E. F. Tuttle (Ravenna: Longo, 1977): 177–89, reprinted in *Il regime delle simmetrie imperfette* (Milan: Franco Angeli, 1988); Giuseppe Mazzotta, "Games of Laughter in the *Decameron,*" *Romanic Review* 69 (1978): 115–31, reprinted in *The World at Play in Boccaccio's "Decameron"* (Princeton: Princeton University Press, 1986); Robert Durling, "Boccaccio on Interpretation: Guido's Escape (*Decameron* VI.9)," in *Dante, Petrarch, Boccaccio: Studies in the Italian Trecento in Honor of Charles S. Singleton,* ed. A. S. Bernardo and A. L. Pellegrini (Binghamton, N.Y.: Medieval and Renaissance Texts and Studies, 1983), 273–304; Victoria Kirkham, "Painters at Play on the Judgment Day (*Decameron* VIII 9)," *Studi sul Boccaccio* 14 (1983–84): 256–77, reprinted in *The Sign of Reason in Boccaccio's Fiction* (Florence: Olschki, 1993).

10. See Janet L. Smarr, "Symmetry and Balance in the *Decameron,*" *Medievalia* 2 (1976): 159–87.

among those (few) of us who experience our frailty consciously. Boccaccio's Dante is not the writer to make such a vision possible, except by inversion; Boccaccio's Dante, in short, has got little that Boccaccio must have except a literary universe to react to. But it is no little help and no little stimulation to have under one's eyes, in all its magnificent articulation, precisely the way not taken.

The road Boccaccio actually did take, it now seems to me, was centrally involved with his large sense of the vision of Roman satire, most particularly the urbane and urban writings of Ovid and Horace. As I and some others have argued, the primary Ovidian texts for the *Decameron* are the early amatory works, not the *Metamorphoses,* the prime Ovidian source for almost all the earlier writings. These poems are formally elegies, but they are inspired by the spirit of satire that yields a picture of Augustan Rome, telling the Romans the truth about themselves: they are not fighters (or anything else) but lovers. The very titles cry Ovid's wares: *Amores, Ars amandi, Remedia amoris.* From the Colosseum to the lady's stone threshold, Romans pursue one another in the agon of "love." The three works form a triptych of Rome's decadence. Juvenal may be more stinging, but he is not necessarily more effective. The "amorous" Ovid was writing, at least in Boccaccio's estimation, brilliant satirical pieces to please and teach (even if he failed on both counts with the one who counted most, his emperor). Boccaccio, who most likely considered himself the Italian Ovid, thought of himself as such not only because he, too, voted early and often for sexuality, but because he, too, was holding the mirror up to an *urbs* (now Florence rather than Rome). What the Italians were to see in the *Decameron* was their nature in all its range, but for Boccaccio, as always for Ovid, mainly in its frequently petty self-seeking. The *Decameron* so pleases us that we tend to make it, in our own image (or in our image of our image), the portrait of the fullness of humanity that stands as our aesthetic progenitor, the first convincing description of what we now call "early modern Europe." Our laughter, however, comes mainly from our recognition of our failings, not our strengths. Boccaccio's Horatian task, then, following the *Ars poetica* (which, I have claimed, as the reader will see, furnished him with his first word as well), is to delight and instruct, but in a way that most resembles the tradition of urbane satire of which Horace is probably the major proponent.

These two subjects, Boccaccio's Dantean borrowings and his desire to shape his work as satire, will be found variously visited in the essays assembled in this book. With the exception of the first piece, which I have put first because of its summarizing bent, they follow the order in which they were written. This course seemed best since the reader may thereby sense the change in focus from Dante to the spirit of satire that first becomes evident in the essay on *utilità*. Thus the first three essays are primarily "Dantean," the last three mainly "Ovidian." These essays have been mostly left as they were when they were first printed. Parts of them would be different were they to have been written now. But they seemed to me better presented as they originally appeared, with only minor changes (e.g., excisions of some material that duplicated itself and additions [generally in square brackets] of a few bibliographical notes).

Boccaccio's Dante

(1986)

Anyone who expounds the texts of Dante's *Commedia* and who is compensated for his labors finds himself in extraordinarily distinguished company. Not many professionals are able to claim that the first practitioner in their specialty was Giovanni Boccaccio. Boccaccio's public lectures (23 October 1373–January 1374, read in the church of Santo Stefano in Badia), for which he was paid by the Commune of Florence, were only the most public sign of his expertise in the matter of Dante Alighieri. His mature years, beginning early in the 1350s, are marked by a continued attention to his great precursor in vernacular eloquence. There are his life of Dante (the *Trattatello in laude di Dante*), which he revised once extensively and in part on still another occasion; the aforementioned public lectures on *Inferno* 1–17 (which we know as the *Esposizioni*); and the transcriptions of various of Dante's letters and poems, the *Vita Nuova,* and possibly even the *Commedia.* No one will dispute Boccaccio's affection for and attention to the works of Dante—at least not when the discussion turns to the "old" Giovanni Boccaccio. For his younger self (and by such a descriptive term most people refer, however loosely, to the author of the *Decameron*) is not widely perceived as having been the sort of *devoté* of Dante whom we find revealed so abundantly in the later works. These, we may reflect, are predominantly of a classicizing bent; indeed, after he completed the *Decameron* the only vernacular texts produced by Boccaccio are either Dantean in their explicit subject or else, as is the case in the sole exception, the *Corbaccio,* clearly Dantean in inspiration and Dantesque in their moral intention (or so, at least, it might seem).

This essay was originally developed from a talk given for the Renaissance Faculty Seminar of the University of Pennsylvania, 27 April 1985.

9

The ample bibliography devoted to this subject, Boccaccio's Dante,[1] is in fact devoted nearly exclusively to the "professional *dantista*"—the "younger" Boccaccio is rarely studied as the avid reader of Dante that he so obviously was. Aside from several brief discussions in the first quarter of the century (perhaps most notably that of Francesco Maggini),[2] which gained support from important studies by the two great figures in Boccaccio scholarship at mid-century, Billanovich and Branca,[3] studies devoted to the first half of Boccaccio's creative life are mainly devoid of interest in what is perhaps the most interesting literary relationship of the early modern period. It is probably fair to suggest that such an obvious and a curious lacuna owes its existence to a preconception—one that would keep asunder two spirits who are perceived as being impossibly related. The poet of God and the novelist of an all-too-human vitality have not seemed to many to be indissolubly joined by the affectionate attention of the latter. Even Billanovich's patient instruction, which revealed how painstakingly Boccaccio imitated Dante's writings in his own first efforts, has not been sufficient to clear the air of supposition. And yet the most cursory study of the so-called minor works of Boccaccio reveals, from his first major effort to his last fiction, that his pages swarm with hundreds of references to the works of Dante, that for him Dante was the single modern in the pantheon of authoritative writers, that indeed Dante's authority—if we are to be guided by the actual use made of the earlier writer by the later one—far outweighed that of anyone else. Simply put, for Boccaccio, Dante was *the* modern writer worthy of emulation. A brief review of Boccaccio's vernacular production—one serving as reminder of what there is rather than as proper introduction to a fairly extensive corpus—helps to make the point.

The *Caccia di Diana* offers eighteen *canti* of *terza rima* which point indelibly to a source for its verse form, as well as for any number of its actual verses, in the *Commedia*.[4]

The *Filostrato* frequently turns to Dante for its inspiration, no more obviously than when its author adapts Dante's simile, which moves the sec-

1. See "Imitative Distance," n. 3, for indication of some of the essential studies.

2. See "Il Boccaccio dantista," *Miscellanea storica della Valdelsa* 29 (1921): 116–22.

3. See Giuseppe Billanovich, "La leggenda Dantesca del Boccaccio," *Studi Danteschi* 28 (1949): 45–144; Vittore Branca, *Boccaccio medievale,* 5th ed. (Florence: Sansoni, 1980 [1956]).

4. Now available in the excellent translation by Anthony Cassell and Victoria Kirkham, perhaps the best edition of any of Boccaccio's vernacular works published in a language other than Italian: *Diana's Hunt/Caccia di Diana* (Philadelphia: University of Pennsylvania Press, 1991).

ond canto of *Inferno* toward its conclusion, to describe Troiolo's renewed enthusiasm for Criseida. Pandarus, as Virgil, encourages Troilus, as Dante, by assuring him that his "Beatrice," Criseida, desires his forward progress. The comic effect of the obvious borrowing is telling, if it has only recently been discussed.[5]

The *Filocolo* includes, among its *danteana,* the spectacle of infantile eroticism based on the fifth canto of the *Inferno:* the youthful Florio and Biancifiore read Ovid's *Ars amatoria* and kiss in such manner as to leave no doubt that Boccaccio has Francesca and Paolo in mind.[6]

Near the end of the *Teseida* Arcita looks down from heaven at this terrestrial sphere in such a way as unquestionably to summon up the downward heavenly vision of Dante in *Paradiso* 22; should we doubt the fact, we need only watch Geoffrey Chaucer, at the end of the *Troilus,* conflate the two scenes with telling effect. Whatever our inclinations in the matter, it is clear that our better was aware of Boccaccio as reader of Dante.

The *Comedia delle ninfe fiorentine,* a work which may be less "serious" than we have all assumed, has, because of its apparent orthodox religious sentiments, frequently been discussed as a Dantean allegory. Its poetic segments are, like the entirety of the *Caccia di Diana,* in *terza rima.*

The same is true for the *Amorosa Visione,* perhaps Boccaccio's most elaborate imitation of Dante, fifty *canti* that seem to put forward Dantean answers to the questions raised by the loves that this world enjoins upon us. The text is shot through with verses and scenes reflecting the verses of the *Commedia.*[7]

(These last two works, because they *seem* to be moralizing instances of a Boccaccio temporarily "gone over to the other side," have had the widest recognition as Dante-inspired texts. Yet it is clear that all of Boccaccio's texts are similarly and abundantly inspired. It is Boccaccio's readers, having determined that his goals are radically diverse from Dante's, who have failed to turn up their hearing aids when they have listened to the other Boccaccian texts.)

The *Elegia di madonna Fiammetta* is awash with the tides of the *Commedia,* if, until recently, most critics saw only a puddle or two—there will be more on this point shortly.

---

5. See Robert Hollander, *Boccaccio's Two Venuses* (New York: Columbia University Press, 1977), 175.

6. For the most recent discussion see Jonathan Usher, "Paolo and Francesca in the *Filocolo* and the *Esposizioni,*" *Lectura Dantis [virginiana]* 10 (spring 1992): 22–33.

7. This work is now available in a bilingual edition, *Amorosa Visione,* trans. Robert Hollander, Timothy Hampton, and Margherita Frankel (Hanover, N.H., and London: University Press of New England, 1986).

The *Ninfale fiesolano,* arguably the least Dantean of Boccaccio's fictions, begins with a word-for-word quotation of Beatrice's words to Virgil in *Inferno* 2, and it, too, makes frequent gestures toward the *Commedia.*

Beyond the *Decameron* there is only the *Corbaccio.* Its vigorous, even strident, anti-venereal pose has helped reveal how much of Dante is reflected in its pages. While it is now my opinion that the *Corbaccio* is more a joke than a serious treatise, along the lines of Ovid's similar unserious attack on love and lovers in the *Remedia amoris,* I would be far more insistent than are most about the sheer amount of *dantismo* which dots its pages. In a study which I am now preparing I will be able to demonstrate that there is far more Dante lurking behind the apparently uncontrolled misogyny than anyone has heretofore noticed: some 120 citations—and the work is roughly half as many pages.[8]

This rapid, incomplete, and partial review of the *opere minori in volgare* is meant only to remind the reader how thoroughly Dantean are the literary practices of Giovanni Boccaccio. I have made no attempt to analyze or describe either what Boccaccio is doing to Dante's text or why he so often turns in its direction. All that I hope the reader will grant is that to underestimate the importance of Dante for Boccaccio—from the beginning of his literary life to its conclusion—is to avoid the force of a fact that is overwhelming and significant.

When we speak of Boccaccio, unless we are the most narrowly focused of scholars, we tend to speak of the *Decameron.* The curious fact is that here, in what all concede is Boccaccio's greatest work, in a text that has become a world classic, in the Boccaccian text which is most pointedly filled with reminiscences of the *Commedia,* we have perhaps the poorest record as critical readers. Let a single citation, chosen to make dramatic what is indeed a widely shared perception, if it is rarely so unguardedly presented, stand for a general attitude of nonchalance or even of aggressive dubiety. Giorgio Padoan's characterization of Boccaccio's view of Dante when he wrote the *Decameron* requires that we believe that for him the *Commedia* was "... a work that Boccaccio interprets rather superficially, struck more by the novelty of its narratives, the vigor of its style, its dramatic power, than by its profound content."[9] Such a perverse judgment is difficult to

---

8. [Now see Robert Hollander, *Boccaccio's Last Fiction: Il "Corbaccio"* (Philadelphia: University of Pennsylvania Press, 1988), 59–71, listing 125 textual confrontations.]

9. See "Mondo aristocratico e mondo comunale nell'ideologia e nell'arte di Giovanni

account for, especially in as intelligent a reader as we here confront. Why, we must ask, should this inclination be so widespread? For Padoan is hardly alone in missing entirely the absolute centrality to Boccaccio's purposes, in his greatest work, of Dante's *Commedia*. The history of criticism of the *Decameron* is thus only necessarily described as having examined most aspects of the work but not what is perhaps one of its most important ones. Crudely put, the problem may be stated as follows: Those who suppose that Boccaccio's work is—as it is so often called—"the comedy of man" are not inclined to believe that it might meaningfully intersect with Dante's "divine" comedy. Such a position is so woefully inadequate, even from a logical point of view, that one can only lament the condition of our science, literary criticism. For even if we assume the critical posture of the most lewd of the "naturalist" explicators of Boccaccio's purposes, we might at least entertain the argument that the author of the *Decameron* would want to imitate the *Commedia* as often as he could, if only to set himself off from the moral purposes of his greatest predecessor. Instead, such as they either neglect entirely the interplay between the two texts (beyond their formulaic assertions that the work makes frequent reference to the *Commedia,* but not in anything like meaningful ways, since Boccaccio's purposes are so entirely different from Dante's) or, as in the case of Padoan, argue that the Boccaccio of 1350 was an unthoughtful reader of Dante (another version of the "young Boccaccio" biographical fallacy which distorts so much of the criticism written about this brilliant and bookish author). This unlikely position forces its followers to assert, in public, that Giovanni Boccaccio, who had been reading Dante from the time of his earliest efforts as a writer, and who would become the first paid professor of Dante studies, was, from the age of thirty-seven to forty, a relatively mindless reader of Dante's texts.

It now seems to me that we have come to a decisive moment in Boccaccio studies, one that has begun to reverse the trend away from recognition of the profound interrelation between Boccaccio's work and Dante's. If Boccaccio thought of himself as the Italian Ovid, as I myself have suggested[10]—since Dante was the Italian Virgil, the opposition must have appealed to him—this did not prevent his far wider use of the texts of

---

Boccaccio," in *Il Boccaccio, le muse, il Parnaso e l'Arno* (Florence: Olschki, 1978 [first in *Studi sul Boccaccio* for 1964]), 31. [For the Italian text of the passage, see "Imitative Distance," n. 43.]

10. See *Boccaccio's Two Venuses,* 112–16.

Dante as "source texts" for nearly everything that he wrote. His Dante is thus both a creature familiar from his habitual inclinations and a source that is consciously visited. In the first case, Dante is heard as one hears an authorizing voice in one's own language; and we do well to remember how new a literary Italian was, even in Boccaccio's day. Steeped in Dante, Boccaccio could not avoid sounding like him. It is in this mode that we so often hear bits and tags derived from Dante regardless of their context. Yet the second and more pointed sort of visitation of Dante's texts is surely the more interesting to study. In our own moment in Boccaccio studies, movement in that direction has been most tellingly accomplished by Carlo Delcorno. His study of the *Elegia di madonna Fiammetta* showed, with patience and skill, that the author of a latter-day version of Ovid's *Heroides* had, over and over again, resorted to Dantean texts with precision, fully aware of their context, manipulating them in ways that make it unmistakably clear that, to resort to the vernacular, "Boccaccio knew what he was doing."[11] If such is the case—and as someone following this argument has surely prognosticated—then the traditional equation ("young" Boccaccio warbles woodnotes wild, devoid of close considera- tion of Dante's texts; "old" Boccaccio has digested their form and mean- ing, since he himself is now interested in "that sort of thing," where in his youth the moral thrust of Dante was simply foreign to his dreams and aspirations) has been quite undone. For if Boccaccio, in the *Elegia,* a work which predates the *Decameron* by a number of years, is an astute reader of *Commedia* and *Vita Nuova,* such as Padoan are forced to abandon their theories or to modify them in ungainly ways (e.g., Boccaccio grew up on Dante's texts, then had a sort of amnesiac lacuna while he was writing the *Decameron,* only to return to close consideration of them in his later works).

The thirteenth volume of *Studi sul Boccaccio*—as does the fourteenth— contains two studies of Boccaccio's awareness of Dante in the *Decameron* that serve to carry the argument considerably further than it had previously gone. For if Vittore Branca has consistently argued for a *Decameron* that is complementary to the *Commedia,* no one had previously claimed that the latter work was so deftly and significantly connected to its precursor. Attilio Bettinzoli has now made it clear that Dante was never far from Boccaccio's mind (or hand?) as he composed the *Decameron.* My own contribution in

---

11. See Delcorno, "Note sui dantismi nell'*Elegia di madonna Fiammetta,*" *Studi sul Boc- caccio* 11 (1979): 251–94. [And now see his edition of the *Elegia* (Milan: Mondadori, 1994).]

both volumes would show the same result.[12] These studies, like a number of current ones undertaken on this side of the Atlantic by such as Robert Durling, Franco Fido, Victoria Kirkham, and Giuseppe Mazzotta,[13] may help to open the question of the *Decameron*'s relationship to the *Commedia* and perhaps the entire "question of Boccaccio." Here I conclude what Dante might describe as the *pars introductiva* of these remarks and turn to the *pars executiva,* in which I shall put forward, in anticipation of the more detailed studies that follow, some evidence and try to move the question toward, if not a global hypothesis, at least some large hypothetical questions.

The significance of the opening gesture made toward the *Commedia* in the very subtitle of the *Decameron* is that Boccaccio would seem to have located the field of meaning for his book in that of the *Commedia*. This is to claim that I believe *not,* as some might suppose (especially if they have read my *Boccaccio's Two Venuses*), that Boccaccio intends that we find his aims to be in accord with those of Dante but rather that Dante's stance as *praeceptor amoris Dei* is the one against which Boccaccio, as Ovidian *praeceptor amoris puellarum/puerorum,* constructs his antithetic position. Nonetheless, we should not, I think, rush into a moralizing understanding, one in which, hearing the echoes of Dante, we simply assume that Boccaccio's purposes are identical with his. Perhaps that intrinsic understanding has been the primary reason that *boccaccisti* have resisted seeing how much Dante there in fact is in the *Decameron,* for to find it might tend to allow that Boccaccio was not a "dirty old man" after all. He may indeed be one, but then, in this formulation, he is one who has made clear that he knows what cleanliness he is opposing.

The presence of a citation of a passage in Dante describing the sun in the sky on the occasion of Boccaccio's own proemial descriptions of sunrise[14] is in itself "value-neutral." If what I think I have observed is truly there, we learn only one thing for certain, that, in the *Decameron,* Boccaccio's allegiance to the text of the *Commedia* is far greater than anyone (except Bettinzoli) had previously come close to fathoming. And that fact, more than whatever secondary considerations flow from it, is, it seems to

12. See Attilio Bettinzoli, "Per una definizione delle presenze dantesche nel *Decameron,*" parts 1, "I registri 'ideologici,' lirici, drammatici," and 2, "Ironizzazione e espressivismo antifrastico-deformatorio," *Studi sul Boccaccio* 13 (1981–82): 267–326; 14 (1983–84): 209–40. My contributions to those two volumes are presented hereafter ("Imitative Distance" and "The Sun Rises in Dante").

13. For all of these see n. 9 in the Introduction.

14. See "The Sun Rises in Dante."

me, of great importance. For what emerges is a picture of a Boccaccio who will rarely make a move without his Dante. And that is a new Giovanni Boccaccio. Let us return to the Day-openings of the *Decameron*.

When we observe that, in ways that may surely be typified as recondite, Boccaccio builds his opening descriptions of sunrise upon similar descriptions to be found in Dante, we are surely surprised. [The evidence for these observations will be offered in the study after next, but I here describe the results briefly.] In each case I have found that one of Boccaccio's appropriations of Dantean text is a *hapax* (or a "pseudo-*hapax*," a word or a phrase that will be used only once again in a passage that reflects its earlier use) and, further, that the passage also includes at least two other citations from the same piece of Dantean text. If the pattern is in fact there, it is also violated on a single occasion. As hard as I looked, I could find no Dantean source for the formulaic dawn-description which opens Day Eight. On that Day, however, Boccaccio, in the second sentence of his Introduction, describes noon in phrases which have long been acknowledged as deriving from Dante. In short, his exception would seem, in typical Boccaccian and playful fashion, to prove his rule.

The question of *hapax* in Boccaccio (and in Dante) is another with which I am currently occupied. I ask the reader, if someone were to ask you how many examples of *hapax* there were to be observed in the *Commedia* and in the *Decameron,* how many do you guess there might be? And by *hapax* I mean only to refer to "hard-core" cases, words that occur a single time in the linguistic universe of a book, not inflected forms or other kinds of formal transformations. I confess that I myself, in part conditioned by the amount of excitement a *hapax* can generate in a critic, would have guessed there were some 200 in either of the two great works. There are in fact roughly ten times that number in each. And if one undertakes to examine the relation of every *hapax* in Boccaccio to the lexicon of the *Commedia,* it develops that, if one does not include several dialectical oddities, words for numbers, place names and proper nouns (with their related adjectives), there are some 1,800 examples of *hapax* in the *Decameron.* Of these, some 500 are words also found in the *Commedia.*

In the first article that I wrote concerning the question of Boccaccio's response to Dante in the *Decameron,*[15] I argued for a telling and contextual use of Dantean text. I proposed that Boccaccio's Cepparello was significantly modelled on Dante's Brunetto Latini, that his Frate Cipolla is

---

15. See the following study, "Imitative Distance."

a burlesque version of Dante himself [I realize that merely hearing such assertions is not likely to make them seem convincing; I hope that the next study will do so]. The view of Boccaccio propounded in that treatment of two of his *novelle* holds that he is, if a fervent admirer of Dante, an admirer who holds his model up to critical examination, and that he does so on two principal grounds: Dante's eupeptic morality and his stance as visionary poet. In both matters I believed—and continue to believe—that Boccaccio had assembled his "human comedy" in such a way as to write a commentary of a kind upon Dante's divine one. This commentary, it seems to me, is meant to be corrective, reminding its author and us, his readers, that while Dante's world may be all well and good to contemplate, we must live in one in which fairy tales do not come true. The Dantean movement from misery to bliss, described in a divinely sanctioned poem, is answered by a Boccaccian account of an attempted escape from mortality that results in neither victory nor defeat (we end where we began, all questions unanswered) and is described in a determinedly and only human prose narrative. Thus, in my own tentative view, Boccaccio's Dante is not the friend or the enemy of Boccaccio's own vision of human life or of the role of art in describing that life. He is, however, the necessary and perhaps unsurpassable precursor. To conclude, I wish to put before the reader a single piece of text which may give a sharper focus to this discussion of Boccaccio's close consideration of Dante and of his insistence on the gulf between their two visions, a gulf which exists, he would seem to want us to infer, only so long as we honor Dante's claims for being different from all other tellers of tales, and not if we see him as no more than a Florentine fabulist, a writer thus not all that different from Giovanni Boccaccio. And to that end I turn to the first tale of the Second Day.

It was only after I had paid close attention to a puzzling verse in *Inferno* 29 that, coming back to the *novella* of "santo Arrigo," I could see a connection. This tale, obviously meant to counterbalance the first *novella* in the collection, with its false saint, Ser Cepparello/San Ciappelletto, puts before us a "true" saint (if the reader enjoys entertaining the notion of German saints from Treviso), the humble Arrigo. Where a false Italian saint is worshipped by foolish Burgundians in the first story, now a "true" foreign saint is worshipped by equally foolish (and rather unpleasant) Italians. Where in the first instance a Florentine trickster is the impostor, here also a Florentine trickster, the travelling actor Martellino, commits an act of self-falsification for similarly self-gratifying and amusing reasons. In each account there is a small group of "insiders," fellow Florentines who are vastly amused by the trick played upon a gullible audience by an impostor. (Martellino, the reader will recall, contorts his body into the shape of a cripple and thus is able to make his way to the bier of saint Harry—a strategem which he devises out of the merest curiosity.) It is an attractive thought that leads one to treat the *novella* as an allegory of Boccaccio's imagined sense of Dante's outrage at his own unsanctified fiction-making. Martellino, as Boccaccio, is unmasked by a nameless Florentine who tells the Trevisans that Martellino is a mountebank (Dante, protector of the truth, revealing Boccaccio as the falsifier that he is?): Marchese, one of the two Florentine friends, makes the (false) claim that Martellino has stolen from him one hundred golden florins (Martellino as Boccaccio, "stealing" by writing his one hundred *novelle,* the one hundred *canti* of the *Commedia*?). But such flights of critical fancy may not be rewarded with certainty. However, that Martellino and his friends are mountebanks who make their living imitating other human beings ("con nuovi atti contraffaccendo qualunque altro uomo" [with uncanny gestures counterfeiting whomever they fancy]—II.i.6) to amuse the courts that they visit for profit and delight may well put us in mind of the tenth pouch of Malebolge, where we find not only Mirra "falsificando sé in altrui forma" [falsifying herself in the form of another] (*Inferno* 30.41) but Gianni Schicchi "falsificando in sé Buoso Donati" [counterfeiting in himself Buoso Donati] (30.44). That Boccaccio here has Dante's *falsadori* of the tenth *bolgia* in mind would not be guaranteed by these similar details were it not for a particular that has occurred a dozen lines earlier. In reporting that Arrigo's sainthood is attested by the Trevisans, the narrator reports that, at the hour of the new saint's death, all the bells of the Duomo of Treviso began to peal of their own accord. The evidence given for the miracle finds expression in the following terms: "according to what the Trevisans affirmed" [*secondo che* i trivigiani af*ferma*vano]. Dante gives similar witness in *Inferno* 29.63: "as the poets hold for certain" [*secondo che* i poeti hanno per *fermo*]. The linguistic similarity joins with contextual resonance to make Boccaccio's point clear. In *Inferno* 29, with its image of falsifiers punished as by a plague—one wishes on many grounds that Boccaccio had lived long enough to finish his commentary on the *Commedia,* and surely one would like to have his remarks on the plague-setting of this canto—Dante compares his true vision of those in the afterworld to Ovid's tale of the plague on Aegina, after which the island had to be repopulated by the Myrmidons, the race of humans born of the eggs of ants—"secondo che i poeti hanno per fermo." Dante's slap at the veracity of pagan truth when it

is compared with the Christian revelation to be found in his *Commedia*
does not go unanswered here. His testimony, to which he swears in verses
55–57 in terms which call to mind the authority of the Bible,[16] would place
his poem beyond the dubieties of pagan myth. Boccaccio, citing him for
lines which undermine the veracity and authority of the populace of Treviso, undoubtedly wanted his own dubiety to read back to Dante's claims
for authority as truth-teller. In fact, he would seem to imply, he himself,
Martellino, Ovid, and Dante Alighieri are all what they seem to be—
mountebanks, peddlers of fiction, capable of changing their own forms to
accommodate their fictional purposes for the amusement of not overly
intelligent observers. That is an ending calculated to delight only those
who are willing to be insulted by their betters. When I deal with Giovanni
Boccaccio I find myself increasingly willing so to be dealt with.

---

16. See Robert Hollander, "Dante's 'Book of the Dead': A note on *Inferno* XXIX 57,"
Studi Danteschi 54 (1982): 31–51.

Imitative Distance (*Decameron* I.i and VI.x)

(1981–82)

That Boccaccio, as he composed the *Decameron,* was keenly aware of Dante's *Commedia* is not (nor do I think it can be) a matter in dispute.[1] However [and as I have been suggesting in the preceding pages], it is fair to say that for the most part the actual relationship between what may be the two greatest works of Italian literature has not been closely studied.[2]

---

1. For significant earlier appreciations of this awareness see remarks of two of Boccaccio's most important critics: Giuseppe Billanovich, "La leggenda Dantesca del Boccaccio," *Studi Danteschi* 28 (1949): 65, discussing the general failure to acknowledge Boccaccio's close awareness of Dante at the time of the *Decameron:* "Per la nostra trascurata ignoranza dei costumi culturali e retorici di questa rigogliosa e complessa età gotica continuiamo a rappresentarci l'artista del *Decameron* solo come un libero pittore di vasti affreschi fantasiosamente spregiudicati" [Because of our negligent ignorance of the cultural and rhetorical habits of this exuberant and complex Gothic age, we continue to consider the artist who wrote the *Decameron* only as a liberated painter of vast, capriciously free-spirited frescoes]; Vittore Branca, *Boccaccio medievale,* 5th ed. (Florence: Sansoni, 1980 [1956]), 23–24: "Il capolavoro del Boccaccio, invece, proprio perché appare nei suoi aspetti più costituzionali e più validi come la tipica 'commedia dell'uomo' rappresentata attraverso i paradigmi canonici alla visione cristiana e scolastica della vita e insieme come una vasta e multiforme epopea della società medioevale italiana colta e ritratta nel suo autunno splendido e lussureggiante, non si oppone alla *Divina Commedia* ma in qualche modo le si affianca e quasi la completa" [Boccaccio's masterpiece, on the other hand, precisely because it reveals itself in its most representative and valid aspects as the typical "human comedy," presented in accord with the canonical paradigms for the Christian and scholastic vision of life, and at the same time as a vast and multiform epic of Italian medieval society, harvested and portrayed in its luxurious and splendid autumn, not only is not set apart from the *Divine Comedy* but in some way moves along with the poem as though to complete it]. Branca's view is shared by Francesco Mazzoni, "Giovanni Boccaccio fra Dante e Petrarca," *Atti dell'Accademia Petrarca* 41–42 (1981), which Professor Mazzoni was kind enough to send me in typescript.

2. But for a welcome recent exception see Franco Fido, "Dante personaggio mancato del *Decameron,*" in *Boccaccio: Secoli di Vita,* ed. Marga Cottino-Jones and Edward F. Tuttle (Ravenna: Longo, 1977), 177–89. See also my n. 16. One day perhaps all of Boccaccio's works

Almost all who have considered the question of Boccaccio's interest in Dante have concerned themselves primarily with the *Trattatello* and the *Esposizioni*.[3] One possible reason for such concentration on the overtly Dantean writings at the expense of Boccaccio's fictions is that these fictions—and especially the *Decameron*—conceal more than they reveal of their dependence on the *Commedia*. Thus the general understanding would seem to be that the *Decameron* may in fact frequently reflect the *Commedia*, if we are left largely to our own labors and experiences in determining where and in what manner.[4] At the same time, aware that Pier Giorgio Ricci has shown that the *Trattatello* itself was almost certainly composed

will have received the sort of detailed concentration on their Dantean sources now to be found in Carlo Delcorno, "Note sui dantismi nell'*Elegia di madonna Fiammetta*," *Studi sul Boccaccio* 11 (1979): 251–94. I need hardly add that Delcorno's painstaking scholarship, which reveals the depth of Boccaccio's grasp of Dante in the *Fiammetta*, offers considerable support to my own view of Dante's presence in and behind the later *Decameron*.

    3. See for each the "Bibliografia essenziale" in the relative volumes in *Tutte le opere di Giovanni Boccaccio*, ed. Vittore Branca (Milan: Mondadori, 1965–): vol. 3, *Trattatello in laude di Dante*, ed. Pier Giorgio Ricci (1974), 856–58; vol. 6, *Esposizioni sopra la Comedia di Dante*, ed. Giorgio Padoan (1965), 728–30. See also Padoan, "Boccaccio, Giovanni," in *Enciclopedia Dantesca*, vol. 1 (Rome: Istituto della Enciclopedia Italiana, 1970), 645b–650b, with bibliography; Carlo Muscetta, *Giovanni Boccaccio* (Bari: Laterza, 1972), 338–40, 365 (bibliography). Modern interest in Boccaccio as *dantista* may be said to begin with Orazio Bacci, *Il Boccaccio lettore di Dante*, Lectura Dantis Orsanmichele (Florence: Sansoni, 1913). In preparing this article I found the following studies, many of which are particularly concerned with the *Trattatello*, of use: Maria Perron-Cabus, "Il Boccaccio per Dante," *Miscellanea storica della Valdelsa* 21 (1913): 86–100; Michele Barbi, "Qual è la seconda redazione del *Trattatello in laude di Dante?*" ibid., 101–41; Francesco Maggini, "Il Boccaccio dantista," ibid. 29 (1921): 116–22; E. G. Parodi, "Il Boccaccio in laude di Dante ossia il Mito del Poeta," in *Poeti antichi e moderni* (Florence: Sansoni, 1923), 176–84; Lorenzo Fontana, "Il culto del Boccaccio per Dante," *La Rassegna* 51–56 (1943–48): 64–89; Giuseppe Billanovich, *Prime ricerche dantesche* (Rome: Storia e Letteratura, 1947); idem, "La leggenda Dantesca del Boccaccio," 45–144; Carlo Grabher, "Il culto del Boccaccio per Dante," in *Studi Danteschi* 30 (1951): 147–56; G. I. Lopriore, "Le due redazioni del *Trattatello in laude di Dante* del Boccaccio," *Studi mediolatini e volgari* 3 (1955): 35–60; Pier Giorgio Ricci, "Le tre redazioni del *Trattatello in Laude di Dante*," *Studi sul Boccaccio* 8 (1974): 197–214; idem, "Dante e Boccaccio," *L'Alighieri* 16 (1975): 75–84; Raoul Blomme, "L'ambiguità dell'esegesi boccaccesca dell'Alighieri," *Revue belge de philologie et d'histoire* 53 (1975): 758–68; Giorgio Padoan, "Il Boccaccio fedele di Dante," in *Il Boccaccio, le Muse, il Parnaso e l'Arno* (Florence: Olschki, 1978), 229–46; five contributions in *Giovanni Boccaccio editore e interprete di Dante*, under the auspices of the Società Dantesca Italiana (Florence: Olschki, 1979): Domenico De Robertis, "La tradizione boccaccesca delle canzoni di Dante," 5–13, Giorgio Petrocchi, "Dal Vaticano Lat. 3199 ai codici del Boccaccio: chiosa aggiuntiva," 15–24; Giorgio Padoan, "Giovanni Boccaccio e la rinascita dello stile bucolico," 25–72; Gioacchino Paparelli, "Due modi opposti di leggere Dante: Petrarca e Boccaccio," 73–90; Aldo Vallone, "Boccaccio lettore di Dante," 91–117.

    4. E.g., Carlo Muscetta devotes one sentence to this subject in his several pages on "il culto dantesco" of Boccaccio: "E si è visto come nelle novelle del *Decameron* (anche se in un

between the summer of 1351 and 1355, we should be increasingly conscious of the close relationship between Boccaccio's public profession of his admiration for Dante and his own work in fiction.[5] For if the strategies which inform his treatment of Dante in the *Decameron,* the *Corbaccio,* and the *Trattatello* are perhaps different, the three works are contiguous vernacular enterprises;[6] they probably contain more common concerns and interests that reflect a renewed involvement with the text of the *Commedia* than is generally suspected.[7]

Whatever his eventual purpose in doing so, Boccaccio seems intent on reminding readers of his *Decameron* that they should keep Dante's great poem near at hand. We need read no further than the subtitle, *Prencipe*

contesto assai diverso) spesso si alluda a personaggi, situazioni, figurazioni della *Commedia*" [And it has been observed that in the *novelle* of the *Decameron* (if in a very different context) there may often be allusions to characters, situations, and scenes of the *Comedy*] (*Giovanni Boccaccio,* 338).

5. Ricci, *Introduzione* to the *Trattatello,* 426. And see his appreciation of Dante's intensified importance to Boccaccio during this prolific period in his career (427). See also his two other contributions referred to in my n. 3.

6. Padoan's arguments for a later *Corbaccio* are now to be found in "Sulla datazione del *Corbaccio*" [1963], in *Il Boccaccio, le muse, il Parnaso e l'Arno,* 199–228. See 199 n. 1, for a list of those who have accepted his thesis. But for an expression of doubt concerning this argument for a later date see *Il Corbaccio,* ed. Tauno Nurmela (Helsinki: Annales Academiae Scientiarum Fennicae, 1968), 18–21. For a still stronger series of counterarguments see *The Corbaccio,* trans. and ed. Anthony K. Cassell (Urbana, Chicago, and London: University of Illinois Press, 1975), 95–98. Mario Marti, who had not yet had the opportunity to see Cassell's translation, supports Padoan's basic position while attacking a central position in his argument: "Per una metalettura del *Corbaccio:* Il ripudio di Fiammetta," *Giornale storico della letteratura italiana* 153 (1976): 63–69. [For the continuing dispute see now Hollander, *Boccaccio's Last Fiction: Il "Corbaccio"* (Philadelphia: University of Pennsylvania Press, 1988); Padoan, "Il *Corbaccio* tra spunti autobiografici e filtri letterari," *Etudes italiennes* 37 (1991): 21–37; and Padoan's edition of the *Corbaccio* in the Mondadori series, vol. 5b (1995), esp. 415–22, 430–34. My attempt once again to relate the *Corbaccio* to Ovid's *Ibis,* presented as a paper in Certaldo on 30 April 1996 and forthcoming in the *Atti* of that conference (see "Day Ten of the *Decameron,*" n. 95), takes issue with some of Padoan's arguments.]

7. But see the appreciation of Francesco Maggini, "Il Boccaccio dantista," 117, of the lasting importance of Dante's work throughout Boccaccio's career: "E dalle opere dei primi anni queste reminiscenze si continuano, attraverso le rime d'amore e la prosa magnifica del *Decamerone* (dove sono anche personaggi danteschi), fino alle fantasie del *Corbaccio,* che dalla *Commedia* deriva, oltre all'espressione, la scena)" [And from the earliest works these reminiscences continue, through the love poems and the magnificent prose of the *Decameron* (where one even finds Dantean characters), right up to the fanciful doings of the *Corbaccio,* which derives, in addition to its vocabulary, its setting from the *Comedy*]; cf. also Enrico Burich, "Boccaccio und Dante," *Deutsches Dante-Jahrbuch* 23 (1941): 45: "Auch nach dem *Decameron* hat Boccaccio die *Commedia,* wie aus dem *Corbaccio* hervorgeht, immer gegenwärtig" [Even after writing the *Decameron,* as is clear from the *Corbaccio,* Boccaccio has the *Comedy* ever on his mind].

Galeotto, to understand that the *Commedia* is to be taken as analogous to the *Decameron* in some respect.[8] And if the subtitle's citation of *Inferno* 5.137 is not urgent enough a signal, the following announcements that the work will contain "cento novelle" are surely meant to remind us of its most recent precursor, also divided into one hundred compositional units.[9] While the *Proemio,* if we leave to one side a possible echo or two,[10] shows less sign of attention to the *Commedia,* the *Introduzione* clearly asks us to remember the grand design of Dante's poem: "Questo orrido comincia-mento vi fia non altramenti che a' camminanti una montagna aspra e erta . . . [This horrible beginning will be like the ascent of a steep and rough mountainside . . .] (*Introduzione* 4). Branca's note to this passage suggests both a textual and an existential connection between the two writers; in this view the *Decameron* exists as a counterpart to the *Commedia,* each of the thirty-five-year-old protagonist/authors thus further linked by the dates of their so different visions, 1300 and 1348.[11] And whatever we choose to make of the innate but clear comparison suggested by Boccaccio's text, it does ask that we entertain (without necessarily accepting) the notion that the *Decameron,* like the *Commedia,* is the record of a spiritual voyage which moves from hell, if not to heaven, at least to the Earthly Paradise.

---

8. This is, of course, a *vexata quaestio.* My own previous attempt to deal with the prob-lem may be found in *Boccaccio's Two Venuses* (New York: Columbia University Press, 1977), 102–6, 225–27. At least two items should be added to the list of works mentioned there: J. H. Whitfield, "Dante in Boccaccio," in the supplement to *Italian Studies* 15 (1960): 30–32; Franco Fido, "Dante personaggio mancato del *Decameron,*" 178–80. Further evidence that Boccaccio had *Inf.* 5 in mind as he wrote the opening pages of the *Decameron* is offered by what seems to me a parodic redoing of *Inf.* 5.138, "quel giorno più non vi *leggemmo avante*" [that day we read no further in it], in I.Int.3: "Ma non voglio per ciò che questo di *più avanti leggere* vi spaventi . . . " (italics added) [But I do not want you to be afraid to read further on this account]. All citations of the *Decameron* derive from *Tutte le opere di Giovanni Boccac-cio,* vol. 4, *Decameron,* ed. Vittore Branca (1976); of the *Commedia* from *La Commedia sec-ondo l'antica vulgata,* ed. Giorgio Petrocchi, Edizione Nazionale under the auspices of the Società Dantesca Italiana (Milan: Mondadori, 1966–67).

9. *Proemio* 1 and 13. That Boccaccio's one hundred mirrors Dante's is a critical com-monplace. For his awareness of the importance of the number in Dante's compositional scheme see *Trattatello* I.224, cited in n. 70.

10. E.g., for the adjective in the phrase "cupi pelaghi navigando" [sailing upon deep seas], Branca's note to *Proemio* 5 (*Note* [= Branca, *Decameron,* 976–1568], 977 n. 1) reminds us of Dante's use of *cupo* at *Inf.* 7.10; *Par.* 3.123.

11. Branca, *Note,* 981 n. 10: "Non si può non pensare alla selva 'aspra' e al 'dilettoso' monte del canto introduttivo della *Divina Commedia:* tanto più che l'azione si svolge per ambedue gli scrittori nel mezzo del cammino della vita, a 35 anni" [One cannot help but think of the *aspra* forest and the *dilettoso* mountain of the introductory canto of the *Divine Com-edy,* all the more because the action takes place when each of these writers is "nel mezzo del cammin di nostra vita," that is, when each is thirty-five years old]. For the rest of the *Intro-duzione* Branca's notes (981–1002) resort to the *Commedia* some dozen and a half times.

In his second and penultimate presentation of his own attitudes as author of the work, Boccaccio's reminiscences of Dante are unmistakable.

> Carissime donne, sì per le parole de' savi uomini udite e sì per le cose da me molte volte e vedute e lette, estimava io che lo 'mpetuoso *vento* e ardente della 'nvidia non dovesse *percuotere* se non *l'alte* torri o le più levate *cime* degli alberi: ma io mi truovo della mia estimazione ingannato. Per ciò che, fuggendo io e sempre essendomi di fuggire ingegnato il fiero impeto di questo rabbioso spirito, non solamente pe' piani ma ancora per le profondissime valli mi sono ingegnato d'andare; il che assai manifesto può apparire a chi le presenti novellette riguarda, le quali non solamente in fiorentin volgare e in prosa scritte per me sono e senza titolo, ma ancora *in istilo umilissimo e rimesso* quanto il più si possono. (IV.Int.2–3; italics added)

> [Dearest ladies, both from what I have heard wise men say and from things I have often seen and read about, I used to think that the impetuous and fiery wind of envy would only batter high towers and the topmost part of trees, but I find that I was very much mistaken in my judgment. I flee and have always striven to flee the fiery blast of this angry gale, by trying to go about things quietly and unobtrusively not only through the plains but also through the deepest valleys. This will be clear to anyone who reads these short stories which I have written, but not signed, in Florentine vernacular prose, and composed in the most humble and low style possible] (trans. Mark Musa and Peter Bondanella)

The citations of *Paradiso* 17.133–34 ("Questo tuo grido farà come vento, / che le più alte cime più percuote" [This cry of yours shall do as does the wind, which strikes most on the highest summits]) and of the *Epistola a Cangrande* ("Nam si ad materiam respiciamus, a principio horribilis et fetida est . . . ; ad modum loquendi, remissus est modus et humilis" [For if we take the matter into consideration, at the beginning it is horrible and stinking . . . ; and if the mode of its speech, it is low and humble]—*Epistola* 13.31) are evident, even obvious.[12] Envy (the word will appear twice again in Boccaccio's next sentence) not only is the true motivation of Boccaccio's detractors but is presented as being utterly out of place as response to the

---

12. Branca, *Note*, 1197–98, with bibliography on the subject of *umiltà* as pose of the medieval author. Boccaccio's "orrido cominciamento" [horrible beginning] (I.Int.4) seems to

ultimately "low" *Decameron,* if it might more reasonably be allowed as a response to the supremely "high" *Commedia.* Every verbal gesture made toward Dante's poem is so flagrantly humble as to invite our delight and suspicious laughter. The "outdoing topos" is redeployed in such a way as to become a claim for having been utterly outdone. If Cacciaguida foretells Dante's huge success in reaching the heights ("le più alte cime"), Boccaccio's poor fictive thing is situated in "profondissime valli"; and if Dante wrote in the vernacular, he at least did so in the noble vehicle of verse, while Boccaccio has limited himself to mere prose; further, if Dante has claimed, disingenuously or not, a style "remissus . . . et humilis," Boccaccio will go still deeper in self-abasement: "in istilo umilissimo e rimesso quanto il più si possono."[13] It is a richly self-conscious moment. And once again, whatever our interpretation of Boccaccio's desire to remind us of Dante's great poem's role in defining his own greatest work, we must admit that the *Commedia* is summoned up as the single most significant vernacular antecedent to the *Decameron.*[14]

While perhaps not enough attention has been given to such Boccaccian tactics as these to draw our eyes to texts of the *Commedia* occasionally evident in the *Decameron,* all of the material referred to above has been noticed in the commentary tradition. And no one, or hardly any one, would wish to claim that Boccaccio composed the *Decameron* without a central awareness of the *Commedia.* Among those who recognize Boccaccio's debt to Dante, the range of understanding runs from a ginger and uneasy feeling that, if Boccaccio does cite the *Commedia,* he is doing so unthoughtfully or casually, the way any writer reprocesses the *lingua franca* of his particular literary tradition, to Branca's claim that the *Decameron* is complementary to the *Commedia.*[15] Branca's notes to

---

have the same locus in the *Epistola* in mind. For the text of the *Epistola a Cangrande* I have used the reprint of Ermenegildo Pistelli's edition for the Società Dantesca Italiana (1921), in *Enciclopedia Dantesca,* vol. 6 (Rome: Istituto della Enciclopedia Italiana, 1978), 815a.

13. Marga Cottino-Jones, "Comic Modalities in the *Decameron,*" *Genre* 9 (1976–77): 430, sees that Boccaccio is echoing Dante's adjectives, but Cottino-Jones does not point to the exaggeration present in the borrowing. For Boccaccio's certain awareness of the *Epistle* (which he is likely to have considered a significant *accessus* by an unknown commentator) see Padoan, *Esposizioni,* 767 nn. 10 and 11. [My own involvement in the current debate over the authenticity of the letter is represented by *Dante's Epistle to Cangrande* (Ann Arbor: University of Michigan Press, 1993).]

14. "Le cose da me molte volte e vedute e lette" of IV.Int.2, surely include, for the second category, first and foremost the works of Dante.

15. For the first view see my citation of Giorgio Padoan in n. 43; for the second see my quotation of Branca in n. 1. See also the latter's *La filologia,* in Vittore Branca and Jean

the *Decameron* are careful to distinguish between what one might call lexicography and citation, that is, between previous uses of various words, phrases, inflections found in Dante which help to understand Boccaccian practice and those words, phrases, inflections which seem intentionally to reflect specific passages in Dante's works. Such distinctions are neither always easily made nor often readily assented to. Yet one may say, with comfortable assurance, that no previous writer is nearly so close to his heart and hand, from the beginning of Boccaccio's career to its close, as Dante. In what follows I hope to persuade students of Boccaccio that we have only begun to appreciate his continuing awareness, not of Dante's grand design alone, but of minute particulars of his work, especially of the *Commedia*. The two cases which I am about to present have this potential virtue: they are both newly observed instances of Boccaccio's reaction to Dante. And they share a common potential defect: they may both be considered over-ingenious. Clearly I would not presume to ask for the reader's patience did I not believe that I have observed phenomena and not phantasms. The only way to test new interpretations is to share them. If the reader is ultimately convinced, he or she will surely agree with my growing conviction that Dante is a far more important and frequent presence in the *Decameron* than we have previously believed.[16]

Starobinski, *La filologia e la critica letteraria* (Milan: Rizzoli, 1977), 52–74. J. H. Whitfield, "Dante and Boccaccio," 17, 19, aligns himself with Branca. For the view that Boccaccio found Dante an "inadequate model" for his own moral stance see Millicent Joy Marcus, *An Allegory of Form: Literary Self-Consciousness in the "Decameron"* (Saratoga, Calif.: Anma Libri, 1979), 110–12.

16. Four of my American colleagues, Robert Durling, Victoria Kirkham, Ronald Martinez, and Giuseppe Mazzotta, are all currently involved in the study of this question. Durling has sent me the typescript of his forthcoming treatment of Guido Cavalcanti (VI.ix) as being deeply reflective of *Inf.* 9 and 10 (see n. 41). Kirkham's recent lecture, "Maestro Simone and the Judgment Day," calls our attentlon to *Inf.* 18–20 in VIII.ix. Mazzotta, "Games of Laughter in the *Decameron*," *Romanic Review* 69 (1978): 115–31, points to Dantean allusions in II.v, V.i, V.viii, VIII.iii, and VIII.ix. Following Mazzotta, Martinez, in a recent lecture, "Calandrino and the Numbers of the Sun," indicates some of the reverberations of *Inf.* 25 in VIII.iii. What all these developing theses, my own included, have in common, beyond their American genesis, is the conviction that the commentary tradition has been too timid in its reception of Boccaccio's awareness of Dante in the *Decameron*. See also Franco Fido's recent contribution, cited in n. 2. I am myself currently preparing a monograph on this subject. [This last promise is in fact fulfilled by this book. At the time I was working on the studies that appear on either side of this one. For bibliographical information about the eventual disposition of three of the four pieces referred to at the beginning of this note, see my Introduction, n. 9.]

Cepparello and Brunetto: "Come l'uom s'etterna"

The first *novella* of the *Decameron* contains a number of Dantean moments.[17] Panfilo, the first *novellatore,* insists on beginning under the sign of God: "Convenevole cosa è, carissime donne, che ciascheduna cosa la quale l'uomo fa, dallo ammirabile e santo nome di Colui, il quale di tutte fu facitore, le dea principio" [It is fitting, dear ladies, that everything that human beings do be prefaced with the wonderful and holy name of Him who was the maker of all things] (I.i.2).[18] His presentation of his tale as an "orthodox" demonstration of God's grace in allowing us to pray to saints depends in part upon various formulations found in the *Commedia.*[19] While the subject is a traditional one, Panfilo's treatment is certainly in accord with Dante's views and, very likely, his precise formulations. Thus the narrative portion of the *Decameron* may be seen as beginning by locating itself alongside the *Commedia.* And once Panfilo's tale proper begins, it situates itself in the event of 1301 that was the prelude to Dante's exile: Boniface's summoning Charles of Valois into Tuscany.[20] One might wish to consider the likely possibility that in Boccaccio's mind the narrated action that initiates the metamorphosis of Cepparello into a saint intersects historically with the very moment that began the terrible series of

---

17. Branca's notes point to more than a dozen verbal parallels or citations of the *Commedia.*

18. Neifile will also insist on a religious enfranchisement of her tale—it too will demonstrate "la benignità di Dio" [God's goodness] (I.ii.3). Filomena will bring us down to earth (". . . il discendere oggimai agli avvenimenti e agli atti degli uomini . . ." [. . . descending to what happens to and what is done by humans . . .]—I.iii.3)—where we will remain at least until Day Ten. For appreciations of this "descent" to the human see Giovanni Getto, *Vita di forme e forme di vita nel "Decameron"* (Turin: Petrini, 1958), 40; Mario Baratto, *Realtà e stile nel "Decameron"* (Vicenza: Neri Pozza, 1970), 19, 53.

19. Branca offers the following juxtapositions from I.i.5 alone: "non potendo l'acume dell'occhio mortale nel segreto della divina mente trapassare in alcun modo" and *Par.* 13.141, "[Non creda donna Berta e ser Martino, / per vedere un furare, altro offerere, /] vederli dentro al consiglio divino"; ". . . Esso, al quale niuna cosa è occulta" and *Par.* 21.50, "nel veder di colui che tutto vede"; "con eterno essilio," "allo essilio del pregato," and *Inf.* 13.126 as well as *Purg.* 21.18, "ne l'etterno essilio."

20. Branca cites *Purg.* 20.70–78 and (for Boccaccio's certain knowledge of this conjunction) *Trattatello* 1.165–66. It is perhaps worth noting that Branca's intriguing and venturesome identification of Cepparello with Judas (in his *Introduzione* to *Decameron,* xvii), questioned by Muscetta, *Giovanni Boccaccio,* 169n, may gain support from the fact that Dante's description of Charles of Valois, in the passage that Branca connects with Boccaccio's treatment of Charles here, associates the French interloper with Judas (". . . la lancia / con la qual giostrò Giuda . . ." [. . . the lance with which Judas did his jousting . . .]—*Purg.* 20. 73–74— is the weapon that he employs against Florence).

events leading to Dante's exile[21] and, not coincidentally, to the completion of the *Commedia.*[22]

In this atmosphere of large-scale political chicanery we are led to focus upon Musciatto Franzesi's choice of Ser Cepparello da Prato to serve as his representative among (and against) the Burgundians. The first thing about him that draws our attention is the difficulty of the French in interpreting the meaning of his name.

> . . . un ser Cepparello da Prato, il quale molto alla sua casa in Parigi si riparava; il quale, per ciò che piccolo di persona era e molto assettatuzzo, non sappiendo li franceschi che si volesse dir Cepparello, credendo che 'cappello', cioè 'ghirlanda' secondo il lor volgare a dir venisse, per ciò che piccolo era come dicemmo, non Ciappello ma Ciappelletto il chiamavano: e per Ciappelletto era conosciuto per tutto, là dove pochi per ser Cepperello il conoscieno. (I.i.9)

> [. . . a certain Ser Cepparello of Prato, who often stayed as a visitor in (Musciatto's) house in Paris. The French, not understanding what *Cepparello* meant and because he was slight of stature and was very well turned out, believing that *cappello* derived from *garland (chapelet)* in their vernacular, and since, as we have said, he was a little man, called him not "Ciappello" but "Ciappelletto." And to everyone he was known as "Ciappelletto" where few knew him as Ser Cepperello.]

While it is clear that Boccaccio invites his Italian reader to know very well what his name means, we cannot be sure whether in his mind it derives from the noun *ceppo* or is a diminutive of *Ciapo,* itself a deformation of *Jacopo.*[23] Since within the economy of Panfilo's narrative he is metaphorically a stump, or dead stock, in that his sexual activity is barren and bears no offspring, it seems to me likely that Boccaccio wants us to read his given name as a diminutive of *ceppo.*[24] In this case not only is the aridity

---

21. For Boccaccio's certain knowledge of the events see *Esposizioni, esp. litt.* 8.39–43.

22. For Boccaccio's sense of the relation of the exile to Dante's completion of the *Commedia,* see his picturesque notion that Dante had left the first seven cantos of *Inf.* behind him in Florence, where Gemma preserved these texts (*Esposizioni, esp. litt.* 8.3–17).

23. Branca, *Note,* 1006 n. 2.

24. Confirming evidence for this hypothesis is perhaps found at VIII.vii.140. There the maid of the widow goes to the aid of her sunburned mistress, who appears "non corpo umano ma più tosto un cepperello inarsicciato . . ." [not so much a human body but a little log consumed by fire . . .]. Branca's note, while not pursuing this connection, glosses "cepperello

of his life made etymologically appropriate (he is a diminutive of a negative entity),[25] but Dante's one use of the word, a *hapax* in the *Commedia,* may serve as the *in bono* counterpart to Boccaccio's root of *Cepparello;* for in *Paradiso* 16.106, we read of "lo ceppo di che nacquero i Calfucci" [the stock from which the Caffuzzi were born]. Thus "il piggiore uomo forse mai nascesse" [the worst man ever to have been born] (I.i.15) is (intrinsically?) compared to one of those Florentine families of "il buon tempo antico," and not to his advantage. Yet the Burgundians, in their unenlightened etymologizing (which parallels their eventual credulity in accepting the gullible friar's sanctification of Cepparello) turn him into something etymologically superior to what he truly is: Cepparello ←cappello ("ghirlanda")→ Ciappelletto ("piccola ghirlanda").[26] He is actually a *ceppo (in malo)* but they take him for a *cappello* ("chapelet"). The use of *cappello* to mean "garland" in the sense of poetic laurel is also a *hapax* in Dante *(Paradiso* 25.9).[27] It is possible that Boccaccio had in mind not only Dante's positive use of the word *ceppo* in *Purgatorio* 16 but this second *hapax* as well. If so, Cepparello is seen as a perverse "author," granted his *cappello* by the credulous populace while the great poet was denied his.[28] Yet the juxtaposition, which at first would seem only to condemn our mortal judgment in rewarding the false poet, having passed over the true one, would also tend to have a polemical undertone that works to

inarsicciato" as "un piccolo ceppo bruciacchiato alquanto arso" [a little log almost consumed by fire] (*Note,* 1441 n. 8). Cepparello's name is once given in this form, as we have just seen (I.i.9). Furthermore, Boccaccio would generally seem to prefer the noun *schiatta* (as opposed to *ceppo*) in order to refer to a fruitful line of descent (e.g., *Ninfale* 454.4, "africhea schiatta"; *Trattatello* 1.13, "nobilissimo giovane per ischiatta de' Frangiapani" [for Dante's ancestor Eliseo]; and cf. *Decameron* I.Int.48, "O quante memorabili schiatte . . .").

25. Cf. Marga Cottino-Jones, "Ser Ciappelletto or 'le Saint Noir': A Comic Paradox," in *An Anatomy of Boccaccio's Style* (Naples: Cymba, 1968), 26–30, discussing "two contrasting linguistic tones, the diminutive and the augmentative . . ." as these are applied to Cepparello. And cf. the similar appreciation of Enrico De Negri, "The Legendary Style of the *Decameron,*" *Romanic Review* 43 (1952): 17, where the first *novella* is seen as ". . . a joke and above all a stylistic joke."

26. See Branca, *Note,* 1006 n. 2: "Il francese 'chapel' aveva il suo diminutivo assai comune in 'chapelet,' cioè 'ciappelletto' pronunziato alla toscana: e anche in italiano 'cappello' s'usava per 'corona, ghirlanda' (*Par.* 25.9) . . ." [French *chapel* had a rather common diminutive in *chapelet,* that is, *ciappelletto* pronounced in the Tuscan way; and in Italian also *cappello* was used for "crown, garland" . . .].

27. See Lucia Onder, *cappello,* in *Enciclopeda Dantesca,* 1:822b, with bibliography; her discussion draws attention to Boccaccio's similar use of the word in this passage.

28. Boccaccio's lament for Dante's non-laureation is expressed in *Trattatello* 2.150 (B): "Lo sforzarsi ad aver delle frondi assai manifesto ne mostra essere stato il disiderio della laureazione però che ogni fatica aspetta premio e il premio dello avere alcuna cosa poetica com-

Dante's disadvantage. For his insistence on the veracity of his *Commedia* is thus to be considered as being nonetheless proximate to Cepparello's totally false confessional autobiography, one which similarly asks to be taken as gospel truth. We shall return to this aspect of Boccaccio's reaction to Dante further on.

The nominal perspectivism of the first *novella* is sure and delightful. Our protagonist is referred to as "Cepparello" and "ser Cepperello" once, as "ser Cepparello da Prato" twice, as "Ciappelletto" three times, as "ser Ciappelletto" thirty-seven times, and as "san Ciappelletto" once. The arrangement of these appellations is instructive. If we may assume that his creator knew his "real" name, it is with that that we begin and end: "ser Cepparello da Prato" (I.i.9 and 89). The Burgundians turn him into "Ciappelletto" (9), to which Panfilo, the narrator, accedes (10), only to retreat to the truer name "Cepparello" (16). Then Musciatto calls him by his transmogrified name, "ser Ciappelletto" (17), to which Panfilo—once again—accedes (18), only to retreat again, this time to plain "Ciappelletto" (19). The next twenty-six times the name appears it is in our narrator's mouth and remains fixed as "ser Ciappelletto" (22–74). At this point the friar names him for the only time—still as "ser Ciappelletto," which the narrator will continue to call him eight more times (76–85).[29] It is but then that the populace is reported as having elevated him to the status of "san Ciappelletto" (88), only to have Panfilo/Boccaccio remind us of the truth and of our point of origin: "ser Cepparello da Prato" (89), significantly enough the name that he is given first and last—and only then. Most commentators yield to the far more frequent use of his falsely derived name and call him "Ciappelletto," thus alerting us to the fact that they have missed the point of all this linguistic play. We should probably insist on calling him "Cepparello," his real name, unless we wish to own ourselves gullible readers of the text which contains him. His final appellation makes that case

---

posta, è l'onore che per la corona dello alloro si riceva" [The clearly evident exertion to have the [laurel's] leaves reveals his desire for laureation. After all, every toil looks for its reward, and the reward for having composed a poem is the honor conferred when one receives the laurel]. Dante's hope was denied him by death, "il che a lui avvenne quando già avea finito quello per che meritamente la laureazione gli seguiva" [which came for him when he had indeed finished that for which laureation deservedly awaited him]. It is difficult to imagine Boccaccio writing these lines without having his perverse "laureate," San Ciappelletto, in mind.

29. The *Concordanze del "Decameron,"* ed. Alfredo Barbina, under the direction of Umberto Bosco, 2 vols. (Florence: C/E Giunti & G. Barbèra, 1969), do not list two of the three uses at 78; also lost track of is the variant "Cepperello" at 9.

secure: "Così adunque visse e morì ser Cepparello da Prato e santo divenne come avete udito" [In this manner did Ser Cepparello da Prato live and die and become a saint, just as you have heard]. And this version of the true and the false is authenticated by our author himself in his *argomento* (I.i.1): "Ser Cepparello con una falsa confessione inganna un santo frate e muorsi; e, essendo stato un pessimo uomo in vita, è morto reputato per santo e chiamato san Ciappelletto" [Ser Cepparello tricks a holy friar by means of a false confession and dies; having been a very bad man during his life, dead he is considered a saint and called Saint Ciappelletto].

This excursus on Ser Cepparello's name leads to a consideration of his profession and his morals. About these we learn two especially significant things: he was a notary ("egli, essendo notaio"—I.i.10), as his title ("ser") would have already indicated; he was a homosexual ("delle femine era così vago come sono i cani de' bastoni;[30] del contrario più che alcuno tristo uomo si dilettava"[31] [he was as fond of women as are dogs of cudgels; in the other sex he delighted more than any other perverse wretch]—I.i.14). Now, if we were to ask ourselves whether there exist any noteworthy literary representations of homosexual notaries in previous medieval texts we do not have far to seek: "Siete voi qui, ser Brunetto?" [Are you here then, Ser Brunetto?] (*Inferno* 15.30). I would suggest that Ser Cepparello da Prato is Boccaccio's parodic version of Dante's Brunetto Latini. It is perhaps surprising that no one has heretofore offered this hypothesis.[32] For

---

30. Cf. another homosexual in the *Decameron,* Pietro da Vinciolo, similarly described at V.x.55 (as Branca points out).

31. Some English translations of the passage have utterly misled their readers—e.g., *The Decameron,* trans. Richard Aldington (New York: Dell, 1973 [1930]), 45: "He was as attractive to women as sticks are to dogs; but he delighted in them more than any other vile man." For a similar sixteenth-century deformation see the edition of Luigi Groto Cieco D'Adria (Venezia: F. and A. Zoppini, 1588): "Delle femmine più che alcun'altro tristo huomo si dilettava" [He delighted in women more than any other miserable man]. This curiosity is pointed out by Luigi Fassò, "La prima novella del *Decameron* e la sua fortuna," in *Saggi e ricerche di storia letteraria* (Milan: Marzorati, 1947 [1931]), 65. Fassò's study remains indispensable for the *fortuna* of I.i.

32. Previous comparisons of Cepparello to figures in Dante have been rather impressionistic. E.g., Luigi Manucci, "La figura di ser Ciappelletto nella prima novella del *Decameron,*" *Miscellanea storica della Valdelsa* 21 (1913): 106: "Possibile che vi possa essere una creatura umana così cattiva? E c'è. C'è ser Ciappelletto del Boccaccio! Egli ha qualche cosa in sé di Farinata, di Sapìa, di Capaneo, di Vanni Fucci!" [Does the possibility exist that there could live a human being as wicked as this? Well, it does. There's Boccaccio's Ser Ciappelletto! He has in him something of Farinata, of Sapia, of Capaneus, of Vanni Fucci!]. Mario Baratto, *Realtà e stile nel "Decameron,"* 299, considers Cepparello ". . . una sorta di Capaneo borghese . . ." [a sort of bourgeois Capaneus]. However, at least one reader of the *novella* has thought of Brunetto Latini as a counterpart to Cepparello, if in a fairly offhand fashion.

instance, we have for some time recognized that Ser Cepparello is modelled on a historical figure, one Cepperello or Ciapperello Dietaiuti ("Maygodhelpyou"—how Boccaccio must have enjoyed that surname!) da Prato.[33] As Branca's notes make clear, nearly all of Boccaccio's particulars but two are fitting: ". . . ma non era notaio, era ammogliato e aveva figli . . ." [. . . but he was not a notary, and he was married with children . . .].[34] Why should Boccaccio have chosen a historical figure as the basis for his literary character and then lent him two peculiarities of which we have no record unless he meant them to serve as iconographic indications which point to a figure whom we might thereby recognize?[35] Even without further evidence or any justifying hypothesis, it nonetheless seems to me a likely interpreta-

---

Felice Tribolati, "Diporto sulla novella I della prima giornata del *Decamerone*," in *Diporti letterari sul "Decameron"* (Pisa: Nistri, 1873 [1863]), 60–61, notes: "Osservate che [Boccaccio] lo fa di professione notaio, onorevolissima a quei tempi, e assai più che nei moderni lucrosa. Notaio fu pure ser Brunetto Latini, il quale avendo commesso un leggero errore nella redazione di un atto, mentre era notaio della Repubblica Fiorentina, amò meglio farsi condannare come falsario di quello, che confessare la sua negligenza; ed ebbe in pena, lo esiglio" [Observe that Boccaccio makes him a notary, a most honorable profession in those days, and much more lucrative than it is today. In fact, Ser Brunetto Latini was a notary. Once, when he served the Florentine Republic in that capacity, having committed a small error in his wording of a deed, he preferred to have himself declared a forger than to confess his carelessness. His punishment was exile]. Tribolati's source for this last incident is Landino's commentary. As we shall see, Boccaccio's own report of the incident is probably the eventual source of Landino's version. And while Tribolati does not suggest anything more than a chance parallel between the two notaries, I am nonetheless pleased not to be the first to think of them as being related. As far as I know, no one else has discussed the possible relationship. In fact Giulio Giani, *Cepparello da Prato (lo pseudo Ser Ciappelletto) secondo la leggenda boccaccesca e secondo i documenti degli Archivi Pratese e Vaticano* (Prato: M. Martini, 1916), 27, complains that Tribolati here ". . . si ferma per esi[bi]re un pizzico di erudizione, su Ser Brunetto Latini pur notaio, non so bene con quanta opportunità" [. . . halts to deliver himself of a nugget of erudition concerning Brunetto Latini as notary, I would not be able to say whether fittingly or not].

33. See Cesare Paoli, "Documenti di ser Ciappelletto," *Giornale storico della letteratura italiana* 5 (1885): 329–69.

34. Branca, *Note*, 1003 n. 1, with bibliography relevant to the question.

35. That Cepparello is portrayed as a notary drew Paoli's puzzled attention ("Documenti di ser Ciappelletto," 331): ". . . dipenda da un errore di fatto o da un equivoco. Ma io non sono alieno dal supporre, che fosse quella addirittura un'invenzione del novellatore, per dare più colorito al quadro" [. . . may depend on an error of fact or on a misunderstanding. But I am not far from believing that this was in fact an invention of the writer, to give a little color to his picture]. Fassò also discusses the matter (*Saggi e ricerche*, 89): "[Boccaccio] può essersi indotto a farne un notaro solamente per accrescere la verosimiglianza del falso supremo in fin di vita" [Boccaccio may have been induced to make a notary of him only to increase the verisimilitude of his supreme forgery as he lay dying]. He also points out (ibid.) that Cepparello's brother was in fact a notary, a circumstance noted by Muscetta as well (*Giovanni Boccaccio*, 167n), also on the authority of Giani *(Cepparello da Prato)*.

tion, one that makes a certain immediate sense. Yet I believe that a justifying hypothesis does exist and that there is further evidence.[36]

Boccaccio's Cepparello, like Dante's Brunetto, is portrayed as a homosexual only upon his author's word or, perhaps, invention; there is no other tradition that associates either figure with homosexuality. Another similarity is apparent when we consider that each of them has left Tuscany to live in France. Here is Panfilo's account of Cepparello's behavior as *notaio*.

> Era questo Ciappelletto di questa vita: egli, essendo notaio, avea grandissima vergogna quando uno de' suoi strumenti, come che pochi ne facesse, fosse altro che falso trovato—de' quali tanti avrebbe fatti di quanti fosse stato richesto, e quegli più volentieri in dono che alcuno altro grandemente salariato. Testimonianze false con sommo diletto diceva, richesto e non richesto, e dandosi a quei tempi in Francia a' saramenti grandissima fede, non curandosi fargli falsi, tante quistioni malvagiamente vincea a quante a giurare di dire il vero sopra la sua fede era chiamato. (I.i.10–11)

> [This fellow Ciappelletto's life was like this: being a notary, he was terribly ashamed if even one of his depositions turned out to be anything but false—something that was rarely the case. And he turned out as many of these as he was asked, and did so as gladly without fee as did another who was well paid for such work. He would give false testimony with the greatest pleasure, whether bidden to do so or not; and since the French in those days had enormous faith in sworn oaths, not caring if he took an oath falsely, he wickedly won his case as many times as he was called on to swear to tell the truth upon his faith.]

And here is Boccaccio as *chiosatore* of Brunetto's life and work (*Esposizioni* 15.17–18).

> Questo ser Brunetto Latino fu fiorentino e fu assai valente uomo in alcune delle liberali arti e in filosofia, ma la sua principale facultà fu notarìa, nella quale fu eccellente molto: e fece di sé e di questa sua fac-

---

36. And I will not force upon the reader such "evidence" as the fact that Dante gives Brunetto the respectful *voi* (along with five other mortals: Farinata, Cavalcante, Pope Adriano, Beatrice, Cacciaguida) while Brunetto returns the *tu*. The resulting parallel between that conversation and Cepparello's confession, in which he addresses the friar as *voi* and receives the fraternal *tu* until the final sanctifying moment (I.i.75), would seem fortuitous.

ultà sì grande estima che, avendo, in contratto fatto per lui, errato e per quello essendo stato accusato di falsità, volle avanti esser condennato per falsario che egli volesse confessare d'avere errato; e poi, per isdegno partitosi di Firenze e quivi lasciato in memoria di sé un libro da lui composto, chiamato il *Tesoretto,* se n'andò a Parigi e quivi dimorò lungo tempo e composevi . . . in volgar francesco . . . il *Tesoro,* e ultimamente credo si morisse a Parigi.

[This Ser Brunetto Latino was a Florentine and a fellow most worthy in several of the liberal arts and in philosophy, but his principal ability was as a notary, in which profession he was absolutely outstanding. And he made for himself and for his notarial abilities such a reputation that, having made, in a deed that he had written, a mistake, for which he was accused of forgery, he preferred to be condemned as a forger than to confess that he had erred. Then, disdainfully having quit Florence, leaving as a token of himself a book he had written, called the *Tesoretto,* he went to Paris. He stayed there a long time and there he wrote . . . in the French tongue . . . the *Tesoro;* and I believe that he died in Paris.

Since Boccaccio, in his *Esposizioni,* never refers overtly to his own fictions, we can only imagine what he felt as he wrote this passage. It is inconceivable that he did not think of his own homosexual notary, Ser Cepparello da Prato, Florentine exile, confessor of his faults, dying in France, leaving his "tesoro" behind him in that foreign land.[37] The two figures are closely related by antithesis, if they share the sin against nature;[38] Brunetto is an honest notary, the very opposite of Cepparello.

---

37. Cepparello's entombment as a saint in Burgundy (I.i.87) is perhaps remembered by antithesis in a passage of the *Trattatello* (1.108) that may serve as a bridge between the conclusion of the first novella and *Esposizioni* 15.18. Describing Ravenna's rich reliquary tradition (tombs of martyrs and emperors), Boccaccio sees the city as also being the "perpetua guardiana di così fatto tesoro come è il corpo di [Dante], le cui opere tengono in ammirazione tutto il mondo . . ." [perpetual guardian of so precious a treasure as the body of Dante, whose works the entire world holds in awe . . .]. The veneration of Dante's body in Ravenna, described in a passage which Boccaccio may have composed within a year of completing the *Decameron,* is thus a glorious counterpart to the foolish veneration of the body of Cepparello in France.

38. For Boccaccio's assurance that Brunetto was a homosexual, see *Esposizioni* 15.18: "E, per ciò che mostra l'autore il conoscesse per peccatore contro a natura, in questa parte il discrive, dove gli altri pone, che contro a natura bestialmente adoperarono" [And, because the author reveals that he knew him as a sinner against nature, he describes him as being here, where he puts the others who acted bestially in their opposition to nature]. Boccaccio's assurance in this matter makes superfluous, in this context, discussion of the claims of André

While more than twenty years intervene between Boccaccio's description of Cepparello and his later encomium of Dante's Brunetto, and while caution urges us against easy assurance that the view of Brunetto found in the *Esposizioni* was operative in the first tale of the *Decameron,* it is nonetheless at the very least possible that Boccaccio's close knowledge of the *Commedia* would have revealed exactly such responses as these in 1348–50. On the evidence, we may say with some certainty that in 1373 Boccaccio thought of Brunetto as a counter-Cepparello; that in 1348–50 he very likely had exactly this Brunettan lore in mind and thought of Cepparello as a counter-Brunetto. And, with or without the possible confirmation offered by the *Esposizioni,* the essential context of Boccaccio's first *novella* is so richly suggestive of Brunetto and his mission—teaching Dante "come l'uom s'etterna"[39] [how man makes himself immortal]—that it seems likely that he built his fictional version of Cepperello Dietaiuti out of an inverse representation of the virtues of Brunetto Latini. And again Boccaccio's later thoughts about Brunetto may be instructive. Near the end of his commentary to *Inferno* 15 he explodes into praise of the true immortality gained in fame by poets or any other "compositore in qualunque altra scienza o facoltà" [practitioner in whatever other science or craft] (99).[40] Brunetto's claim that he still lives on in his *Tesoro* (15.119–20) offers Boccaccio a final occasion on which to sing the praises of poetry. Yet it also must have reminded its author of his Cepparello, perverse achiever of another kind of immortality. Boccaccio's gloss may thus be seen to be pertinent both to Dante's poem and to his own *Decameron.*

Panfilo's concluding reflections upon the tale that he has told rehearse dutifully the dual possibilities that Christians, as a matter of doctrine (and on the authority of Dante as well), must entertain: Cepparello may have

---

Pézard *(Dante sous la pluie de feu* [Paris: Vrin, 1950]) and Richard Kay *(Dante's Swift and Strong* [Lawrence, Kansas: Regents Press, 1978]) that Dante did not intend us to conceive of the denizens of *Inf.* 15 as homosexuals. Both these stimulating and important studies have their beginnings in what must be considered implausible readings of the literal sense of the text. [For more in this vein, with indication of more recent bibliography on the question, see my "Dante's Harmonious Homosexuals," *Electronic Bulletin of the Dante Society of America,* 27 June 1996 (http://www.princeton.edu.~dante)].

39. A student in my seminar on Boccaccio, Gerald Dal Pan, Princeton 1982, first suggested to me the aptness of this phrase to Cepparello's own "teaching."

40. It is the longest *postilla* to this canto, running over three pages (15.86–100). As Giorgio Padoan points out *(Esposizioni,* 968 n. 104), it is a continuation of the similar fervent pleading on behalf of poetry found in *Genealogia* 14.8. It is in fact Boccaccio's last utterance of this kind in a lifetime devoted to the cause of glorifying poetry.

been taken up into heaven or down into hell. It is not a matter which we in this life may know.[41] And no matter how much more likely the second alternative seems, it is significant that Panfilo, despite his own opinion that the false saint has most likely been damned, insists on presenting the issue as an open question (". . . per avventura Idio ebbe misericordia di lui e nel suo regno il ricevette" [. . . perchance God had mercy on him and received him into his kingdom]—89). As we reflect on this most dubious of possibilities, considering whether or not Cepparello has won immortality in heaven as he has won it in the credulous minds of the Burgundians, do we hear a distanced reformulation of Dante's final vision of Ser Brunetto ("e parve di coloro / quelli che vince, non colui che perde" [and among them he seemed the one who is winning, not the loser])? If so, the resonance serves as a mild rebuke to the poet who claimed to know the denizens of hell and heaven. For surely, in Boccaccio's sense of Brunetto's work in *Esposizioni* 15 there is better ground to think of Brunetto as saved than as damned. A damned Brunetto (on Dante's authority) and a potentially saved Cepparello (on Dante's own formulation of what *Donna Berta* and *Ser Martino* explicitly cannot know) tend to call into question Dante's poetic stance as *vates,* while at the same time making his Brunetto a figure of the poet worthy of emulation. Boccaccio's Cepparello thus serves to remind the attentive reader that the way in which man may make himself immortal has been debased in a leaden age.

If Boccaccio has rooted prolusory passages of his *Decameron* in Dante's *Commedia* by means of a continuing series of allusions that most readers will readily accept as being immediately evident, he has in his first *novella,* in the formulation offered here, raised an at once more general and more delicate series of allusions to a specific Dantean text: *Inferno* 15. He has

---

41. Branca's notes (*Note,* 1014 nn. 2 and 3) remind us of the applicability of the surprising salvations of Manfred (*Purg.* 3) and Buonconte (*Purg.* 5) as well as of the probably still more relevant damnation of Buonconte's father, Guido (*Inf.* 27). Perhaps even more to the point is the full context of a verse that Branca has already cited (see my n. 19), *Par.* 13.141, where "donna Berta e ser Martino" are warned that they predict God's future plans for us with merely human sight. (The passage was seen as relevant to this theme in I.i as long ago as 7 March 1750—see Giovanni Bottari, *Lezioni sopra il "Decamerone,"* vol. 2 [Florence: G. Ricci, 1818], 3.) The Dantean provenance of Panfilo's framing remarks serves both to continue Dante's doctrine concerning the limited nature of human foresight and to open a polemic that will run the length of the *Decameron,* one that calls into question Dante's own poetic claim that he possesses exactly such knowledge. This is a point made by Robert Durling in his as-yet-unpublished article (see my n. 16 [and n. 10 of my Introduction for bibliographical details]), "Boccaccio on Interpretation: Guido's Escape (*Dec.* VI, 9)," where *Par.* 13.112–42 is lodged against Messer Betto's attempt to judge Guido Cavalcanti.

done so without once directly quoting the text in question,[42] relying instead on his reader to be reminded by several rather vivid, if general, likenesses and parallels to appreciate first the overall appositeness of Dante's Brunetto to his Cepparello, then the antithetic nature of the resemblance. If we conclude by considering Cepparello a "false Brunetto" (and I am aware that the evidence for doing so is not so much conclusive as suggestive), we must also consider that such a delicate art of citation, of summoning up the presence of an earlier text, leaves us wondering at Boccaccio's intent. I suggest that in the *Decameron* the *Commedia* is not only a revered text, one which authorizes Boccaccio's choice of words, characters, and events, but is also a text which is being gingerly scrutinized for its possible failings on two main grounds, its poetic truthfulness and its moral applicability.[43] It is my growing sense that Boccaccio's Dante is seen first of all as a maker of fictions, no matter how

---

42. But for a later instance of Boccaccio's actual reworking of a text in *Inf.* 15 (34–39) see *Corbaccio* 129 (p. 58): "e se la natura del luogo il patisse, io direi in servigio di te, ché stanco ti veggio, che noi a seder ci ponessimo, ma perché qui far non si può, ragioneremo in piede" [and if the nature of the place allowed it, I would say as a courtesy to you, for I can see that you are fatigued, that we should sit down; but since we are not allowed to do that here, we shall speak while standing]. Anthony Cassell's note to the passage, in his English translation (89 n. 61), credits Attilio Levi, *Il "Corbaccio" e la "Divina Commedia"* (Turin: Loescher, 1889), 16, with being the first to suggest the presence of this echo.

43. Such a view is at odds with that of Giorgio Padoan but is not very distant from the opinion of Franco Fido. Here are these two critics responding to the problem of Boccaccio's interpretation of *Inf.* 5.137, which he has subsumed in his subtitle (see my n. 8), as that reveals a larger dimension of his reception of the *Commedia*. Padoan, "Mondo aristocratico e mondo comunale nell'ideologia e nell'arte di Giovanni Boccaccio" [1964], in *Il Boccaccio, le muse, il Parnaso e l'Arno*, 31, writes: "Il Boccaccio non coglie insomma l'intimo ed appassionato messaggio della *Comedìa*, che egli interpreta assai superficialmente, colpito più dalla novità delle storie, dallo stile vigoroso, dalla potenza drammatica che dal contenuto più profondo" [Boccaccio, in the end, does not grasp the inner passionate message of the *Comedy*, a work that he interprets rather superficially, struck more by the novelty of its narratives, the vigor of its style, its dramatic power, than by its profound content]. Fido, "Dante personaggio mancato del *Decameron*," 189, writes that Boccaccio's use of *Prencipe Galeotto* as his subtitle reveals "insieme rispettoso omaggio e voluta deviazione semantica. Un'ammirazione e un'indipendenza di giudizio, in altre parole, che paradossalemnte potrebbero farci riconoscere nell'irriverente autore del *Decameron* un lettore della *Commedia* più acuto e felice del devoto scoliasta delle *Esposizioni*" [at once respectful homage and knowing semantic deviation. An admiration and an independence of judgment, in other words, that paradoxically might have made us recognize in the irreverent author of the *Decameron* a reader of the *Comedy* both more acute and lighthearted than the pious scholiast of the *Esposizioni*]. Fido believes, as do I, that the Boccaccio of the *Decameron* is not a neophyte reader of the *Commedia* and that he is reading Dante's poem simultaneously with and against the grain.

strongly he wishes to be taken as veridical reporter of the news from the otherworld,[44] and second as an incurable optimist in his insistence that his moral vision is applicable in a world populated by scoundrels, from Cepparello to Gualtieri, Griselda's pitiless husband. If such an appreciation is at all correct, Boccaccio's Dante becomes a different figure from the one that he is generally perceived as being, a precursor who is always poetically relevant, yet not eventually to be trusted. On Dante's home ground Boccaccio is usually content to be the dutiful commentator whose disputes with his *auctor* are unintentional, the result of an early humanist's misperceptions of Dante's poetic first principles. On his own turf, however, Boccaccio's gentle attacks on Dante are wholly intentional, deriving from the position of a man of the world who respects but cannot accept the idealistic zeal of the *Commedia*. If this view is correct, it would suggest that Boccaccio's great work is far more bitter than it is generally perceived to be, that it reveals us as we are, interested primarily in our personal *utilità* (the perverse version of Horatian and Augustinian usefulness), our motto present in the Introduction, as though waiting to become a description of Cepparello himself, a man "non curando d'alcuna cosa se non di sé . . ." [a man caring for nothing except for himself . . .] (I.Int.25).[45]

Frate Cipolla in Certaldo: The Friar as Poet (VI.x)

Only two of Dioneo's ten tales are not concerned primarily with sexual license, those that conclude the Sixth and Tenth Days of the *Decameron*. And while my own discussion of I.i and VI.x, as tales which contain hitherto unremarked presences of Dante, is but a result of my recent readings and is put forward without prejudice to eventual more wide-ranging investigations, there is some likelihood that Boccaccio thought of Day Six as

---

44. Is not this the friendly polemic to be found behind every pastiche of the Dantean afterworld found in the *Decameron*? There are many such (e.g., Simone in Hell, Ferondo in Purgatory, Tingoccio in Paradise, etc.).

45. Such a view of the *Decameron* is already available. See T. K. Seung, *Cultural Thematics: The Formation of the Faustian Ethos* (New Haven and London: Yale University Press, 1976), esp. 207–16, "The Sovereign Individual in the *Decameron*." While I have many differences with my brilliant friend, I have not read elsewhere as central an appreciation of the dark formulation of man's egotism and depravity that lies just beneath the smiling surface of the *Decameron*.

being particularly closely connected with Dante's poem and with his own Day One.[46] For, while the ten-day structure of the *Decameron* is of course prior, there are also several indications that Boccaccio thought of Day Six as bringing a large aesthetic unit of his work to a formal, if temporary, conclusion:

1. The title *Decameron,* intrinsically at least, invites us to keep in mind the more usual medieval title, *Hexameron,* used for a treatise on the six days of creation.[47]

2. Days One and Six both are Wednesdays and are thus associated with Mercury *(mercoledì),* the god of eloquent speech and thus, in general, of writers.[48]

3. Days One and Six are linked by being the only two Days devoted primarily to *motti;* for even if Day One is nominally a "free day," starting with Filomena's third *novella* all the *novellatori* tell tales which demonstrate the force of a ready wit put into clever words.[49]

---

46. And for a previous appreciation of the relatedness of these two particular tales (I.i and VI.x) see Luigi Russo, *Letture critiche del "Decameron"* (Bari: Laterza, 1967 [1956]), 51: "Il Boccaccio ammira ser Ciappelletto perché è un artista delle sue imbroglierie, come ammira frate Cipolla che è un altro virtuoso della ciarlataneria apostolica e predicatoria" [Boccaccio admires Ser Ciappelletto because he is an artist in his swindling intrigues, as he admires Cipolla, who is another virtuoso in his apostolic, sermonizing hoodwinkery]; and see Russo's p. 226. See also Giuseppe Mazzotta, "The *Decameron:* The Marginality of Literature," *University of Toronto Quarterly* 42 (1972): 69–75, where these two tales are considered in sequence.

47. See Branca, *Note,* 976 n. 1. See also Mazzotta, "Marginality," 67.

48. Cf., e.g., Boccaccio's own *Esposizioni,* 5.*litt.*19: "Vogliono adunque i poeti sentir per Mercurio, mandato a far venire gli armenti d'Agenore dalla montagna alla marina, alcuna eloquente persona . . ." [Thus the poets like to understand in Mercury, sent to get the herds of Agenor to come from the mountain to the seashore, an eloquent person . . .]. See *Metamorphoses* 2.841–42: Jupiter, masquerading as a bull among the kine, soon seduces Europa as a result of this "eloquence."

49. This fact is made manifest in Fiammetta's formulation at I.v.4, "quanta sia la forza delle belle e pronte risposte" [how great may be the force of pleasing and ready answers]; in Emilia's reference to "un motto" (I.vi.3); in Pampinea's "leggiadri motti" [graceful witty remarks] (I.x.3). But it is also evident throughout I.iii–x. Elissa's proleptic remark (V.Conc.3) to the Sixth Day, "Noi abbiamo già molte volte udito che con be' motti o con risposte pronte o con avvedimenti presti molti hanno già saputo con debito morso rintuzzare gli altrui denti . . ." [We have heard many times that with clever sayings or ready answers or nimble wit many have known how with a well-deserved bite to repel the teeth of another or to fend off danger before it overtakes them . . .], as Branca remarks, also points specifically to Day One.

Thus Day Six seems to have had for Boccaccio the function of rounding out, of completing, an important secondary unit of composition.[50] To put this into a more speculative light for a moment, we might try to imagine how satisfying a composition the *Decameron* might have been had it contained only its first six Days. I think we can sense that, had Boccaccio in fact written only his *Hexameron,* we would not find it an aesthetically disharmonious artifact.[51]

Day Six is also more than usually reminiscent of Dante's *Commedia.* All of its first nine tales take place in Florence or its environs[52] and probably reveal a greater feeling for the city during Dante's time than the tales of any other Day. (Surely the presence of Giotto and Cavalcanti as exemplary makers of *motti* is enough to make us think of Dante's treatments of these two figures in the *Commedia.*) And if we pause to think of Day Six as rounding out a Boccaccian week (Wednesday to Wednesday) of tale-telling, we will probably consider that the action of the *Commedia* also takes precisely a week (Thursday to Thursday).

With these brief and tentative remarks serving as introduction, let us turn our attention to Dioneo's account of Cipolla's successful deception of the populace of Certaldo.[53] The fact that the friar is of the order of St.

50. Janet L. Smarr, "Symmetry and Balance in the *Decameron,*" *Medievalia* 2 (1976): 159–87, has shown convincingly what the actual structure of the work as a whole entails, a division of nine-plus-one that is very likely based on Dante's similar structural arrangements, particularly that of *Paradiso* (nine heavens plus Empyrean). Smarr's discovery of the perfect chiastic structure of Days One through Nine represents, in my opinion, the single most successful treatment of the vexed problem of Boccaccio's structuring of the *Decameron.* [But see also Pamela D. Stewart, "La novella di madonna Oretta e le due parti del *Decameron,*" *Retorica e mimica nel "Decameron" e nella commedia del Cinquecento* (Florence: Olschki, 1986 [1977]), 19–38. I confess that I am now far more convinced by the view, advanced by Stewart, that Days One and Six are aligned as parallel beginnings than by my own argument that Day Six acts as an ending. I nonetheless decided not to withdraw these few pages, despite the temptation a second printing offered.]

51. That Dioneo's tale is, for the first time, not centrally concerned with sexual matters would also tend to support this hypothesis. His final novella, which ends the telling of tales, is similarly without prurient interest.

52. See Franco Fido, "Boccaccio's *Ars Narrandi* in the Sixth Day of the *Decameron,*" in *Italian Literature Roots and Branches: Essays in Honor of Thomas Goddard Bergin,* ed. Giosé Rimanelli and Kenneth John Atchity (New Haven and London: Yale University Press, 1976), 229.

53. See Ciro Trabalza, "L'arte nella novella di frate Cipolla," in *Studi sul Boccaccio* (Città di Castello: Lapi, 1906), 223: "Il narratore della novella è Dioneo (il Boccaccio medesimo, ciò che importa moltissimo, perché il teatro dell'azione è Certaldo) . . ." [The narrator of the *novella* is Dioneo (Boccaccio himself, which is particularly significant because the theater of the action is Certaldo) . . .]. While his positivistic identification of Boccaccio with Dioneo is to be treated circumspectly, I do think that the conjunction of Dioneo's narration and the

Anthony has drawn some commentary attention to Dante's invective against that order in *Paradiso* 29.124–26.[54] But the entire passage is likely to account for details found in Cipolla's sermon and in the responses of his credulous auditors. Beatrice, having explained the angelic hierarchy to Dante (28.98–29.66), turns her attention to those who misrepresent angelic nature to mankind (29.67–96). Such malevolent preachers are described as follows.

> Per apparer ciascun s'ingegna e face
> sue invenzioni; e quelle son trascorse
> da' predicanti e 'l Vangelio si tace.
>
> (94–96)

[Everyone seeks to dazzle in his own inventions, and these are divulged by the preachers—but the Gospels are silent.]

Her words are not without relevance to Cipolla. She continues in a similar vein:

> Non ha Fiorenza tanti Lapi e Bindi
> quante sì fatte favole per anno
> in pergamo si gridan quinci e quindi:
>   sì che le pecorelle, che non sanno,
> tornan del pasco pasciute di vento,
> e non le scusa non veder lo danno.
>
> (103–8)

[Florence has not so many Lapos and Bindos as there are tales like these told from the pulpit all through the year and repeated hither and thither, so that the poor sheep, knowing nothing, come home from the pasture fed on wind; and not knowing their loss excuses them not.]

---

only tale set in Boccaccio's hometown is decidedly important and that Dioneo's stance as narrator and commentator, worldly and enigmatic, exactly parallels Boccaccio's own.

54. Russo, *Letture critiche del "Decameron,"* 243; Fido, "Dante personaggio mancato del *Decameron,"* 187n; Branca, *Note,* 1345–46 n. 10, 1351 n. 11. As for other links between the *Commedia* and VI.x, Branca cites Scherillo's notice of the similarity between Guccio's beard and Cerberus's (*Inf.* 6.16) at VI.x.18; he also suggests reminiscences of *Inf.* 17.16 at VI.x.23 and of *Par.* 15.107 at VI.x.27. Russo (227) compares Cipolla's title as *barone* (VI.x.44) with *Par.* 24.115, 25.17. Bottari, *Lezioni,* vol. 1 (Florence: G. Ricci, 1731), 67, cited *Purg.* 22.49–51 as being germane to the situation of the credulous Certaldesi.

Boccaccio's Certaldo also has its share of Lapos, Bindos, and *favole*. After reminding Dante that Christ did not teach the apostles to preach silly tales *(ciance)* to the world (110), she concludes her anti-fraternal outburst with the following.

> Ora si va con motti e con iscede
> a predicare, e pur che ben si rida,
> gonfia il cappuccio e più non si richiede.
>   Ma tale uccel nel becchetto s'annida,
> che se 'l vulgo il vedesse, vederebbe
> la perdonanza di ch'el si confida:
>   per cui tanta stoltezza in terra crebbe,
> che, sanza prova d'alcun testimonio,
> ad ogne promession si correrebbe.
>   Di questo ingrassa il porco sant'Antonio,
> e altri assai che sono ancor più porci,
> pagando di moneta sanza conio.

                                                      (115–26)

[Now they preach with clever sayings and low puns, and all they require is a good laugh to swell their cowls out. But such bird makes nest in the cowl's tip that, if the people were to see it, they would see what sort of "pardon" they have put their trust in. From it has sprung such foolishness on earth that they will rush to every kind of unproved promise. With this grows fat the swine of St. Anthony, and many another that is still more swinish, paying debts with unstamped coin.]

Beatrice's "digression" (see v. 127: "Ma perché siam digressi assai . . ." [But because we have much digressed . . .]) was surely both to Boccaccio's purpose and on his mind as he developed his portrait of Frate Cipolla. Like Beatrice's prevaricating preachers, he too uses *motti;* and Dante's words probably yield a helpful gloss to Guccio Balena-Imbratta-Porco: is he not a pig fattened by Saint Anthony?

Boccaccio's closeness to Dante's text here is palpable, and if it is not the sort of obvious literary theft one can so easily perceive in Thomas Mann's later appropriation of Cipolla's name for his magician in *Mario und der Zauberer,*[55] where it simply seems impossible to read Mann's story without

---

55. Cf. Percy Matenko, "The Prototype of Cipolla in *Mario und der Zauberer*," *Italica* 31 (1954): 133–35; Hans Wagener, "Mann's Cipolla and Earlier Prototypes of the Magician," *Modern Language Notes* 84 (1969): 800–802; Giuseppe Mazzotta, "Marginality," 73–74.

recognizing the borrowing, it is perhaps still richer in its implications. Frate Cipolla becomes, on the authority of Dante's text, the very emblem of fraternal fraudulence. Had Boccaccio's purpose been merely to continue Dante's values, however, he surely would have made his borrowing more evident. His imitation is a distanced one, visible enough once we have learned to see it, but not at once before our eyes. Clearly, Boccaccio agrees with the moral force of Beatrice's denunciation. Yet he does so, it seems to me, with two disclaimers tugging at him. First, he must have desired to challenge Dante's firm sense of the gulf that separates false rhetorical extravagance from truthful rhetorical expression;[56] second, he is more willing than Dante to explore the pleasures to be found in human behaviors that he admits are immoral. Thus Beatrice's outburst is used as a ground text for the situation of this *novella* but does not completely control its final significance. Instead, and as we have seen in the first *novella* of the *Decameron,* Dante's *Commedia* becomes a text at issue, fervently admired, yet considered over-optimistic in its epistemological and moral assertions. Frate Cipolla, at our first perception of his Dantean provenance, is but a false Antonine, circumscribed by *Paradiso* 29. Yet, once we consider him more closely, does not this antithetic representative of Dante's most dearly held values as truth-teller and moralist become increasingly recognizable as the itinerant lying rhetorician who is a latter-day version of the world's greatest itinerant poet, Dante Alighieri?

Cipolla's perversely lengthy *motto*[57] is devoted to a description of his voyage, along the crusaders' route, to visit the patriarch of Jerusalem (VI.x.37–43).[58] Branca has demonstrated that the place names pronounced during the first stage of his narrative of the voyage (37–39) respond to a series of *loci* in Florence itself, moving from east to west.[59] Do we not think of Dante, who describes a visionary journey to still-more-distant worlds

---

56. For a general sense of Boccaccio's recognition of the necessary untruth of the writer's art see Guido Almansi, *The Writer as Liar* (London and Boston: Routledge & Kegan Paul, 1975), passim: e.g., "The story of Cepperello suggests itself as a model of art's systematic and high-handed deformation of the truth" (29); the *Decameron* is seen in general as ". . . a glorious defence of the prevarications of writing" (ibid.). But see Marcus, *An Allegory of Form,* 23–26, for the sounder view that the Boccaccian writer lies in such ways as to make manifest his deceitfulness to his readers.

57. Boccaccio's jest in expanding a *motto* from a line or two to three pages (VI.x.37–52) has been appreciated by his readers; see, e.g., Manlio Pastore Stocchi, "Dioneo e l'orazione di Fra Cipolla," *Studi sul Boccaccio* 7 (1973): 203.

58. For the relevance of some travel literature to Cipolla's fantastic voyage see ibid., esp. 207–11.

59. *Note,* 1350–51 n. 4.

and who might have tested our credulity less had he been content to describe his (and Boccaccio's) city, a city so present in the preceding tales of Day Six? Cipolla continues on his way, through Truffia and Buffia and finally to "terra di Menzogna," before leaping the sea. Do we not again think of Dante, who so frequently and emphatically swears to us that his journey was a true, not an imaginary, experience? Small wonder that Guccio's wardrobe of shreds and patches includes an item reminiscent of Dante's Geryon. His *farsetto* ". . . con più macchie e di più colori che mai drappi fossero tartareschi o indiani" [. . . with more spots and colors than were ever found on cloth of Tartary or India] (23) almost certainly reflects the coloration of Dante's beast of fraud: "Con più color, sommesse o sovraposte / non fer mai drappi Tartari né Turchi . . ." [More colors, whether in the background or standing up in the fabric, were never found on cloth from Tartary or Turkey . . .] *(Inferno* 17.16–17).[60] Is not the *Commedia* in Boccaccio's genially pugnacious view precisely a "terra di Menzogna"? Is not the relationship between Boccaccio and Dante in VI.x nearly identical to that between the "due giovani astuti molto" (one of whom, Giovanni del Bragoniera happens to share the Christian name of his author) and Frate Cipolla? Boccaccio and the two Certaldesi are witty and playful audiences for marvellous rhetorical performances that they know are literally false, but which they admire for their sheer magical audacity.

With this much as indication of Boccaccio's probable desire to put us in mind of Dante when we consider Frate Cipolla, I would now like to turn to the two key words of this *novella: penna* and *carbone.*[61] (These words occur a total of thirty-two times in Dioneo's tale, thus offering a qualitative judgment some quantitative support.) It is my contention that both are used with a lively awareness of their previous presences in the *Commedia,* where each does important service as a signifier of success or failure in aesthetic enterprise. Let us begin with *penna.*

---

60. Cf. my n. 54. This is the last passage on which Boccaccio's *commento* was to pause. His previous remark on Dante's "giuramento" *(Espos.* 16.82), in which Dante expresses his fear that he won't be believed when he claims that he has seen Geryon, would have us believe Dante to have been concerned lest "color che l'odono si fanno beffe di lui e dicono lui essere grandissimo bugiardo" [those who hear it make fun of him and say that he is a colossal liar]. Is not this exactly the sort of playfulness about Dante's claim for truth-telling that we so frequently encounter in the *Decameron*? [For the most recent discussion of the Dantean connections of this *novella* see Jonathan Usher, "Pieces of Dante among Cipolla's Relics," *Lectura Dantis [virginiana]* 13 (fall 1993): 22–31.]

61. As is clear from the *argomento* alone, where they are seen as significant and related objects. (The text is reproduced below, just after n.72.)

Penna occurs in twenty-five *loci* in the *Commedia;* it appears twenty-eight times in the *Decameron.* In both works its most usual meaning is "feather," the *penne* found on wing of bird or of angel. In the *Commedia,* however, the word five times signifies "pen," the tool of writer or painter; in Boccaccio it has such meaning six times.[62] This meaning of the word is introduced to the *Commedia* in the extended simile that presents a peasant being at first discouraged by the hoarfrost *(brina)* that "copies" the snow: "ma poco dura a la sua penna tempra" [but his pen's sharp edge lasts but a little while] (*Inferno* 24.6). This remarkable image of nature imitating nature yields to a more usual sense for the word *penna* in *Inferno* 25.144. Dante, describing the super-Ovidian transformations of the thieves, begs our indulgence: "e qui mi scusi / la novità se fior la penna abborra" [and here let my excuse be the novelty if my pen makes a botch of things]. The word returns in the celebrated passage in which Dante's poetic superiority is acceded to by Bonagiunta Orbicciani: "Io veggio ben come le vostre penne / di retro al dittator sen vanno strette, / che de le nostre certo non avvenne" [I see clearly that your pens followed the speaker's words closely; such was not the case with ours (*Purgatorio* 24.58–60)]. Without pausing on the complex problems raised by this passage, we may simply note that the word has the same meaning here as in *Inferno* 25, the authorial pen, made from a bird's feather, a natural object become the very sign of poetic making. Yet is it not Dante's claim that *his* pen is capable of faithful and truthful imitation? Justinian, retelling the history of Rome in terms of the flight of the imperial eagle, claims that its development under Julius Caesar was such "che nol seguiteria lingua né penna" [that neither tongue nor pen might follow it] (*Paradiso* 6.63). At *Paradiso* 24.25 the word is employed with this signification a final time: "Però salta la penna e non lo scrivo" [wherefore my pen skips and I do not write this].[63] Dante's use of

---

62. *Inf.* 24.6, 25.144; *Purg.* 24.58; *Par.* 6.63, 24.25; *Dec.* VI.v.5, VII.viii.46, VIII.vii.99 (twice), *Conc. Aut.* 1 and 6. In addition, Dante three times refers to the *penne* necessary for his heavenward "flight" in such a way as to remind us of the pun available in the word; his *penne* are metaphors for the *penne* with which he inscribes his vision (*Purg.* 27.123; *Par.* 25.49, 33.139).

63. It is perhaps worth speculating on the fact that *penna,* with this significance, enters the poem in the twenty-fourth canto of *Inf.* and departs after the twenty-fourth canto of *Par.* It is used once in *Purg.,* again in the twenty-fourth canto. Kevin Brownlee has identified two similar programs of repetition in the *Commedia,* both based in Dante's reading of Ovid: Dante refers to Narcissus in the thirtieth canto of each *cantica;* see his "Dante and Narcissus," *Dante Studies* 96 (1978): 205–6. (R. Allen Shoaf, "Dante's *Commedia* and Chaucer's Theory of Mediation," to appear in *New Perspectives in Chaucer Criticism,* ed. Donald M. Rose

penna, then, with the sense of recording instrument of reality, is obviously of some importance in the *Commedia.* Boccaccio's deployment of the word is no less striking and, as we shall see, cognizant of Dante's. It first appears in the description of Frate Alberto, interestingly enough a self-disguiser who assumes the role of the angel Gabriel, punished as "uom salvatico" [a wild man], covered with honey and "empiuto di sopra di penna matta" [plastered over with tiny feathers] (IV.ii.52). Not only does the punishment fit the crime, but the criminal looks forward to the similarly deceitful Friar Cipolla, who also seeks to identify himself with Gabriel. At V.ix.37 the "penne, piedi, e becco" [feathers, feet, and beak] of Federigo's falcon become the sad and tangible sign of the poor man's love for Giovanna. The third use of the word in the *Decameron* occurs at VI.v.5, when we are introduced to Giotto.

> E l'altro, il cui nome fu Giotto, ebbe uno ingegno di tanta eccellenzia, che niuna cosa dà la natura, madre di tutte le cose e operatrice col continuo girar de' cieli, che egli con lo *stile* e con la penna o col *pennello* non dipignesse sì simile a quella, che non simile, anzi più tosto dessa paresse, in tanto che molte volte nelle cose da lui fatte si truova che il visivo senso degli uomini vi prese errore, quello credendo esser vero che era dipinto. (italics added)

> [And the other, who was called Giotto, was so great a genius that there was nothing in nature, mother and instigator of all things with her continual wheeling of the heavens, that he with stylus and pen or brush could not paint so like its original that it seemed not like it but the thing itself, in evidence of which it befell many times that eyes of men were fooled by things he had created, taking for real what was only a painting.]

The passage draws on Dante's exclamation of his wonder at God's art in the figurations on the pavement at *Purgatorio* 12.64–69.

[Norman, Okla.: Pilgrim Books, 1981], 86–88, will also make this point [after n. 10—Professor Shoaf has shared his galley proofs with me], if without reference to Brownlee's earlier work). Brownlee has also pointed out, in a paper delivered at the Sixteenth International Congress on Medieval Studies at Kalamazoo, Michigan, on 8 May 1981, that there is a program of reference to Phaeton in the seventeenth canto of each *cantica.* [Now see his "Phaeton's Fall and Dante's Ascent," *Dante Studies* 102 (1984): 135–44.]

Qual di *pennel* fu maestro[64] o di *stile*[65]
che ritraesse l'ombre e ' tratti ch'ivi
mirar fariemo uno ingegno sottile?
    Morti li morti e i vivi parean vivi:
non vide mei di me chi vide il vero,
quant'io calcai, fin che chinato givi.
    (italics added)

[What master of brush or stylus could have drawn the figures or the outlines there that would have astounded a subtle mind? Dead the dead and
living seemed the living; he, who sees the truth, sees no better than I that
which I trod upon as I walked along, head bent.]

Perhaps no two passages in the *Decameron* and the *Commedia* more
intensely present our authors' enthusiasm for the mimetic nature of art.
Yet Dante insists on the inadequacy of even the greatest human sculptor or
painter when his art is confronted with God's mimetic magnificence; Boccaccio, in evident polemic with his *maestro e autore,* insists on Giotto's
supremacy as perfect mimic of nature. This is the sole mimetic task that
Boccaccio would seem to be willing to admit to a human aesthetic capacity. Dante's passage itself reflects his judgments of painters pronounced
some hundred lines earlier: Oderisi, having praised Franco Bolognese, goes
on to report that Giotto has now surpassed Cimabue (11.94–96).[66] Thus
Dante's encomium of God's art in *Purgatorio* 12 is implicitly a criticism of
Giotto's merely human art. Boccaccio, imitating Dante's discussion of imitation and undoubtedly understanding the limited nature of Dante's praise
of Giotto, now turns the argument back on its author.

Of Boccaccio's twenty-seven uses of *penna* in the *Decameron,* nineteen
occur in VI.x. There it always has the meaning "feather," always referring
to the parrot's feather (VI.x.46) that Cipolla claims is a feather from a wing

---

64. Giotto is referred to as *maestro* by Panfilo at VI.v.6; the latter goes on to recount that
in life Giotto modestly refused this title.

65. For this *stile,* or sculptor's stylus, Branca cites *Purg.* 12.64 (*Note,* 1333 n. 11) along with
Petrarca *Canzoniere* 78.5. I do not find in him or elsewhere a larger sense of the dependency
of Boccaccio's text on Dante's here.

66. [I no longer would say this as I have phrased it here, for Giotto has surpassed
Cimabue only in the favor of the populace. That is a different thing and does not mean that
Dante necessarily considered Giotto a better painter than Cimabue—that is not the issue
here. See Hollander, "Dante's Self-Laureation: *Purgatorio* XI, 92," *Rassegna Europea di Letteratura Italiana* 3 (1994): 41–42.]

of the angel Gabriel. We shall return to this *penna* shortly, after completing our inventory of *penne* in the *Decameron*. The next one we find is at VII.viii.46, where the deceived husband Arriguccio is rebuked by his scathing mother-in-law; her description of him includes the following details of his appearance: "con le calze a campanile e colla penna in culo" [with cut-off stockings and a pen up his ass]. Branca's note here refers us to the practice of a merchant or a notary who carries his *pennaiuolo* in his back pocket.[67] Arriguccio's mercantile pen is a scabrously sorry object to imagine, the antithesis of Giotto's "stile . . . penna o . . . pennello," the petty bourgeois's pitiful (and probably falsifying) instrument for carrying out his *mercatura*. The word occurs four more times in the *Decameron*. Its next two uses are in the mouth of the vindictive scholar, boasting to the roasted widow of the power of his satiric *penna* (VIII.vii.99) in ways that look forward to the *Corbaccio*.[68] The *Conclusione dell'Autore* finally places the *penna* in the hand to which it most truly belongs: ". . . da dare alla penna e alla man faticata riposo" [. . . to give my pen and my wearied hand their rest] (1). His last use of the word asks that we grant his pen an authority equal to that which we allow the painter's brush: "Sanza che alla mia penna non dee essere meno d'auttorità conceduta che sia al pennello del dipintore . . ." [Unless less authority is to be granted to my pen than to the painter's brush . . .] (6). We are reminded again of Giotto and of Boccaccio's sense of identity with him; and we have seen how much authority we should grant Giotto's mimetic capacity in the passage quoted earlier (VI.v.5).

Thus Boccaccio's varying uses of *penna* as the instrument of the artist would seem to establish a hierarchy. One's pen may resemble Giotto's brush (and Boccaccio's is obviously meant to be perceived as doing exactly that), or it may be the poor instrument of an inept merchant (VII.viii), even the angry and wounding engine of a spurned scholar/lover (VIII.vii). In Boccaccio's hand it is the tool of the artist who has the power, like Giotto, to set before us the world as it is; this implicit claim has been honored by nearly all Boccaccio's enthusiasts.

Let us return to Cipolla. The parrot's feather that the friar would hold up as a relic is not referred to in terms that at first remind us of the six *loci* in the *Decameron* in which *penna* means "pen." Yet the fact that the actual object is the feather of a parrot is itself instructive, for that creature is the

---

67. *Note,* 1390 n. 2.

68. Cf. Branca's *Note,* 1438 n. 9, and see Almansi, *The Writer as Liar,* 97–98, for several citations of *Inf.* in this tale.

most talkative and mimetic of fowl.[69] Cipolla is himself a sort of *pappagallo,* whose "tail feather" is redeployed by his fraudulent imagination on Gabriel's wings.[70] This feather is metamorphosed by Cipolla's "pen," his artist's capacity for colossal untruth. As I have suggested earlier, Cipolla is presented as a sort of Dante run amok, a poetic wild man, if one, unlike Dante, who is willing to admit to his two Certaldese admirers that his "poetry" is *fabula* and not *historia.* It is the latter only for the groundlings at 3:00 P.M. on one 8 August[71] in the early fourteenth century at Certaldo.

To conclude, we return to the second key word of *Decameron* VI.x: *carbone.* It appears fifteen times in the work, fourteen of these here.[72] Boccaccio's *argomento* to VI.x runs as follows: "Frate Cipolla promette a certi contadini di mostrar loro la penna dell'agnolo Gabriello; in luogo della quale trovando carboni, quegli dice esser di quegli che arrostirono san Lorenzo" [Brother Cipolla promises certain peasants that he will show them a feather of the angel Gabriel; finding coals in its place, he says that these were among those that roasted Saint Lawrence]. The struggle faced by Cipolla is to turn the *carboni,* left him in place of the parrot's feather by his inimical friends, into spiritualized relics for the multitude. If a parrot's feather is, by comparison, fairly easy to pass off to the gullible as angelic, to make *carboni* seem sacral objects involves greater sleight of mind.

We have already seen how central to Dioneo's tale is Beatrice's assault on false preachers in *Paradiso* 29. Another of Dante's texts also beckons. *Purgatorio* 2.25–51 chronicles the advent of the Mercury-like angel who

---

69. For Dante's thoughts about the limited mimetic capacities of birds see *Conv.* 3.7.9 and *DVE* I.2.7. Francesco Mazzoni, "Per il 'tópos' della gazza e del pappagallo," in *Contributi di filologia dantesca* (Florence: Sansoni, 1966), 202–4, shows that Dante's remarks depend on Uguccione of Pisa.

70. See Marcus, *An Allegory of Form,* 70, who also sees Cipolla as a parrot. Does his parrot's feather anticipate the "penna in culo" leant Arriguccio by his angry and imaginative mother-in-law? Boccaccio also thought of Dante as being a bird and as having *penne.* See *Trattatello* I.221–25, where he discusses the meaning of Dante's mother's dream of her as-yet-unborn *Wunderkind,* seen as a peacock. This bird has "penna angelica" (221, 223); and by these *penne* Boccaccio understands "la bellezza della peregrina istoria, che nella superficie della lettera della *Comedia* suona . . . distinta in cento canti, sì come alcuni vogliono il paone avere nella coda cento occhi" [the beauty of the strange tale that is heard in the superficial literal sense of the *Comedy,* divided into one hundred cantos, just as some insist that the peacock has one hundred eyes in its tail] (224). The second redaction (*Trattatello* 2.153 [B]) firms the analogy: "E i cento occhi, chi non intenderà i cento canti [della *Comedia*] . . . ?" [And by the one hundred eyes, who will fail to understand Dante's one hundred cantos . . . ?]. If each canto of the *Commedia* is a peacock's feather, *Decameron* VI.x is the feather of a parrot.

71. Branca, *Note,* 1353–54 n. 10.

72. Its previous use, in IV.vi.16, "una veltra nera come carbone," is seen by Branca (*Note,* 1238 n. 5) as remembering *Inf.* 13.125, 33.31.

guides the triumphant crusading souls of the saved to the shore of Purgatory. Virgil orders Dante to kneel and pray in reverence before his "etterne penne, / che non si mutan come mortal pelo" [eternal wings, which do not moult like mortal plumes] (35–36). This "uccel divino" (38) presides over a boatload of singing pilgrims. He leaves them after he has made the sign of the cross over them (49)—with his *penne,* we may reflect. Cipolla has described his crusade/pilgrimage to the Holy Land, where he was given his angel's feather. After he sings a hymn of praise, "una laude di san Lorenzo" (VI.10.53), he too makes the sign of the cross on his auditors[73] (a large one, requiring arduous laundering, we must reflect). Dante's arrival in Purgatory, a scene reflective of medieval pilgrimage to the Holy Land,[74] probably stands behind Cipolla's false "pilgrimage" and his behavior as fraudulent angelic intercessor.

The *carboni* that he employs to sign these "crusaders" of Certaldo are also, it seems to me, of Dantean provenance. As he reveals them to the multitude, Cipolla refers to them as "carboni spenti" (51). The phrase, as far as I have been able to determine, has occurred only once before in Italian literature,[75] at *Inferno* 20.100–102: ". . . son sì certi e prendon sì mia fede, / che li altri mi sarien carboni spenti" [. . . are so sure and so persuade me that all others would be burnt-out coals to me]. Dante, seduced by Virgil's own denunciation of a passage in the *Aeneid* (10.198–203), which would make Manto the mother of Mantuans, agrees to "desacralize" those verses of the *Aeneid. Carboni spenti,* in this formulation, become the very emblem of dead poetic activity.[76] For a text to be a "carbone spento" is for it to contain no truth. Has not Cipolla given the final twist possible to Dante's phrase and its meaning? He has taken worthless objects, *carboni spenti,* and revivified them, made them, as it were, "penne." They even become,

---

73. Will each thus appear "beato per iscripto" (*Purg.* 2.44) as a result? But see Petrocchi, *Introduzione* to *La Commedia secondo l'antica vulgata,* 189–90, for the possibility of an alternate reading (which he adopts), "beato pur descripto."

74. See John G. Demaray, *The Invention of Dante's "Comedy"* (New Haven and London: Yale University Press, 1974), passim.

75. The entry *carbone* in Salvatore Battaglia, ed., *Grande Dizionario della lingua italiana,* vol. 2 (Turin: UTET, 1962), 744c–746c, shows the phrase appearing elsewhere only in *Cantari cavallereschi* 97: "tre carboni spenti." Consultation of fourteen volumes (excluding, of course, those dedicated to the works of Dante) of Mario L. Alinei, ed., *Spogli elettronici dell'Italiano delle origini e del Duecento* (The Hague: Mouton, 1968), turns up no incidence of the phrase.

76. See my treatment of the significance of these lines and of their resonance in the two uses of *carbone* in *Par.,* "The Tragedy of Divination in *Inferno* XX," *Studies in Dante* (Ravenna: Longo, 1980), 196–98.

and specifically, instruments for writing, indeed for writing the most sacrosanct of "words," the cross. Such is the nature of Boccaccio's supremely artful little joke at the expense of his beloved Dante.

If these reflections upon Boccaccio's reading of Dante have merit—and I confess that I myself am not so much convinced by evidence as intrigued by possibility—then there is a good deal more to be studied in the relationships between two of the greatest texts that mankind has received from its masters.

Decameron: The Sun Rises in Dante

(1983–84)

[As I have argued in the two preceding studies,] the apparently antithetic nature of the *Commedia* and the *Decameron* is the probable cause for the lack of concerted attention to Boccaccio's constant and significant borrowings from Dante.[1] The complexity of the problem is perhaps also to some degree responsible for the nearly total lack of careful consideration of the nature and extent of the references to and citations of Dante in the *Decameron.* And while both the broad contours of the obvious resemblances between the two works and some of the minute philological particulars—an "echo" here and there—have received some notice, it is fair to say that the systematic study of the relationship between two of the greatest works of Italian literature, one written by the champion and commen-

---

Since most of the Italian texts cited in this study are put to the service of establishing linguistic connections, I have not translated them. However, the reader will find other Italian texts Englished.

1. But for perception of the diverse cultural preparation of the Boccaccio of the *Decameron*—and especially his renewed close attention to the texts of Dante—see Giuseppe Billanovich, "Dalla *Commedia* e dall'*Amorosa Visione* ai *Trionfi,*" *Giornale storico della letteratura italiana* 123 (1946): 14: "La revisione accalorata dell'*Amorosa Visione* subito dopo l'aprile del 1351, e quindi la composizione del *Trattatello in laude di Dante* e il riordino del corpo poetico dantesco a cui egli attende allora laboriosamente per un altro stimolo immediato dei colloqui e della corrispondenza col Petrarca, si accompagnarono e si accavallarono, incredibilmente per noi, intellettuali mediocri e perciò frigidi e lenti, colla esecuzione a pennellate larghe e fiammeggianti del *Decameron*" [His feverish revision of the *Amorosa Visione* just after April 1351, and thus just after the composition of the *Trattatello,* and his reordering of the Dantean poetic corpus, to which he studiously turned his attention, stimulated by the immediacy of his conversations and correspondence with Petrarch, accompanied and were teamed with, amazing to us, intellectuals of middling worth and, as a result, cold and slow, the composition, in broad, fiery strokes, of the *Decameron*].

tator of the other, remains to be undertaken.[2] In what follows I shall put forward a series of texts which seem to me to reveal a systematic, if at times fairly well concealed, program of references to the *Commedia* in the *Decameron*. My aim here is not to solve a problem but to discover whether or not it exists. Nor is it my intention even to suggest the possible global nature of the phenomenon which I examine. Thus the treatment offered is both tentative and partial. If, in the judgment of competent authorities, there is basis in fact for what I believe I have observed, then there is a great deal of new thinking to be done. But before considering its possible consequences, one does better to analyze the issue itself.

It is currently my opinion that, after the first, each Day of the *Decameron* begins with, partially obscured from our view in its formulaic description of the rising sun, a nonetheless precise reference to a passage in the *Commedia* (see fig. 1). If I am correct, the first sentence of the Introduction to each *giornata* that begins with the sunrise, with a single exception (VIII), involves a deliberate recollection of Dante, one that is located in the most mechanical—some might say banal—passages of Boccaccio's prose, his opening descriptions of dawn. First, however, we should examine the "odd Day out," the First Day—the only one not to begin with such a formulaic gesture.[3] However, if it breaks from the pattern by not opening with an astronomical setting, it is not without its Dantean moment.

---

2. [For discussion and bibliography see the opening pages of the preceding study.] Perhaps the single most persuasive treatment yet offered of the closeness of a Boccaccian text to its Dantean sources is Carlo Delcorno's "Note sui dantismi nell'*Elegia di madonna Fiammetta*," *Studi sul Boccaccio* 11 (1979): 251–94. [And now see his edition of the *Elegia* in *Tutte le opere di Giovanni Boccaccio*, ed. Vittore Branca (Milan: Mondadori, 1994).] (As this article went to press I received from its author a welcome and major development in the study of the *Decameron*'s debt to the works of Dante: Attilio Bettinzoli, "Per una definizione delle presenze dantesche nel *Decameron*," part 1, "I registri 'ideologici,' lirici, drammatici," *Studi sul Boccaccio* 13 (1982): 267–326. A number of the juxtapositions cited here will also be found in Bettinzoli's discussion [see esp. Bettinzoli's pp. 269–71, 278–80, 282, 289].)

3. The "action" of the *Decameron* begins, *in medias res*, "un martedì mattina" (I.Int.49) and thus without a sunrise. Daybreak of the Wednesday on which the *brigata* removes to the country thus occurs well into the Introduction (89) and is described with less detail than will be the case when daybreak is presented as the frontispiece of each Day: " . . . la seguente mattina, cioè il mercoledì, in su lo schiarir del giorno, le donne . . . si misero in via." Sunrise of the last Day, that of the return to Florence, is similarly understated (X.Conc.16): "E come il nuovo giorno apparve, levati, verso Firenze si ritornarono." These are atypical in that they do not occur as the first detail of a *giornata* and in that they are without rhetorical flourish. It is still possible that they reflect passages in the *Commedia*. For the first see *Inf.* 26.26, where the sun is referred to as "colui che 'l mondo schiara"; for the second, *Purg.* 7.69 and 28.3: "il novo giorno." Yet the absence of rhetorical signals that the description seeks our close attention makes it unlikely that any reference to Dante is intended (even if Boccaccio had already cited the passage in *Purg.* 28 at II.Int.2—see ensuing discussion).

Decameron I.Int.2–3:

Quantunque volte, graziosissime donne, meco pensando riguardo quanto voi naturalmente tutte siete pietose, tante conosco che la presente opera al vostro iudicio avrà grave e noioso principio, sì come è la dolorosa ricordazione della pestifera mortalità trapassata, universalmente a ciascuno che quella vide o altramenti conobbe dannosa, *la quale essa porta nella sua fronte* [*Conc. Aut.*19]. Ma non voglio per ciò che questo di *più avanti leggere* vi spaventi, quasi sempre tra' sospiri e tralle lagrime leggendo dobbiate trapassare.

Inferno 5:

. . . tante *volte | quantunque* gradi . . .

(11–12) [Branca]

quel giorno *più* non vi *leggemmo avante.*

(138)

See also:

Sette P ne *la fronte* mi descrisse
col punton de la spada . . .

(*Purg.* 9.112–13)[4]

I have previously discussed the subtitle of the *Decameron, Prencipe Galeotto,* as constituting the first citation (of many) of Dante in Boccac-

---

4. All citations of the *Decameron* derive from *Tutte le opere di Giovanni Boccaccio,* vol. 4, *Decameron,* ed. Vittore Branca (Milan: Mondadori, 1976); of the *Commedia* from *La Commedia secondo l'antica vulgata,* ed. Giorgio Petrocchi, Edizione Nazionale under the auspices of the Società Dantesca Italiana (Milan: Mondadori, 1966–67). Naturally I have made use of concordances to the two works: *Concordanze del "Decameron,"* ed. Alfredo Barbina, under the direction of Umberto Bosco (Florence: C/E Giunti & G. Barbèra, 1969); *A Concordance to the "Divine Comedy" of Dante Alighieri,* ed. Ernest Hatch Wilkins and Thomas Goddard Bergin for the Dante Society of America, associate editor Anthony J. De Vito (Cambridge, Mass.: Harvard University Press, 1965). Here and in all following quotations my procedure has been to put the words of Boccaccio that seem to me to be derived directly from those of Dante in italics; when a word or phrase, reflecting Dante's in the pertinent passage, is also a *hapax* in the *Decameron* (or if it occurs in a later passage that also involves an astronomical indication, one which looks back to the phrase in question), I have put it not in italics but in boldface; Branca's previous notice of a Dantean source is signalled by the presence of his name in brackets.

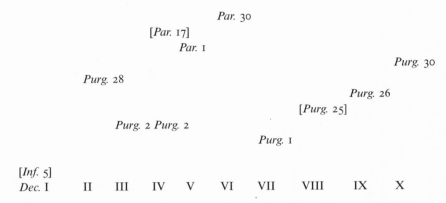

Fig. 1. Sources in the *Commedia* for Boccaccio's "beginnings." Passages not related to descriptions of sunrise are in brackets.

cio's book;[5] I would like here simply to register the opinion that Boccaccio's *proemium* is a perfectly balanced rhetorical exercise in the first half of which the author assumes the role of Dante (the references are mainly to *Inferno* 1 and 2), while in the second he plays the part of Ovid.[6] Thus, in my view, every opening gesture made by Boccaccio in the *Decameron (incipit, proemio, introduzione)* has its Dantean analogue. Further, and not surprisingly, given the amorous nature of so many of the tales, the canto which he revisits on the first and third of these occasions is *Inferno* 5.

The *Decameron* begins as a double hell on earth, first that of a lovesick, indeed nearly moribund, narrator in the *Proemio,* then that of a plague-stricken city in the *Introduzione.* Boccaccio's witty reminiscence of Francesca's last words[7] reminds us of the relation he has developed

---

5. See *Boccaccio's Two Venuses,* 102–6, and pp. 4, 23–24, and 38 in the present book.

6. [Now see "The Proem of the *Decameron*" in the present book.] I would offer this much argumentation here. The *Proemio* is divided into two parts of seven periods each (2–8, 9–15). In the first the narrator speaks of his own newly won freedom from subjection to love; in the second he offers his compassion and aid to ladies who are still under love's sway. In the first part there are several references to the *Commedia;* in the second, to the *Remedia amoris.* Perhaps the key word of the *Proemio* is *noia* (it appears half a dozen times), associated primarily with love, but also—if indirectly—with plague (a role that it will take on in evident ways in the *Introduzione*). The two parts are joined in their common concern for locating a problem—or a painful symptom, and then offering a solution—or medicament. Boccaccio's pose here, as it will be in the subsequent *Corbaccio,* is that of a post-Ovidian, indeed of a Boethian, purveyor of remedy. [For my later views of the *Corbaccio* see *Boccaccio's Last Fiction: Il "Corbaccio"* (Philadelphia: University of Pennsylvania Press, 1988).]

7. See previous brief notice in "Imitative Distance," n. 8.

between sexual desire and plague; the victims of either disease are worthy of our compassion.[8] The "ladies" whom he addresses, he hopes, *will* read further. His book, we are led to surmise, is thus being presented as antidote to lust and plague. Whatever its eventual resolution of this aim (and that is a matter of some complexity and will not be broached here), it is important that we become aware of the parallel treatment given two apparently rather different phenomena, love and plague. The opening sentences of the Introduction to Day One thus remind the alert reader that Boccaccio wants his work to be read with the *Commedia* in mind, and even close at hand.[9]

With these remarks serving as introduction, I now turn to the opening descriptions of sunrise which begin each Day of the *Decameron.*

Decameron II.Int.2:

Già per tutto aveva il sol recato con la sua luce **il nuovo giorno** [X.Conc.16] e *gli uccelli* su per *li verdi rami cantando* piacevoli *versi* ne davano agli orecchi testimonianza, quando parimente tutte le donne e i tre giovani levatisi ne' giardini se ne entrarono, e le rugiadose erbe *con lento passo* scalpitando d'una parte in un'altra, belle ghirlande faccendosi, per lungo spazio diportando s'andarono.

Purgatorio 28:

. . . *il novo giorno* . . .

(3)

---

8. For a helpful treatment of the presence in the *Decameron* of the tradition that considers love a disease see Massimo Ciavolella, "La tradizione dell'*aegritudo amoris* nel *Decameron,*" *Giornale storico della letteratura italiana* 167 (1970): 496–517.

9. The next sentence is generically Dantean in its inspiration: "Questo orrido cominciamento vi fia non altramenti che a' camminanti una montagna aspra e erta [a *hapax*—see *Inf.* 1.31], presso alla quale un bellissimo piano e dilettevole sia reposto, il quale tanto più viene lor piacevole quanto maggiore è stata del salire e dello smontare la gravezza" (I.Int.4). Branca's note to this passage is entirely to the point: "Non si può non pensare alla selva 'aspra' e al 'dilettoso' monte del canto introduttivo della *Divina Commedia:* tanto più che l'azione si svolge per ambedue gli scrittori nel mezzo del cammino della vita, a 35 anni. . . ." [One cannot help but think of the 'aspra' forest and the 'dilettoso' mountain of the introductory canto of the *Divine Comedy,* all the more so because the narrated action takes place, for both these writers, 'nel mezzo del cammin' of life, when they were thirty-five years old]. See also the similar discussion of Aldo S. Bernardo, "The Plague as Key to Meaning in Boccaccio's *Decameron,*" in *The Black Death: The Impact of the Fourteenth-Century Plague,* ed. D. Williman (Binghamton, N.Y.: Medieval and Renaissance Texts and Studies, 1982), 39–64.

. . . li augelletti . . .

(14)

ma con piena letizia l'ore prime,
cantando, ricevieno intra le foglie,
che tenevan bordone a le sue *rime,*
    tal qual di ramo in ramo si raccoglie
per la pineta in su 'l lito di Chiassi, . . .

(16–20)

. . . i lenti passi . . .

(22)

See also:

. . . i verdi rami . . .

(29.35)

Perhaps remembering his pledge at I.Int.4, which mirrors the *Comme-dia*'s movement from "orrido cominciamento" to "bellissimo piano e dilet-tevole," Boccaccio's first auroral beginning seems certainly to have Dante's Earthly Paradise in view.[10] It is difficult to imagine that the context and the very words of the first moments of Dante's Edenic scene are not being closely reflected in this text.

Decameron III.Int.2:

L'aurora già di *vermiglia* cominciava, appressandosi il sole, a *divenir* **rancia,** quando la domenica, la reina levata e fatta tutta la sua com-pagnia levare e avendo già il siniscalco gran pezzo davanti mandato al luogo dove andar doveano assai delle cose oportune e chi quivi preparasse quello che bisognava, veggendo già la reina in cammino, prestamente fatta ogni altra cosa caricare, quasi quindi il campo lev-ato, con la salmeria n'andò e con la famiglia rimasa appresso delle donne e de' signori.

---

10. For "cantando piacevoli versi" Branca cites *Inf.* 16.19–20, "Ricominciar . . . l'antico verso," and Petrarch *Rime* 239.3, "E li augelletti incominciar lor versi." The "belle ghirlande" which members of the *brigata* make for themselves (near the end of this sentence) probably reflect Lia's similar behavior at *Purg.* 27.102: "a farmi una ghirlanda."

Purgatorio 2.7–9:

> sì che le bianche e le *vermiglie* guance,
> là dov' i' era, de la bella *Aurora*
> per troppa etate divenivan *rance.*

[Branca]

Bernardino Daniello was the first of Dante's commentators (there have been several after him) to look up from Dante's *rance* and think of this passage in Boccaccio.[11] I think there can be no doubt that his text remembers Dante closely here. Boccaccio's Day, like Dante's, is Sunday—a small detail that might have further pleased him. And while *salmeria* here means "baggage" (see Branca's note), we may reflect that the opening stanzas of *Purgatorio* 2 are filled by the sound of another kind of "salmeria," the singing of the 113th Psalm. If Boccaccio was in fact conscious of the context of the borrowing, the resultant pun would be typical of his deflating procedures in his more quizzical visits to Dante's texts.[12]

Decameron IV.Int.2–3:

> Carissime donne, sì per le parole de' savi uomini udite e sì per le cose da me molte volte e vedute e lette, estimava io che lo 'mpetuoso *vento* e ardente della 'nvidia non dovesse *percuotere* se non l'*alte* torri o *le più* levate **cime** degli alberi: ma io mi truovo della mia estimazione ingannato. Per ciò che, fuggendo io e sempre essendomi di fuggire ingegnato il fiero impeto di questo rabbioso spirito, non solamente pe' piani ma ancora per le profondissime valli mi sono ingegnato d'andare; il che assai manifesto può apparire a chi le presenti novellette riguarda, le quali non solamente in fiorentin volgare e in prosa scritte per me sono e senza titolo, ma ancora *in istilo umilissimo e rimesso* quanto il più si possono.

---

11. In this, and in many another particular, Daniello, it is now clear, is repeating the opinions of his teacher, Trifon Gabriele. See *Annotationi nel Dante fatte con M. Trifon Gabriele in Bassano,* ed. Lino Pertile (Bologna: Commissione per i testi della lingua, 1993), 120.

12. While my purpose here is to discuss only a very limited number of Boccaccian texts, his "beginnings," as it were, I would merely point out in passing that the Introduction to Day Three is particularly reminiscent of Dante. E.g., in III.Int.8–9, the phrase *nel mezzo* occurs three times and probably reflects the opening verse of the *Commedia:* in 8, *Purg.* 7.79–80 [Branca]; in 9, *Purg.* 10.30–32; in 15, *Inf.* 5.131–32.

Paradiso 17.133–34:

> Questo tuo grido farà come vento,
> che *le più alte cime* più *percuote;*

[Branca]

Epistola a Cangrande 30, 31:

> Similiter differunt in modo loquendi: elate et sublime tragedia; come-
> dia vero remisse et humiliter . . . ad modum loquendi, *remissus est*
> *modus et humilis,* quia locutio vulgaris in qua et muliercule comuni-
> cant. [Branca]

The beginning of Day Four is clearly Dantean,[13] thus maintaining the
pattern which we have come to expect. Yet this authorial interruption does
not yield the customary auroral description, which is delayed until Boccaccio stops defending himself; it finally occurs as the penultimate sentence
of the Introduction.

Decameron IV.Int.44:

> **Cacciata** aveva *il sole* del *cielo* già ogni stella e dalla terra l'umida
> ombra della notte, quando Filostrato levatosi tutta la sua brigata fece
> levare. . . .

Purgatorio 2.55–57:

> Da tutte parti saettava il giorno
> *lo sol,* ch'avea con le saette conte
> di mezzo 'l *ciel cacciato* Capricorno.

We remain in *Purgatorio* 2, the locus of the preceding Day's description of
the sunrise. Needless to say, "cacciare" is not, as its boldface letters would
indicate, in fact a *hapax* in the *Decameron* (the word occurs some sixty-
three times). However, it is—as is its probable source in the *Commedia*—

---

13. [For my earlier comments on Boccaccio's reshapings of these two centrally important
statements of Dante's *ars poetica* see "Imitative Distance," at n. 12.] Commenting on a draft
of this article in July 1983, Professor Margherita Frankel suggested that *Purg.* 5.13–15 may
have been even more in Boccaccio's mind here than *Par.* 17.133–34.

used only once in the work to refer to the sun's effect on the dwindling light of the stars at dawn, that is, in an astronomical context. The image, which has the sun "chasing" stars from the sky, occurring once in each work, is probably striking enough to make Boccaccio's reliance on Dante's text here a near certainty, at least in a work that has so much evident concourse with its precursor.

Decameron V.Int.2:

> Era già l'oriente tutto *bianco* e li *surgenti* raggi per tutto il nostro **emisperio avevan fatto** chiaro, *quando Fiammetta* da' dolci canti degli uccelli, li quali la prima ora del giorno su per gli albuscelli tutti lieti cantavano, incitata sù si levò e tutte le altre e i tre giovani fece chiamare;

Paradiso 1.37–38; 43–46:

> *Surge* ai mortali per diverse foci
> la lucerna del mondo; . . .

> *Fatto avea* di là mane e di qua sera
> tal foce, e quasi tutto era là *bianco*
> quello *emisperio,* e l'altra parte nera,
> *quando Beatrice.* . . .

Entering *Paradiso* may have seemed to Boccaccio a fitting moment as analogue to the beginning of the happiest Day of the *Decameron.* The *hapax* "emisperio" would seem, in conjunction with the other likely echoes and the syntactically similar structures (pluperfect + "when" + woman's name), to leave little doubt as to Boccaccio's precise reference here, especially given the resulting equation of the two women in question, Fiammetta and Beatrice.[14]

Let us pause here for a moment, since the second half of the *Decameron* will at times yield results that seem to me less immediately convincing than those which we have heretofore explored. If the evidence up to now seems encouraging for my thesis (and I am aware of the fragility of such enter-

---

14. Here Branca cites, only for the passage "uccelli . . . cantavano," *Purg.* 28.14–17, verses which seem more closely followed in the Introduction to Day Two.

prises as these), can we extract from it any "rules" which might be of assistance in pursuing the question of Boccaccio's rather recondite, if apparently programmatic, citations of the *Commedia*? In each case we have found that one of his alleged appropriations of Dantean text is a *hapax* (or a "pseudo-*hapax*," a word or a phrase that will be used only once again in a passage which reflects its earlier use)[15] and, further, that the passage also includes at least two other citations from the same piece of text. As I have suggested, the trail becomes still more difficult to follow in some of the instances which we will soon examine, two of which offer fewer possible confirmations than those that we have found in each of the passages previously discussed.

Decameron VI.Int.2:

> Aveva la luna, essendo **nel mezzo del cielo** [VI.x.4], *perduti i raggi suoi,*
> e già per la nuova luce *vegnente* ogni parte del *nostro mondo* era
> *chiara,* quando la reina levatasi fatta la sua compagnia chiamare, . . .

Paradiso 30.1–9:

> Forse semilia miglia di lontano
> ci ferve l'ora sesta, e *questo mondo* [Branca][16]
> china già l'ombra quasi al letto piano,
>   quando '*l mezzo del cielo,* a noi profondo,
> comincia a farsi tal, ch'alcuna stella
> *perde il parere* infino a questo fondo;
>   e come *vien* la *chiarissima* ancella

---

15. As a parallel experiment one might wish to examine the relation of every *hapax* in Boccaccio to the lexicon of the *Commedia.* If such a study is undertaken, it develops that there are some 1,800 examples of *hapax* in the *Decameron.* Of these, some 500 are words also found in the *Commedia.* Since in all of the descriptions of sunrise which occur in Days Two through Nine—as will be seen—we find at least one Boccaccian *hapax* that is also a word found in the *Commedia,* this high percentage of shared vocabulary is surely striking when it is compared with the general case. One should also observe that the sheer number of words which coincide in this particular instance, a *hapax* in the *Decameron* which is also a part of the linguistic field of the *Commedia,* tends to indicate a close sense of Dante's poetic arsenal—all the more so since in at least 227 instances a *hapax* in the *Decameron* is also one in the *Commedia.* [See the Appendix for the list of *hapax* in the *Decameron.*]

16. Branca's note attaches the phrase *nostro mondo* to *Par.* 30.2 but does not seem to indicate a larger dependence than that.

del sol più oltre, così 'l ciel si chiude
di vista in vista infino a la più bella.

If Boccaccio's text is a deliberate recasting of the opening of *Paradiso* 30, it is accomplished in so complex a manner as to make his desire to begin each Day with such citations seem even more deliberate than we may have hitherto ascertained. Dante's simuletic pre-dawn moment in *Paradiso* seems to have been reformulated by Boccaccio as follows.

1. The aurora of the sun:
   "vien la chiarissima ancella / del sole"
   "per la nuova luce vegnente"
2. begins to bring light back to the world:
   "questo mondo / china già l'ombra al letto piano"
   "ogni parte del nostro mondo era chiara"
3. with the consequence that heavenly bodies do not shine as far as earth:
   "'l mezzo del cielo . . . / comincia a farsi tal, ch'alcuna stella / perde il parere infino a questo fondo."
   "Aveva la luna, essendo nel mezzo del cielo, perduto i raggi suoi. . . ."

Boccaccio's identification of *alcuna stella* and *luna* is certainly a possible reading of Dante's verse, but not a necessary one. If he has intentionally made specific what is only general in the passage in *Paradiso,* we may surmise that for one reason or another he has wanted to have the moon "preside" over his Sixth Day. (Indeed the moon is mentioned in no other Introduction.) Whereas at first glance the claim that this Boccaccian fragment has a Dantean source may have seemed less convincing than most of the previous ones, close examination reveals that it is among the most careful and studied borrowings we have yet encountered.

Decameron VII.Int.2:

Ogni stella era già delle parti d'*oriente* fuggita, se non quella sola la qual noi chiamiamo **Lucifero** che ancora luceva nella biancheggiante aurora, quando il siniscalco levatosi con una gran salmeria n'andò nella Valle delle Donne. . . .

Purgatorio I.19–21:

> *Lo bel pianeto che d'amar conforta*
> faceva tutto rider l'*orïente,*
> velando i Pesci ch'erano in sua scorta.

Displacements similar to those that we have seen in the preceding passage confront us here. Dante's morning star, the "bel pianeto che d'amar conforta," becomes the single shining star of Boccaccio's description, "Lucifero," the alternate name for Venus as morning star; and Dante's "veiled" constellation of Pisces, blotted from our vision by the effulgence of Venus, becomes all the stars in the eastern sky. It should also be observed that the concluding phrase, "biancheggiante aurora," very likely reflects a text that we have already seen cited in Day Three, *Purgatorio* 2.7–9.[17]

Where Days Six and Seven offer some difficulties but still seem to continue the pattern of citation, Day Eight interrupts it.

Decameron VIII.Int.2:

> Già nella sommità de' più alti monti apparivano, la domenica mattina, i raggi della surgente luce e, ogni ombra partitasi, manifestamente le cose si conosceano, quando la reina levatasi con la sua compagnia primieramente alquanto su per le rugiadose erbette andarono, e poi in su la mezza terza una chiesetta lor vicina visitata, in quella il divino oficio ascoltarono.

One might attempt to argue that "i raggi della surgente luce" reflect (for a second time—see V.Int.2: "li surgenti raggi") Dante's verses at *Paradiso* 1.37–38: "Surge ai mortali per diverse foci / la lucerna del mondo. . . ." On the previous occasion there were better grounds to support such a claim

---

17. *Purgatorio* 2.7–9:

[la notte . . . uscia di Gange . . .]
   sì che le bianche e le vermiglie guance,
là dov' i' era, de la bella Aurora
per troppa etate divenivan rance.

Boccaccio's "biancheggiante" (a *hapax*) may remember "le bianche . . . guance" here, where his "vermiglia" at III.Int.2 remembered the "vermiglie guance" as they yield to the orange hue of dawn.

(other verbal similarities and the shared *hapax* "emisperio"). If we are to follow the tentative procedures outlined previously (see the discussion that follows the examination of V.Int.2), we must simply admit that Day Eight does not begin—at least not immediately—with a citation of Dante. That Boccaccio should have suddenly decided to depart from his program is puzzling. The Introduction to Day Eight is the shortest in the *Decameron* and takes the *brigata* to church (for their only such visit since they assembled in Santa Maria Novella at the outset; the preceding Sunday, Day Three, includes no mention of religious observances—quite the contrary). Yet neither a desire to be brief nor the recording of churchgoing offers in itself an obvious reason to depart from the usual opening citation of Dante.[18] However, if we do not find the *Commedia* remembered at the outset, we do not have long to wait.

Decameron VIII.Int.3:

> Ma *avendo* il *sol* già passato **il cerchio di meriggio** come alla reina piacque, al novellare usato tutti appresso la bella fontana a seder posti, per comandamento della reina così Neifile cominciò.

Purgatorio 25.2–3:

> che 'l *sole avëa il cerchio di merigge*
> lasciato al Tauro. . . .

[Branca]

If Boccaccio's description of sunrise is here Virgilian, his noontide seems Dantean enough. The astronomical phrase, once more a *hapax,* seems in itself conclusive, if it is aided by the other similar elements as well. Why should Boccaccio have turned from Dante to Virgil for this description of the sunrise? The Dantean resonance of the ensuing description of the hours after midday comes hard enough upon to keep the pattern nearly intact. One might suspect that Boccaccio had "run out" of Dantean sunrises. As we have seen, he does not repeat his borrowings in his opening passages (his revisitation of *Purgatorio* 2 in IV.Int.44 is of a different passage from the one cited in III.Int.2). Yet there are others for him to have

---

18. Branca's note proposes that the opening description indeed does have a "source," *Aeneid* 12.113–14: "Postera vix summos spargebat lumine montis / orta dies. . . ." The citation surely seems apt—and certainly more so than any passage in Dante.

chosen from, for instance, the splendid opening of *Purgatorio* 9. It is difficult for me to believe that Boccaccio was not aware of the Dantean provenance of every other "beginning" in the *Decameron*. Why should, on this Day uniquely, his source lie elsewhere? With the hope that others may have hypotheses which may help to answer this question, I turn to the next passage, which offers fewer difficulties.

Decameron IX.Int.2:

> *La luce,* il cui splendore la notte fugge, aveva già l'ottavo cielo d'az-zurrino in color **cilestro mutato tutto,** e cominciavansi i fioretti per li prati a levar suso,[19] quando Emilia levatasi fece le sue compagne e i giovani parimente chiamare;

Purgatorio 26.4–6:

> feriami *il sole* in su l'omero destro,
> che già, raggiando, *tutto* l'occidente
> *mutava* in bianco aspetto di **cilestro;**

While Dante's sky changes from sky blue to white and Boccaccio's from azure to sky blue, both observers look into the western sky to observe the transmutation. And each text involves its author in a *hapax*, "cilestro," in itself a fairly certain sign that Boccaccio meant to mirror his Dante here. Indeed, without the presence of the shared *hapax* (the only example we find in these passages) it might be difficult to make the case for an "echo" here. It is, however, present.

Decameron X.Int.2:

> Ancora eran vermigli certi nuvoletti[20] nell'*occidente,* essendo già quegli dello *oriente* nelle loro estremità simili a oro lucentissimi divenuti per li solari raggi che molto loro avvicinandosi li ferieno, quando Panfilo, levatosi, le donne e' suoi compagni fece chiamare.

---

19. Branca notes the relation of this clause to *Inf.* 2.127–29.

20. For Boccaccio's *nuvoletti* Branca cites *Vita Nuova* 23.25 and Petrarch *Rime* 115.12–13. While the word is a *hapax* in Boccaccio, it does not reflect a word in the text that seems most appropriate to this final description of daybreak.

Purgatorio 30.22–27:

> Io vidi già nel cominciar del giorno
> *la parte orïental* tutta rosata,
> e l'altro ciel di bel sereno addorno;
>   e la faccia del sol nascere ombrata,
> sì che per temperanza di vapori
> l'occhio la sostenea lunga fïata:

Perhaps none of Boccaccio's redoings of descriptions of sunrise in Dante is as complex as this one. What makes the ascription seem most probable is the double focus of each passage. In *Purgatorio* 30 Dante remembers an earthly dawn when he looked first toward the roseate east, then to the unclouded western sky; the east has its color because clouds cover the sun. Boccaccio repositions Dante's clouds so that all the sky is occluded. He looks first to the west, where the clouds are vermilion, then to the east, where their borders are turned to gold by the rising sun. This is the only case that we have examined in which there is not a Boccaccian *hapax* (or a "pseudo-*hapax*") found in an apposite text in the *Commedia.* Yet the two glances (one to the western heavens, one to the east) and the mutually shared attention to the relation of sun to clouds are common details which help to confirm Boccaccio's awareness of Dante's text.

There has been little attempt in what has gone before to analyze what such borrowings might signify. Indeed, even assuming that they are all justly observed, I would find it very difficult even to begin to account for their significance. Do they, for instance, reveal a Boccaccio who worships Dante or who holds him at arm's length, a challenging precursor who must be dealt with, if not in a public way (as, perhaps, for Chaucer Boccaccio himself was shortly to serve as lion in the roadway)?[21] Do they show close attention to Dante's contexts, or are they torn from the pages of the *Commedia* as mere philological appurtenances? Do they form a pattern of development, or are they random?[22] Such questions as these are surely of interest. Before they can even be asked by Boccaccio's readers in meaning-

---

21. The word *Dante* is itself a *hapax* in the *Decameron* (IV.Int.33)—but that is an infinite improvement on Chaucer's acknowledgment of Boccaccio, whom he never names but continually uses.

22. See fig. 1 for a review of the citations noted previously. If there is a pattern to them, it is not readily ascertainable.

ful terms, these readers must be satisfied that what is put forward here is not imagined but observed.

It is probably fair to say that if Boccaccio has done what it seems to me he has, namely, to begin every Day (or nearly every Day) of the *Decameron* with a citation of a specific text in the *Commedia,* there is a far closer relationship between the two texts than anyone has hitherto fathomed. My hope is that this brief analysis will help to widen our understanding of Boccaccio's extraordinary debt to Dante.[23]

---

23. During the summer of 1982 I offered a Faculty Seminar at Dartmouth College in the course of which the phenomenon studied here first caught my interest. I hope that my colleagues at Dartmouth, who were the first to hear these ideas, remember them and me as warmly as I remember them. I would like to offer my gratitude to the National Endowment for the Humanities for the fellowship year (1982–83) which enabled me to proceed with this and other projects relating to Boccaccio and Dante. My research assistant at Princeton, Tim Hampton [now Professor Timothy Hampton of the University of California at Berkeley], was his usual helpful self; his efforts on behalf of this project are closely reflected in n. 15.

Utilità

(1985–86)

In the penultimate sentence of the *Decameron*'s *Proemio* its author promises its feminine readership certain rewards: "... parimente diletto delle sollazzevoli cose in quelle [novelle] mostrate e utile consiglio ..., in quanto potranno cognoscere quello che sia da fuggire e che sia similmente da seguitare"[1] [... at once delight in the pleasing things set forth in them and useful advice ..., insofar as they will be able to recognize what should be avoided and, likewise, what should be sought]. Given the nature of the ancient and continuing debate over the purposes of the *Decameron,* this passage invites close consideration, since either a moralist's or a naturalist's interpretation of the overall conception of the work must (or at least ought to) take this statement of purpose into account. The passage in Horace's letter on poetry, known to posterity as his *Ars poetica,* which nearly automatically comes to mind in this context is familiar to all students of the history of criticism.

Aut prodesse volunt aut delectare poetae
aut simul et iucunda et idonea dicere vitae. ...

[This essay, departing from the first three, does not consider Boccaccio's use of Dantean text but centers attention on another literary element that has been present in the first two essays especially: the satirical nature of Boccaccio's vision. As I believe the Tenth Day finally makes plain, that has been the primary generic affiliation of the *Decameron* from its beginning.]

1. *Tutte le opere di Giovanni Boccaccio,* ed. Vittore Branca, vol. 4, *Decameron* (Milan: Mondadori, 1976). Other primary texts cited are Horace, *Satires, Epistles, and "Ars Poetica,"* trans. H. R. Fairclough (London: Heinemann; Cambridge, Mass.: Harvard University Press, 1970 [1929 rev. ed.]); *Ovid in Six Volumes,* trans. J. H. Mozley, vol. 2, *The Art of Love, and Other Poems* (London: Heinemann; Cambridge, Mass.: Harvard University Press, 1979 [1939 rev. ed.]).

ficta voluptatis causa sint proxima veris. . . .
omne tulit punctum qui miscuit utile dulci,
lectorem delectando pariterque monendo.

(vv. 333–34, 338, 343–44)

[Poets aim either to benefit, or to amuse, or to utter words at once both
pleasing and helpful to life. . . . Fictions meant to please should be close
to the real. . . . He has won every vote [i.e., both that of the elderly sage
and the pleasure-seeking youth] who has blended profit and pleasure, at
once delighting and instructing the reader.] (trans. Fairclough; my inter-
polation)

Whether the penultimate period of Boccaccio's *Proemio* resorts to the
text of Horace directly or to the tradition of that text, which is so widespread that its *dictum* may surely be said to have achieved the status of a
commonplace, probably cannot be ascertained. What we can say with
some certainty is that Boccaccio expects his reader to be conscious of this
tradition and perhaps of its Horatian origin.[2]

Attached to this Horatian or pseudo-Horatian *caput* is a perhaps
ungainly body. With little doubt, the concluding two clauses of the
promise of advice to the ladies in love ("quello che sia da fuggire e che sia
similmente da seguitare") reflect the admonition of Ovid near the conclusion of his *Remedia amoris:* "quos fugias quosque sequare, dabo" (796). To
be sure, Ovid, in his usual disingenuous way, is describing what foods to
choose and which to avoid in order to be in control of one's sexual appetite.
Yet I think we can be sure that Boccaccio is here quoting this specific text.[3]

---

2. If Boccaccio meant us to consider the *Ars* as a generative text here, he might also have
expected us to notice that his book begins with the same word as Horace's: *human.* "Umana
cosa è aver compassione degli afflitti" [It is human to take pity on those who suffer affliction];
"Humano capiti cervicem pictor equinam / iungere si velit . . ." [Should a painter choose to
put a human head atop the neck of a horse . . .]. If the contexts are not similar, the fact that
both works—uniquely?—begin with that most significant word, so important to their eventual meanings, may reflect a conscious decision on Boccaccio's part. [Subsequent consultation of the corpus of Latin literature represented in the database prepared by the Packard
Humanities Institute has indeed revealed that no other Latin work begins with this word.]

3. One is even more attracted to an already likely hypothesis when one considers the precise and witty appropriateness of the context. Ovid goes on, with a wry deadpan shot at the
opening lines of the *Aeneid,* to single out the onion as a food to be avoided.

Daunius, an Libycis bulbus tibi missus ab oris
  An veniat Megaris, noxius omnis erit.

(797–98)

One might wish to argue that it, too, had attained the status of a common-place, that Boccaccio was merely resorting to its tradition as well. The fact that so much else in the second half of his *Proemio* is also derived from the *Remedia* makes what might otherwise seem a reasonable argument an unlikely one.[4]

In itself there is little surprising in Boccaccio's decision to make this proemial statement of so traditional a classical definition of the role of fiction. What author would not claim that his work was intended not only for your delight but for your instruction as well? And we expect to hear the claim as comfortably as he is prepared to make it, since readers are as much creatures of convention as are authors. What is surprising is that so little has been made of the passage, even by those (comparatively few) students of the *Decameron* who believe that it purveys the traditional Christian morality of its time. What I hope to demonstrate in the following pages is that the classical notion of "utility" does not inform either the behavior of the characters or the attitudes of most of the narrators of the *Decameron* and that, as a result, we have a difficult task ascertaining exactly what is meant by the claim made, here and in its *Conclusione,* by its author, who, as we shall see, is insistent in pressing it upon us.

If most students of the *Decameron* agree that it does have a "moral" pur-pose, I need hardly report that there is sharp disagreement between those who see it as championing the "new morality" that it so amply portrays (surely the majority opinion) and those who argue that it is a work pro-moting traditional religious and moral values. This description of the broad and general contours of the continuing debate does not do (nor does it attempt to do) justice to its layers of partial agreement and disagree-ment, the differences over the moral tone of one form of behavior or another, in short over the manifold complexities of what all can agree is an extraordinarily subtly-woven literary fabric. Indeed, one has to look only as far as the first *novella* to find behaviors and situations which are consid-ered in very different lights by those who agree on a basic interpretive posi-

---

[The onion, whether Italian or sent from Libyan shores, or even from Megara, will always be noisome.]

The *bulbus daunius* might have struck Boccaccio as an amusing emblem for the food that inhibits love; it is his own "emblem," that "Italian onion" which was the main product of Certaldo.

4. [See my treatment of this series of citations in the next study.]

tion. For example, is Cepparello's self-creating "confession" to be condemned or admired? Does he go to heaven or hell, or are we not supposed to attempt such judgment? Does the fact that gullible Frenchmen pray to him confirm God's mercy in allowing intercession through even such flawed vessels as he, or does it call into question the very efficacy of prayer? Such questions are invited by the text; answers to them are virtually impossible to confirm in the text. The author of the *Decameron* prefers to formulate questions rather than to answer them, perhaps aware that the first generation of Dante's enthusiastic readers would find his work a hard nut to crack. Subsequent generations have not had an easier time with it. And whether a particular disputant is a "naturalist" or a "moralist" does not require that answers to such questions as just adduced will follow a party line. We know, in fact, that they have not done so in the past, and we have little reason to expect that they will do so in any imaginable future.

We probably all agree—all of us who like the work—that the *Decameron* breeds delight in its readers. What is the nature of its *utile consiglio*? Is it that of traditional morality? We may wish to remember that, in the medieval West, superadded to conventional Roman morality in some generalized form (Aristotle's *Ethics* in solution with Stoicism?) are the Augustinian distinctions concerning things to be used *(uti)* and those to be enjoyed *(frui)*. Surely no fourteenth-century user of this terminology would be innocent of the magnificent reversal employed by the great apologist in *De doctrina christiana,* by which classical wisdom was accepted in an inverted form. Where such as Horace would, in writing, make pleasure the vehicle for instruction, Augustine makes the useful merely the agency for what alone is truly pleasing—the love of God. In one developed argument he has reduced mere pleasure and mere utility to the condition of trash, leaving us to acquire learning only if it is useful in the pursuit of the true faith. Few will choose to argue that Boccaccio's *Decameron* shares this view of "utility."[5] Most, however, will agree that the word, as it is presented in his *Proemio,* does urge us to think in terms of a conventional ethical framework, one without necessary reference to a particular theology. *Utile consiglio* in this understanding means no more than advice which is physi-

---

5. Not even those who put forward a theologically based understanding of the *Decameron.* Recent works of which I am aware are Florinda M. Jannace, *La religione del Boccaccio* (Rome: Trevi, 1977); Aldo S. Bernardo, "The Plague as Key to Meaning in Boccaccio's *Decameron*," in *The Black Death: The Impact of the Fourteenth-Century Plague,* ed. D. Williman (Binghamton, N.Y.: Medieval and Renaissance Texts and Studies, 1982), 39–63. For brief descriptions of some earlier studies in this vein see Robert Hollander, *Boccaccio's Two Venuses* (New York: Columbia University Press, 1977), 236–37.

cally and morally helpful. Thanking his benefactors—the ones who
showed him how to fall out of love—he now proposes to share what he has
learned with others less fortunate than he, since it will be of greater use
(utilità) to those who are still under Love's sway *(Proemio. 8)*. That kind of
utilità helps us to understand what is meant by the word *utile* in the passage
with which we began. The ladies to whom it is addressed—it seems clear
enough—are thus promised that the hundred *novelle* will teach them how
to follow reason and shun lust.[6] That is the apparently clear meaning of
the promised aid. It is no wonder that so many of Boccaccio's commentators—even those who expressly set out to examine the *Proemio*—have chosen to disregard the passage utterly.[7] It violates everything that they have
been taught about this book as well as every feeling they have developed in

---

6. The most recent attempt to see the *Decameron* as a conventionally moralizing text
which champions reason in its battle against the appetitive soul is that of Victoria Kirkham,
"An Allegorically Tempered *Decameron*" (forthcoming in *Italica,* 1985). [Now see Kirkham's
book, *The Sign of Reason in Boccaccio's Fiction* (Florence: Olschki, 1993), 131–71.]

7. It is common to find those who devote a study to the *cornice* not even mentioning the
Proemio as constituting a part of that frame. Some of those who have recently dealt with the
Proemio without even referring to, much less discussing, the pointedly moralizing statements
examined here are Luigi Russo, "Proemio alle donne," in *Letture critiche del "Decameron"*
(Bari: Laterza, 1967 [1938]), 9–15; Guido Di Pino, "Il *proemio* e l'*introduzione* alla quarta *gior-
nata,*" in *La polemica del Boccaccio* (Florence: Vallecchi, 1953), 209–20; Carlo Muscetta,
"Esposizione critica del *Decameron:* I modelli, il Proemio, l'Introduzione, i novellatori," in
Giovanni Boccaccio (Bari: Laterza, 1972), 156–60; Pier Luigi Cerisola, "La questione della
cornice del *Decameron,*" *Aevum* 49 (1975): 148–51; Lucia Marino, *The Decameron "Cornice":
Allusion, Allegory, and Iconology* (Ravenna: Longo, 1979), 25–36. This list is not exhaustive,
nor is it intended to castigate those mentioned, but only to indicate the difficult condition of
our comprehension of the *Decameron*. For example, the chapter entitled "Orientamenti
morali del Boccaccio" in Mario Baratto's *Realtà e stile nel "Decameron"* (Vicenza: Neri
Pozza, 1974 [1970]), 49–68, which offers an "analisi degli ideali morali e dei gusti sociali del
Decameron" [analysis of the moral ideas and social tastes of the *Decameron*], does not even
mention the *Proemio*. One of the few major treatments of the *Proemio* known to me which
even mentions the passage is that of Giovanni Getto: "La cornice e le componenti espressive
del *Decameron,*" in *Vita di forme e forme di vita nel "Decameron"* (Turin: Petrini, 1958), 1–9.
On p. 2 Getto does deal fleetingly with the passage in question, but he does not consider it
more than conventional or of any real importance; he goes on to contrast this merely conventional treatment of Boccaccio's purpose with the only elements in the *Proemio* for which
he feels any fondness, ". . . quello spunto, più risentito e personale, del ricordo di una vissuta
scartata esperienza . . ." [. . . that hint, more felt, more personal, of the remembrance of a
lived experience that has been laid aside . . .]. Among the few recent discussants who have
taken even brief notice of the monitory binome is Antonio Prete, "Ritmo esterno e tempi
spirituali nella cornice del *Decameron,*" *Aevum* 28 (1964): 37; Prete concludes his four-page
analysis of the *Proemio* (pp. 34–37) by taking the language of the *Proemio* as "sincero." And
also see the paragraph in Marga Cottino-Jones, *Order from Chaos* (Washington, D.C.: University Press of America, 1982), 9, which briefly discusses the traditional phrase "diletto . . . e
utile consiglio" [delight . . . and useful advice] and its varied formulations in the words of
Dioneo (I.iv.3), Pampinea (I.x.8), and Filomena (I.Conc.9).

themselves as they have read it. Their critical behavior is not to be applauded; but their instincts are not, in my opinion, wrong. Reading the passage straight, they find it an embarrassment (as is indeed the entire *Proemio,* which may account for the fact of the nearly universal neglect of the most important indicator we may have of the work's announced intention). Had they taken the time to consider the likely source of Boccaccio's literary behavior here, Ovid's *Remedia amoris,* they might have been willing to grapple with the significance of this apparently moralistic entreaty and seen the smile behind it. Before attempting to make the case for Boccaccio as Ovidian ironist, I would like to examine the numerous ensuing references to "utility" which dot the pages of the *Decameron.* They offer a context for the understanding of the *Proemio* and, I am convinced, of the moral stance of the work as a whole.

Our views of the meaning of "utility" in Boccaccio's text are, strikingly enough, given the fact that we live in the wake of utilitarianism, untinged by such an appreciation as our historical situation might afford. Instead, good historicists, we are content to hear in the word what we think we should hear, namely, the "orthodox" humanistic re-creation of classical values, with their promise of moral uplift. As we shall see, as we follow the career of the word and its cognates through the *Decameron,* it only rarely has such meaning. And even when it does, its seriousness is frequently at least questionable.

The *Decameron* contains thirty-nine occurrences of the word *utile* (27) and its related forms *utilità* (11) and *utilmente* (1).[8] While the context of the present discussion emphasizes the importance of those passages that examine the capacity of fiction to instruct, consideration of the nature of *utilità* within the *novelle* themselves is not without significance for the former concern. Of these twenty "internal" occurrences of *utile* and *utilità,* the words have mostly to do with the acquiring of money or other worldly possessions, as a glance at the tabular display at the conclusion of this study will affirm. Once, and only once, is it coupled with *consiglio,* as it was in the *Proemio:* Nathan, in disguise, offers to give Mithridanes the information that the would-be champion of magnanimity seeks—the whereabouts of the current champion, Nathan himself. And it is indeed Nathan who describes this information as "utile consiglio." In this, then, the only

---

8. According to the *Concordanze del "Decameron,"* ed. A. Barbina, vol. 2 (Florence: C/E Giunti & G. Barbèra, 1969), 2059–60. See my Addendum for a tabular display of this material.

reappearance of this phrase in the *Decameron,* useful advice consists in learning how to be able to murder the most magnanimous man on the face of the earth. Whatever we may choose to think about the nature of Nathan's own version of magnanimity (and surely its perverse imitation of the self-sacrifice of Jesus should have caught our attention before now), we must surely conclude that Mithridanes' eager acceptance of this counsel reveals the depravity of his spirit and utter unsuitability for the public role he seeks to play.

If *utilità* has, then, little to do with wise or good counsel in the tales themselves, it has a single presence of this kind in the so-called one-hun-dred-and-first tale of the *Decameron,* the author's detailing of the thwarted moralizing urge of Filippo Balducci. Then, and only then, does a character in one of the *novelle* (or in the sole "meta-*novella*") use the adjec-tive *utile* as a moralist would warrant: "Il padre, per non destare nel con-cupiscibile appetito del giovane alcuno inchinevole disiderio men che utile, non le volle nominare per lo proprio nome, cioè femine, ma disse: 'Elle si chiamano papere'" [The father, in order not to rouse in the concupiscible appetite of the youth any inclination or desire that might be other than for good purpose, did not want to call them by their real name, that is, women, but said: "They are known as geese"] (IV.Int.23). The entire scene, reflective of the simile in *Purgatorio* 26.67–70, which compares the stupefied amazement of the heterosexual penitents on the Terrace of Lust when they look upon a living soul to that of the "montanaro . . . rozzo e selvatico" [the man from the mountains . . . uncouth and untutored] when he first enters a city (and surely Florence is the city in Dante's mind as it is in Boccaccio's text), reverses the Dantean priorities. In the *Commedia* reformed heterosexual lovers behave like bumpkins upon seeing a living soul who betokens God's grace and the possibility of undoing the sin of lust; here a country bumpkin discovers his sexual appetite with a similar amazement.[9] The subliminal presence of Dante's text thus informs the moralizing lie told by the elder Balducci. But what might seem good advice in the *Commedia* seems a useless and foolish attempt to bridle nature here, as Filippo himself realizes: "sentì incontanente più aver di forza la natura che il suo ingegno; e pentessi d'averlo menato a Firenze" [at once he under-stood that nature had more power than his contrivance; and he was sorry to have brought the lad with him to Florence].

---

9. I do not find reference to this conjunction in Attilio Bettinzoli, "Per una definizione delle presenze dantesche nel *Decameron,*" part I, "I registri 'ideologici,' lirici, drammatici," *Studi sul Boccaccio* 13 (1982): 267–326.

Thus, within the 101 *novelle* we find the words *utile* and *utilità* used only once with their traditional moral sense, and then only to demonstrate that a morality which totally opposes nature cannot interact with the conduct which is natural to humanity. In all other cases these words are devoid of any traditional moral tone; in the only occurrence which preserves that tone, such morality is seen to be a foolish intrusion upon the preserve of human reality.

What of the nineteen instances in which these words appear in passages that purport to represent the purposes of the individual *novelle,* of groups of them, or of the assemblage which constitutes the *Decameron*? As we have seen, our author starts us out believing that he at least might mean to be taken in a serious and traditional moral vein. If he will relieve ladies of their pain in love, if he is writing a *remedium amoris,* do not his formulations sound "orthodox" enough? His book offers, we may remind ourselves, ". . . parimente diletto delle sollazzevoli cose in quelle [novelle] mostrate e utile consiglio . . . , in quanto potranno cognoscere quello che sia da fuggire e che sia similmente da seguitare" [. . . at once delight in the pleasing things set forth in them and useful advice, insofar as they will be able to recognize what should be avoided and, likewise, what should be sought]. Yet once the *novellatori* themselves begin to account for their motives as makers or retailers of fiction, their formulation of the *utilità* of their tales begins to take on a quite different coloration.

Filomena calls for the *brigata,* for the literary part of its second day's activity, to return to *il novellare,* "nel quale mi par grandissima parte di piacere e d'utilità similmente consistere" [the purpose of which seems to me to be constituted in large part in pleasure and, in equal measure, profit] (I.Conc.9). Horace may yet apply. But when she further defines their task, determining as their subject the happy results obtained by one who begins in a difficult situation, the lessons to be learned from Day Two begin to evade a simple moral formulation. This *giornata,* as comic in its pervading spirit as the fourth is tragic, reveals that the unjust and the foolish are as likely to be victorious as the just and the wise. What kind of *utilità* has Filomena in mind? Undoubtedly, hers is not distant from that envisioned by Filostrato (II.ii.3), whose tale about lucky Rinaldo is introduced as follows: "Belle donne, a raccontarsi mi tira una novella di cose catoliche e di sciagure e d'amore in parte mescolata, la quale per avventura non fia altro che utile avere udita; e specialmente a coloro li quali per li dubbiosi paesi d'amore sono caminanti, ne' quali chi non ha detto il paternostro di san

Giuliano spesse volte, ancora che abbia buon letto, alberga male"[10] [Lovely ladies, there draws me to tell it a tale of things holy, with misfortunes and love mixed in; to have heard it perhaps will be nothing but profitable, especially for those who walk the uncertain lands of love, where the one who has not said, again and again, the Our Father of Saint Julian may very well find a good bed, but not a good stay]. The author's insistence on "diletto e utile consiglio," reformulated by Filomena as "piacere e utilità," has now become *utilità* in the service of pleasure; Filostrato, seeming to be the moralist *tout court*, all utility and no pleasure, is the very opposite. His witty subversion of the topos is answered by Pampinea, who tells her tale of Alessandro and the at-first-apparently-homosexual abbot who is actually the daughter of the king of England—a tale that could have been as wittily carnal as Filostrato's, but which is "cleaned up" to include a marriage presided over by the pope and the eventual rumored kingship of its protagonist. Her opening sally (II.iii.4), with its serious tone and conventional moral attitudes, is a homily on Fortune, concluding with a restoration of Horace's binome, "utilità e . . . piacere." However, when Neifile ordains that the tales of the Third Day should be "utile o almeno dilettevole," she may be siding with Filostrato's view of the pleasing as being what is useful. Whatever her intention, the tellers, with the exceptions of Lauretta and Dioneo, relate tales which concern successful cuckolders (all of mortal husbands except for Masetto). And all of them take the "alcuna cosa molto disiderata" [something that is greatly desired] (II.Conc.9) to signify genital enjoyment. And Fiammetta's introductory remarks (III.vi.3) concerning her own tale of extramarital love are meant at once to warn the ladies, by Catella's example, against the wiles of men and give delight in the things narrated (while her formulation does not use a word for *utilità*, its "cautela," paired with "diletto," has a similar effect). Elissa's governance of Day Six, with its return to *motteggiare*, this time on the themes of an insult turned back or a bad situation avoided, seems "cor-

---

10. The phrase "una novella di cose catoliche e di sciagure e d'amore in parte mescolata" [a tale of things holy, with misfortunes and love mixed in] may be meant to remind us of *Ars poetica* 343–44: "omne tulit punctum qui *miscuit* utile dulci, / lectorem delectando pariterque monendo" [he who has mixed together the useful and the pleasing wins every vote, delighting as much as he instructs the reader], thus offering still another dimension to the parodistic elements noted by Branca, *Decameron*, 1051: "L'ironia linguistica introduce tutta la narrazione ironica, equivoca fra enunciati religiosi e realtà ben materiali e sensuali" [The linguistic irony introduces the narrational irony, playing ambiguously between religious pronouncements and down-to-earth, sensual occurrences].

rect" enough. And her formulation balances the moral and the pleasing in good Horatian ways (one might argue that Day Six, the most "Florentine" and "ethical" of all the *giornate,* encompasses Boccaccio's most Horatian satire), as does Neifile's iteration of the rubric for all the tales which precede her own about Chichibio (VI.iv.3): "Quantunque il pronto ingegno, amorose donne, spesso parole presti e utile e belle, secondo gli accidenti, a' dicitori, la fortuna ancora, alcuna volta aiutatrice de' paurosi, sopra la lor lingua subitamente di quelle pone che mai a animo riposato per lo dicitore si sareber saputo trovare" [Amorous ladies, however often a ready wit may lend a speaker words both useful and pleasing to meet a particular situation, it also falls out that even Fortune, at times the helpmeet of the fearful, suddenly puts into their mouths words that a speaker enjoying peace of mind would never find it in himself to speak].

It is in Day Seven that Filostrato's reduction of the frame to *utilità* in the service of sexual pleasure returns—both Emilia (VII.i.3) and Filostrato (VII.ii.4) resort to exactly that mode in presenting their tales in defense of female license. And this theme is continued by Pampinea (VIII.vii.3), whose widow's insufficient ingenuity in tricking her scholar-lover will offer the ladies of the *brigata* a negative example "per ciò che meglio di beffare altrui vi guarderete" [so that you will become aware how better to play tricks on others]; in this way her tale will be of use to them.

Day Nine, presided over by Emilia, is a second "free day." The queen insists, ever since their bondage to a set topic after the First Day, that freedom will be *utile* before they again put themselves under the yoke of a restraining topic. Her own tale, which perhaps surprisingly accords with Solomon's misogynist views that women should be beaten, is put forward as *utile.* Neifile, beginning Day Ten, recurs to the traditional formula ("una novelletta assai leggiadra . . . [e] utile" [a little tale delightful . . . and helpful]). In the world of petulant courtiers Ruggieri's urinary wit shows the way to profit in the king's largesse.

Until Filomena's response to her own tale of Tito and Gisippo (X.viii), and as we have seen, the words *utile* and *utilità* have had either the conventional Horatian significance or else a particularly Boccaccian one: that which is useful is exactly that which brings pleasure or the avoidance of pain. Filomena's lengthy outburst (X.viii.111–19), one of the longest of such "intrusions" by a narrator into the tale which she tells,[11] is the first

---

11. It is in fact the longest to occur at the conclusion of a *novella* and is only slightly shorter than the longest moralizing "glosses" which precede their fictions, Emilia's "sermon" on female inconstancy (IX.ix.3–9) and Pampinea's discourse on the fitting use of *motti* by

occasion on which we find ourselves forced to think of *utilità* in a patently negative way. The word, which has hitherto been used with comfort by all who have uttered it (and, with the exception of Fiammetta, every narrator will use it at least once, whether in framing material or in a tale itself), is now savaged. Against the magnanimous friendship shared by Tito and Gisippo (the uniquely classical setting of this tale, that of ancient Greece and Rome, may have been meant to call to mind the moral vision of a golden—or at least a better—age), Filomena sets the world of the fourteenth century. It is only very rarely, she says, that we observe the most sacred effects of shared friendship, "colpa e vergogna della misera cupidigia de' mortali, la qual solo alla propria utilità riguardando ha costei [l'amistà] fuor degli estremi termini della terra in essilio perpetuo rilegata" [fault and shame of the wretched cupidity of mortals, which, thinking only of its own profit, has bound friendship in perpetual exile beyond the ends of the earth] (X.viii.112).[12] The lady may protest too much, but her point is well taken once we consider most of the behavior exemplified in the pages of the *Decameron*. The *Proemio* presents an author who is grateful for the generosity of a friend whose "piacevoli ragionamenti" brought him, from what seemed the brink of death in his passionate attachment to a lady, back into a social group in which he finds still other friends who support him in his newfound freedom from the tyranny of love. This opening might well lead us to believe that the *Decameron* will be a text that demonstrates the power of friendship. Yet, from the *Introduzione*'s picture of a plague-stricken time in which familial and social ties are unbound, through all the *novelle,* it is a topic that we rarely confront. And most of the "friends" whom we do encounter are those who share the pleasure of watching another's misfortune (e.g., the pairs of onlookers in II.i and VI.x; Bruno and Buffalmacco in the several *novelle* concerning Calandrino; etc.) or who work together in order better to achieve the personal advantage of each (beginning with the two transplanted Florentine brothers who are visited by Cepparello in I.i; the murderous brothers of Elisabetta in IV.v; Cimone and Lisimaco in V.i; Pinuccio and Adriano in IX.vi; etc.). Filomena's last

women (I.x.3–8); it is still longer than any of the loquacious Panfilo's four lengthy prefatory discourses (I.i.2–6, II.vii.3–7, IV.vi.3–7, VI.v.3–8). [See the similar discussion of this passage in the last essay in this collection, just after n. 52. A number of the details from Day Ten considered here are given a larger treatment there.]

12. As Bettinzoli realizes ("Per una definizione," 323), the passage closely reflects *Par.* 1.30 and 27.121: "colpa e vergogna de l'umane voglie" [fault and shame of human wills], "O cupidigia, che i mortali affonde . . ." [O cupidity, that thrusts into the depths all mortal beings . . .].

novella, with its nostalgic championing of *amistà* (the word has ten of its twenty-eight occurrences in the *Decameron* in X.viii [one, retrospective, in X.ix]), reminds us how little true friendship we have found in the cento *novelle.* Life in the pages of the *Decameron* is predominantly the life of what Seung has called "the sovereign individual."[13] The plague-stricken city is not only the initial image of this condition but the place to which the temporary exiles must and do return. The plague, from which, following Dioneo's condition for his joining the *brigata* (I.Int.93), they have withdrawn their attention, is nonetheless referred to by Lauretta (VI.iii.8), who refers gratuitously to "una giovane la quale questa pistolenzia presente ci ha tolta donna" [a young girl whom this present pestilence has taken from us now that she had become a woman] (the very parenthetic nature of the inserted and offending phrase underlines its unseemliness—and its importance). Further, our author takes pains to remind us that the unusual peace accorded the small animals of the neighboring woodland is the result of the plague's negative effect on the hunters who would normally be in chase of them (IX.Int.2). And the "moral symptoms" of the plague have also been increasingly making themselves felt among the members of the *brigata.* We learn in Day Ten—that Day devoted to presentations of liberality—that one of the ladies in the *brigata* is a Ghibelline (vii.2; viii.2) and that her aesthetic sense is governed by her political allegiances. Thus the apparently innocent debates, the jealous maneuverings among the lovers in the group, the rivalries in storytelling which are most apparent (and most inappropriate) in Day Ten—all these insistences on self to which we have been witness may offer a more telling sign of disharmony among the *brigata* than has generally been recognized. Readers of the *Decameron* perhaps are too willing to accept at face value Panfilo's sunny praise of the attitudes and behaviors of the *novellatori* (X.Conc.4–5). Dioneo's last tale may be read as the Judeo-Christian allegory which Petrarch claimed to find in it, one which makes Gualtieri God the Father, or it may be read along the lines which Dioneo himself seems to be proposing (X.x.68), in which case Gualtieri (whose name is perhaps meant to remind the contemporary reader of the tyrant Walter of Brienne, who ruled Florence in the early 1340s) is one of those "più degni di guardar porci che d'avere sopra uomini signoria" [more worthy of keeping pigs than of having lordship over men]. We learn that the ladies are divided in their responses to the tale (X.Conc.1). Whether the last tale is to be regarded as praise of the virtuous

---

13. See T. K. Seung, *Cultural Thematics: The Formation of the Faustian Ethos* (New Haven and London: Yale University Press, 1976), esp. 207–16.

Griselda, blame (or even praise) of the excessive *signoria* of her husband, or as a blending of both, the point that I think it is most important to grasp is that the tale does not leave either its auditors or us, its readers, with a sense of resolution. Nor does the conclusion of the text's "action." The *Decameron* is an exquisitely formed text, as Janet Smarr has demonstrated more adequately than perhaps anyone else.[14] The only element not present that seems to have been called for by the demands of symmetry is an answering "frame" to that given in the *Introduzione*. The rounded unit of the one hundred tales is itself surrounded at the outer boundary by the mutually reflective *Proemio* and *Conclusione dell'Autore*. Imagine a *Decameron* with a fully developed Conclusion, one in which, for example, the *brigata* returns to find the plague departed from their city and their surviving co-familiars welcoming them. That would be a very different book from the one which we possess—even if it is frequently read in the optimistic spirit which that putative ending might have afforded. That the return is accomplished as briefly and enigmatically (if with evident recourse to the concluding phrases of the *Proemio*) as it is tells us more than we perhaps wish to acknowledge.

E come il nuovo giorno apparve, levati, avendo già il siniscalco via ogni lor cosa mandata, dietro alla guida del discreto re verso Firenze ritornarono; e i tre giovani, lasciate le sette donne in Santa Maria Novella, donde con loro partiti s'erano, da esse accommiatatosi, a' loro altri piaceri attesero, e esse, quando tempo lor parve, se ne tornarono alle lor case. (X.Conc.16)

[And when the new light appeared, risen from sleep, the seneschal having already sent their belongings on ahead, they made their way back to Florence under the leadership of their prudent king. The three young men, having left the seven ladies in Santa Maria Novella, whence they had set out with them, and bidden farewell by them, attended to their other cares; and the ladies, when it seemed time, went back to their houses.]

The three men, attending to their other business, leaving the women to their unattended lives in their houses, remind us of the similar situation referred to in the *Proemio* (10), where ladies in love ". . . il più del tempo nel

14. See, again, Janet L. Smarr, "Symmetry and Balance in the *Decameron*," *Medievalia* 2 (1967): 159–87.

piccolo circuito delle loro camere racchiuse dimorano e quasi oziose seden-
dosi, volendo e non volendo in una medesima ora, seco rivolgendo diversi
pensieri, li quali non è possibile che sempre sieno allegri" [. . . most of the
time remain shut up within the limited dimensions of their rooms and,
seated as though at their ease, desiring and not desiring at the same
moment, turning over various thoughts; it is not possible that these may
always be joyful]. The *Decameron* has come almost full circle (the next sentence, the first of the *Conclusione dell'Autore,* will begin the completion of
that circle, looking back to the *Proemio* in still more evident ways). In this
text the human animal lives within the limited circle of its own desires,
mainly unaided by its fellow creatures. Boccaccio, claiming that he writes
for otiose women in love,[15] actually describes us all, with few exceptions,
exercising our wills in pursuit of the goods of the world as we perceive
them good. In this pursuit it is *utilità* that we seek—that alone is *dolce* to
us, whether it be money, power over others, sexual pleasure.

The word *utile* is thus of considerable consequence in the work. The tale
in which it appears most often (VI.x.37, 39, 55) is set in Certaldo, thus perhaps associating it, more than any other *novella,* with Boccaccio's message.
Its protagonist, that lying itinerant friar, offers an emblematic portrait of
the upper portion of the Boccaccian centaur (his companion, Guccio, sup-
plies a related anatomy for the bottom). The rational soul, as it actually
operates, does not control the appetitive and concupiscible appetites but
uses its *ingegno* to satisfy these urges. Whether in *chiesa* or in *cucina,* there
are gullible fellow creatures on whom to work one's wiles. Cipolla perverts
the function of small-town preaching, which traditionally offers delight
and instruction, by himself taking *utilità* from the crossed Certaldesi as the
fruit of his preaching (VI.x.55). As we have seen before, within the tales the
concept of "utility" has been bared of its classical and wholesome conno-
tations and seen for what it is: gaining advantage for oneself. In Filomena's
formulation, *amistà* has been exiled by *cupidigia,* which seeks only its own
utilità. That root sin ("radix malorum est cupiditas" [cupidity is the root of
all evil]) is generally presented, in the pages of the *Decameron,* as the end
of rational choice, not its defeated enemy. If such *utilità* is the aim of

---

15. Victoria Kirkham, "Boccaccio's Dedication to Women in Love" (unpublished), which
the author has kindly shared with me in typescript, argues that we should take this announced
purpose at face value and seriously—a conclusion from which I dissent. [The article was sub-
sequently published in *Renaissance Studies in Honor of Craig Hugh Smyth,* ed. A. Morrogh et
al. (Florence: C/E Giunti & G. Barbèra, 1985), 333–43, and republished in Kirkham's *The Sign
of Reason in Boccaccio's Fiction,* 117–29.]

behavior, it is not necessarily what we are meant to conceive of as the consummation of our thought about such behavior.

If we hear the words *utile* and *utilità* from Day One to Day Ten, we hear them most often in the mouth of the author at the boundaries of his text, twice in the *Proemio,* four times in the *Conclusione dell'Autore.* What *utilità* does Boccaccio propose that we take from his text? The opening claims for its *utilità* seemed, as we have seen, conventional enough in a context that appears at once Horatian, Ovidian, and Boethian[16] in its offering of pleasure and instruction to offset the pains of love in granting consolation. And while these claims have received little enough attention, two recent readers give interesting and widely divergent interpretations that have in common a sense of the importance of the gesture. According to Aldo Bernardo, "These stories will not only be a source of enjoyment, but a source of useful advice."[17] And surely that is what the text says. But is that what it means? Bernardo sees the work as joining the tradition of Saint Augustine, Dante, and Petrarch in upholding traditional Christian values; Giuseppe Mazzotta takes a totally different view of the passage.

> The audience itself that Boccaccio chooses, the "oziose donne," exposes the trap of the literary act: writing for the ladies, however coy a claim it can be, is concomitantly an admission of estheticism and futility. Even St. Augustine's esthetic doctrine of the "uti et frui" . . . is depreciated: women who will read the tales "diletto delle sollazzevoli cose in quelle mostrate e utile consiglio potranno pigliare. . . ." The world of pornography is revealed as the essential structure which supersedes the impossible effort to write serious literature.[18]

While I have quarrels with this formulation (it does not confront the possibility of the more obvious reading that the text so clearly seems to call for; nor does it include reference to the key Ovidian phrase with which the passage concludes and which would still more strongly seem—even if it may not eventually do so—to gainsay the interpretation put forward), I can more readily agree with its perception of an ironic author than with Bernardo's view that Boccaccio is here a serious Christian apologist. What

---

16. For discussion of the Boethian consolatory purposes of the text see Millicent Marcus, *An Allegory of Form* (Saratoga, Calif.: Anma Libri, 1979), 112–25.

17. "The Plague as Key to Meaning," 41.

18. "The *Decameron:* The Marginality of Literature," *University of Toronto Quarterly* 42 (1972): 69.

does one follow and what does one flee as a reader of the *Decameron*? One seeks *utilità;* one flees *noia.* But in what does that *utilità* consist? It depends. If you are a Cepparello or a Gualtieri, it consists in one thing; if a Griselda, in another. The *Conclusione dell'Autore* preserves this sense of ambiguity that pervades the Ovidian resonances of the *Proemio.* Thus we are told that the text is like fire, *utilissimo* to mortals, though it may also be destructive (9). The formulation returns us to the *Proemio.* But Boccaccio's full restatement of that opening gambit is reserved for a slightly later passage.

> Chi vorrà da quelle [novelle] malvagio consiglio e malvagia operazion trarre, elle nol vieteranno a alcuno, se forse in se l'hanno, e torte e tirate fieno a averlo: e chi utilità e frutto ne vorrà, elle nol negheranno, ne sarà mai che altro che utile e oneste sien dette o tenute, se a que' tempi o a quelle persone si leggeranno per cui e pe' quali state son raccontate. (14)

> [If one would draw from those stories bad advice and evil actions, they will not prevent anyone from doing so, if perhaps they have such in them, or are twisted and stretched in order to seem to do so; and one who would take profit and fruit from them will not find them preventing that, nor should they be said or considered other than useful and honorable, as long as they are read at those times in which or by those people for whom they have been told.]

What is *utile,* what *malvagio, consiglio?* What is *malvagia,* what *buona, operazion?* Not only the choice but the very definition is left to the reader. Are you, gentle reader, one of the "happy few" for whom they have been told? Or are you one, like Diderot's nephew of Rameau, who will read Molière's *Tartuffe* as a source for immoral behavior? In the latter case, you will read the tales as aid and comfort to your own *malvagia operazion.* The moral and epistemological possibilities here are surprisingly "modern"; the tales themselves seem to be put forward as amoral (or, better, "pan-moral"), while the reader's moral predilections will govern his understanding. Implicit to Boccaccio's complex and difficult sentence is the position that the tales have in fact no effective instructive purpose, that is, the bad will remain evil and the good stay good. In any case, the morality here seems to be one that governs perception rather than behavior. And thus the shot at his detractors who hold that some of the tales are overlong allows Boccaccio to take a swipe at his eventual commentators as well: we who "utilmente adoperare il tempo faticano" [exert ourselves to use the time profitably] (21) will not bother with these tales written for otiose, amorous ladies. The claim that these are not fit objects for scholarly attention forces us to consider whether we are good or evil people, good or bad readers. Certifying the correctness of Filomena's praise of friendship and lament for its absence in the present age, Panfilo speaks to Boccaccio's purpose (X.ix.4).

E se noi qui per dover correggere i difetti mondani o pur per riprender-gli fossimo, io seguiterei con diffuso sermone le sue parole; ma per ciò che altro è il nostro fine, a me è caduto nell'animo di dimostrarvi, forse con una istoria assai lunga ma piacevol per tutto, una delle magnificen-zie del Saladino, acciò che per le cose che nella mia novella udirete, se pienamente l'amicizia d'alcuno non si può per li nostri vizii acquistare, almeno diletto prendiamo del servire, sperando che quando che sia di ciò merito ci debba seguire.

[And if we had assembled here dutifully to correct worldly errors or to criticize them, I would follow her words with a lengthy lecture. But since our aim is other, it has come into my mind to reveal to you, with a tale that is perhaps too long, but no less pleasing for that, one of the magnificent deeds of Saladin, so that through the things that you will hear in my *novella,* [you will learn that] if we cannot fully acquire the friendship of another because of our vices, let us at least take pleasure in service, in the hope that, whenever it may be, our reward for this may follow.]

This disclaimer of the conventional Horatian purpose helps us to interpret these passages that apparently claim such a purpose in the work's *Proemio* and *Conclusione.* The ladies and we may read the text as a *Galeotto* (Maz-zotta's position) or as a "counter-*Galeotto*" (Bernardo's view)—it depends entirely on their, and our, natures.

In the view of the *Decameron* sponsored here, Boccaccio is most con-cerned with our governance of our intellectual response to life. Unlike Dante, he does not wish to make us live or pray better; rather he wants to enable us to think more clearly about our human nature. About human behavior, he would seem to be saying, there is nothing to be done. The only attribute of human behavior explicitly approved of in the *Decameron* is thus *ingegno,* but not that wit which serves appetite so much as the one which is the property of the minds of those who escape the social condition of humankind in order to reflect upon the follies of the herd, the *ingegno* of the great solitary figures who appear in coruscating moments in this masterpiece of the depiction of human selfishness: Giotto, Cavalcanti, and Giovanni Boccaccio himself.

Addendum: *Utilità* in the *Decameron*

Proemio		8	**author**	those in greater need will have *utilità* from his comforting
Proemio		14	**author**	tales will grant "diletto . . . e *utile* consiglio"
I	vii	7	**Bergamino**	hopes for *utilità* from Can de la Scala (gets robe, money, horse—28)
I	Conc.	9	**Filomena**	tales of Second Day "di piacere e d'*utilità* similmente consistere"
II	ii	3	**Filostrato**	tale about Rinaldo will be *utile* for ladies to hear
II	iii	5	**Pampinea**	her tale will offer *utilità* (concerning our subjection to fortune) "e dovrà piacere"
II	vii	102	**Antigono**	hopes king will grant him "grande *utile*" for having had Alatiel in his charge (he is well rewarded when he returns her to the sultan)
II	ix	56	**Ambruogiuolo**	is set up in business by Sicurano, who thus grants him "*util* grande"
II	Conc.	9	**Neifile**	instructs each to tell a tale "*utile* o almeno dilettevole"
III	Int.	10	**author**	the two mills are not without *utilità* to the owner of the villa
III	vii	33	**Tedaldo**	disguised as friar warns Ermellina against friars "a *utilità* di voi"
III	ix	8	**Giletta**	herbs with which she cures the fistula of king of France are *utili*
IV	Int.	23	**author**	Filippo Balducci does not want his son to have "desiderio men che *utile*"
IV	iv	23	**Gerbino**	changes military tactic, seeing previous actions "poco *util* fare"
V	x	22	**old woman**	promises to be *utile* in helping wife of Pietro di Vinciolo take a lover

V	Conc.	3	**Elissa**	of next Day's *motti:* "la materia è bella e può essere *utile*"
VI	iv	3	**Neifile**	fortune, as well as wit, may supply "parole presti e *utile* e belle"
VI	x	37	**Cipolla**	"i privilegi del Porcellana . . . molto più *utili* sono a altrui che a noi"
VI	x	39	**Cipolla**	friars "poco dell'altrui fatiche curandosi dove la loro *utilità* vedessero seguitare"
VI	x	55	**Cipolla**	his *utilità* in making the mark of the Cross on the Certaldesi
VII	i	3	**Emilia**	her tale, telling how to exorcise a ghost (= successfully cuckold a husband), "vi possa essere *utile* nell'avvenire"
VII	ii	4	**Filostrato**	his similar account of Peronella cannot be anything but *utile* to the ladies
VIII	i	5	**Gulfardo**	the noun *utile* is used for the interest which he charges on loans
VIII	i	10	**Gulfardo**	the *utile* which he must pay to Guasparuolo
VIII	vii	3	**Pampinea**	her tale will teach the ladies how to play better tricks than the widow, not "senza *utilità* di voi"
VIII	vii	89	**the scholar**	his life is more *utile* than that of one hundred thousand of the likes of the lady
VIII	Conc.	4	**Emilia**	having a free choice of subject for the next Day's tales will be *utile*
IX	ix	7	**Emilia**	the advice of Solomon in her tale (women should be beaten) is "*utile* medicina"
X	i	2	**Neifile**	her tale will be "assai leggiadra, la quale . . . non potrà esser se non *utile*"
X	3	21	**Natan**	disguised, he offers Mitridanes "*util* consiglio"—how to find (and kill) Natan
X	iv	38	**Gentile**	asserts that Catalina was considered "non *utile*" by Niccoluccio, who rejected her
X	viii	70	**Tito**	he will be "*utile* . . . padrone" if Sofronia marries Gisippo
X	viii	112	**Filomena**	friendship has been exiled by cupidity, which seeks only its own *utilità*

X	ix	30	**Torello's wife**	her advice (that her guests accept gifts) will be *utile*
X	Conc.	8	**Panfilo**	his advice (that they now return to the city) is finally judged "*utile* e onesto" by the rest of the company
Conc. Au.		9	**author**	fire, though it destroy, is *utilissimo* to mortals
Conc. Au.		14	**author**	the tales may be construed as counseling evil deeds; nonetheless, one who wants to will find in them "*utilità* e frutto"
Conc. Au.		14	**author**	the truth is that they are to be held as "*utile* e oneste" if the circumstances and the tellers are kept in mind
Conc. Au.		21	**author**	length of tales no burden for the otiose; only scholars need short texts, for they do not wish to pass the time, but to use it *utilmente*

The Proem of the *Decameron*

(1993)

Points of departure are signs that lead to arrivals; finishing anything, we tend to look back to its inception, for only with the sense of the relation of those two events or moments do we feel we come in contact with whatever it is that constitutes wholeness, integrity. Given the fact that beginnings are of undisputed importance, we should be more than a little surprised that Boccaccio's *Proemio* is probably the most neglected part of the *Decameron*. Robbed of wide recognition of its rightful and important place as introduction to the whole by the (justly) closely studied *Introduzione*,[1] it is frequently forgotten and almost always underattended. Even those who announce their intention to study it at some length (e.g., Di Pino, Getto, Russo) do not offer either close analyses or particularly insightful larger understandings. Indeed, the *Proemio* tends to suffer from the same sort of subjective and impressionistic responses that the *Decameron* as a whole tends to receive.

Perhaps because of the extraordinary complexity of its wholeness (even Dante's *Commedia* is easier to keep in mind in some orderly fashion), the pieces of the *Decameron* are allowed to serve us, in our hunger for mean-

[An earlier and shorter version of this essay was given as the first *Lectura Boccaccii Americana* in Washington, D.C., in December 1984 under the auspices of the American Boccaccio Association. I thank Professor Elissa Weaver, the editor of the volume of the twelve papers dedicated to the First Day of the *Decameron* that is under contract to the University of Pennsylvania Press, for permission to print my work in the volume dedicated to the memory of Silvio Pasquazi (published in 1993), and I thank both publishing houses for permission to republish it here, in a form somewhat abbreviated from that it had in the Pasquazi volume.]

1. Gibaldi is but one of the more recent students of the frame to spend all his attention on the second beginning of the work. Here and elsewhere the reader may find bibliographical information in the list of works consulted at the conclusion of this study.

ing, as adequate specimens from which to draw our totalizing generaliza-
tions. Without wishing to offend, I would merely suggest that the
Decameron is one of the worst read masterpieces that the world possesses.
Unlike the vast, often contradictory, but generally useful hoard of scholarship that we have concerning the first two cantos of the *Commedia,* or even
the less imposing amount of interesting matter dedicated to Boccaccio's
difficult and fascinating *Introduzione,* the unconcerted and fleeting attention paid to his *Proemio* is itself a primary indication that, as readers, most
of us are not ready for the demands made on us by Boccaccio's text. In the
group of those who do not understand it I unhesitatingly include myself.

In her recently published study, "An Allegorically Tempered
Decameron," Victoria Kirkham reminds us of how few of the *Decameron's*
riddles we have been able to solve. Her opening paragraph reminds us how
poorly we have responded to the following difficult and necessary objects
of attention: the hidden "real" names of the ten narrators, the significance
of the pseudonyms which Boccaccio says he has supplied them, the identi-
ties of those who are lovers among the *brigata,* the reason for the uneven
distribution of servants among the ladies and gentlemen, the meaning of
the evidently allusive ballads sung at the conclusion of each Day. That is a
short list, its own potential for elaboration not even slightly developed.
And we can all add to it our own small heap of miseries—things in the text
which seem to call out for the critic's solving balm but resist our ministra-
tions. Kirkham's inventory suffices to remind us how little we have accomplished in six hundred years in our attempts to grasp Boccaccio's intentions. And one wishes that more studies of Boccaccio had the good grace
to insist that the texts which they purport to clarify are, at the very least,
resistant to their clarifiers. We do the truth a disservice when we make Boccaccio sound "easy." The *ballate,* for instance, remain a closed book to the
vast majority of critics who concern themselves with the *Decameron.* Can
we not all see that they are obviously of importance, that they call out for
interpretation? Yet how many of those who would tell us what the
Decameron means even confront the fact of their puzzling presence? Very
few do. And some of those who have had concourse with them have produced results which are so unconvincing that those who remain silent may
feel that, in some circumstances, silence is indeed golden. Yes, this text is
enjoyable, so comforting, so "user-friendly," that we are allowed to believe
we have understood it. We may, I would agree, have felt its spirit. Understanding the way in which it was put together and what it may signify—

these are desires which, in my experience, remain nearly totally unfulfilled. Let me offer only one example of the sort of difficulties encountered by an ideal Boccaccian reader. Such a reader—unlike most of the work's actual audience—comes to the book from Boccaccio's preceding vernacular fictions and Latin texts with certain expectations of the techniques and preoccupations that he or she will encounter in a fabulist who owes his major intellectual allegiance to classical forebears and to Dante. He is, as he is often said to be, a "pre-humanist." What of the author who now confronts us? Everything is changed—or nearly everything (at least we may say that everything seems to be changed): gone is the narrator-in-love-who-by-this-book-woos-his-sweetheart; gone are the mythological figures who populate the earlier texts. While there has been a "comico-borghese" element in some of the earlier works, at least for moments at a time, now that style gives the dominant tone to many of the one hundred tales and surely sets the scene for our reaction to the work as a whole. The motives for the conscious choice (for surely it must have been one) which accounts for these major changes remain obscure to us and probably will always do so. Our most usual form of response is to look upon the considerable earlier production of Boccaccio as little more than an apprenticeship, despite the fact that the author himself repeatedly looks back to the antecedents which he created for himself. We tend to deny the importance of the continuum and, as a result, the extraordinary nature of his change of course within it. Like native inhabitants of the New World, we stare in wonder or alarm at this new vehicle without knowing anything about Genoa or that its captain came from there. Were we to know these things, we would still be amazed that he and it had been capable of such a voyage.

While some have argued that the *Decameron* is a work void of moral concern or purpose, almost all who deal with it argue with some zeal that it puts forward a vision of human life that urges a moral choice upon us. Without reviewing the centuries of debate (we are aware with what difficulty those who defended Boccaccio in the Renaissance did so, forced to tell his detractors—and themselves—that he really was a good Christian), we can make a simplified outline of the positions which have grown up alongside the book. I would describe the three major and competing views of the *Decameron* which have emerged since the Second World War as follows. (I would also be quick to insist that I am aware that my three schools force together some interpretive positions that in fact reveal wide divergences of opinion). It is variously held that the *Decameron* may be characterized as embodying one of the following central positions:

1. a traditional Christian/humanist moral vision, one which essentially maintains the Augustinian/Dantean continuum (e.g., Branca, Bernardo, Kirkham);
2. a literature of "escape," of pure amusement (e.g., Singleton, Olson);
3. a new moral vision which is in polemical relation to the old moral order (e.g., Di Pino, Getto, Scaglione, Baratto).

I do not now believe that any of these approaches enables us to understand what the *Decameron* is most centrally concerned with, if I believe that each of them contributes an important element of understanding to a better working hypothesis. The first view is undoubtedly correct in understanding that whatever is "new" in Boccaccio's vision, that vision was produced out of an existing set of cultural and moral givens; the second, if less convincing in its total premise than either of the other two, at least has this much on its side: Boccaccio's art is more aware of itself as an aim in itself and of the possibility of an art for mere delectation's sake than that of most of his medieval precursors; the third, with which I disagree most strongly because it leads to the most inhibiting final perceptions, has on its side Boccaccio's palpable hostility to the representatives of the social and religious institutions which are ostensibly charged with the maintenance of morality. Thus I would put forward a fourth possibility for a general understanding of Boccaccio's purpose in the *Decameron,* which I now see as a text that combines the following elements in the following ways:

4. an exploration of humankind's inability to be governed or to govern itself in accord with traditional morality, or to find a harmonious way of living within nature; yet the work does envision a human capacity to develop an aesthetic expression that is fully capable of examining our own corrupt and unameliorable being (in this formulation one finds elements of Mazzotta and Seung).

If Boccaccio is "new" in his *Decameron,* I think that some such combination of negative observations of human behavior and the pleasing development of the aesthetic means to portray such behavior may help to account for his novelty.

Boccaccio's presentation of his book as Ovidian text, with particular relevance to the *Amores,* has received some brief notice.[2] What has gone
almost totally unnoticed, as far as I have observed, is the way in which he
carefully connects his own role as narrator who wishes to ease the pains of
love to the Ovid of the *Remedia amoris.*[3] The textual evidence for this rap-
prochement seems to me so inviting that one can only wonder that it
requires demonstration. There is a single likely reason for the existence of
so crucial a lacuna in our understanding of the *Decameron.* We have
tended to decide two issues before we begin to read the text: first, that Boccaccio, as champion of an erotic sensibility, could not possibly uphold the
values of a text which is anti-erotic; second, that the *Remedia* is in fact a
seriously anti-erotic text. Both of these assumptions, like the baseless (and
still occasionally present) notion that the phrase "Iohannes tranquillita-
tum" [sunshine Johnny] means to praise Giovanni's good nature (rather
than condemn his fickle friendship), require better analyses.

It is true that in the Middle Ages the *Remedia* was generally understood
as an anti-venereal text.[4] Those who knew it by its name alone or through
the instructions of others or by means of anthologized fragments may well
be excused this questionable assumption. However, anyone who reads the
text with smiling attention realizes that it is a joke at the expense of the
foolish and vituperative detractors of the *Ars amatoria.* In brief, I would
describe this problem as follows: Ovid, in the *Ars,* had in fact meant to
demonstrate (as he had frequently done in what is surely one of the greatest first works ever written, the *Amores*) that lovers are foolish. Having
assumed the role of *praeceptor Amoris,* Ovid allows us to read him lascivi-
ously if we are so inclined, but he hopes that the wiser of us will understand that his text is in fact a witty and devastating revelation of the follies
of lovers. The *praeceptor Amoris* is really the *magister de amore,* an ironist,

---

2. For discussion of the phrase "senza titolo" of *Dec.* IV.Int.3 as suggesting a generic
resemblance between the two works (since the *Amores* was often referred to, and indeed twice
by Boccaccio in the *Esposizioni,* as *Sine titulo*) see Hollander 1977, 115–16, 235; see also
Branca 1976, 1197; Padoan 1978, 93–94.

3. Since I first advanced this hypothesis, Janet Smarr, who, I believe, was the first person
ever to have made the suggestion that the *Remedia* is significantly linked to Boccaccio's strategy of self-presentation in the *Decameron* (Smarr 1976, 176–77), has repeated and developed
her observation (Smarr 1986, 166; 1987, 252); see also Kirkham 1985b, 337. The latter, however, privileges the resonance of the *Heroides.* See my n. 12.

4. For a detailed account of the *Remedia* (considered alongside of the companion *Ars*) as
object of the medieval scholiast's attention see Hexter 1986, 15–82.

even a satirist, pulling what we must refer to, in polite conversation, as our leg.[5] If that is so, we can readily understand the reaction of such a writer to what to him must have seemed the ludicrous reactions of Roman bluenoses. His polished witty verses display the nonsense of carnality; the bluenoses cry out against his prurience. The only form of response to such unenlightened critics was to write a companion piece which would apparently give them what they wanted: the remedies of love.[6] The latter work was thus intended to take revenge upon a critical response that showed neither grace nor acumen.

Where the earlier work pretended to praise the god of love and actually revealed his damaging effects, the *Remedia* pretends to counter the god of erotic activity but actually tells lovers how to get what they want. Lovers in the *Ars* are plangent losers; in the *Remedia* they are cool and collected exploiters of the objects of their desires. Boccaccio, I believe, not only carefully observed the reversals in Ovid's two complementary works but found them utterly germane to his own purposes. The *Decameron* is presented as a *remedium amoris*—in the root sense of Ovid's title. Its task, as we must agree, if we read its *Proemio* with any care, is apparently to offer ladies who are unhappily amorous "utile consiglio" [helpful advice] by which they may understand what they should flee, what they should seek. But his unenlightened detractors, like Ovid's, do not understand (or even observe) this patent overall intention of the work, stamped clearly into its *Proemio*. The Introduction to the Fourth Day and the *Conclusione dell'Autore* both spend considerable time trying to convince these *morditori* (whether these actually existed or are invented is of little moment to this argument) that the tales and the intentions of their author are, if not chaste, not libidinous either.[7] It seems that Boccaccio did not believe that the *Decameron* was acceptable to the outraged sensibilities of its real or imagined detractors. And thus the *Corbaccio* had to be put forward as the companion piece of the *Decameron* and as the overtly remedial text which their small imaginations required (I have recently published a study that attempts to return to the notion that the *Corbaccio* was in fact written soon after the *Decameron*,

---

5. Hexter points out that Ovid's phrase "ego sum praeceptor Amoris" [I am Love's teacher] was simply too eloquently ambiguous for most of his readers. In Hexter's words (1986, 21) "it seems Ovid misjudged either the effectiveness of the image or the capacity of his readers."

6. For Boccaccio's awareness that the *Remedia* was written early in Ovid's career and as a companion to the *Ars* see Hollander 1977, 114.

7. An article by Janet Smarr (1987) demonstrates that Boccaccio's self-defense in the *Conclusione dell'Autore* is modelled on Ovid's in the second book of the *Tristia*.

noting that it, like the *Decameron*, begins with a hitherto-unnoticed citation of the *Remedia*, and that it, like Ovid's apparent palinode, mocks the
opposers of love even more than lovers).[8] Before we begin to examine the
evidence for an Ovidian presence in the text of the *Proemio*, I should like to
examine the binary arrangement which typifies its development.

The *Proemio* is divided into two parts, one of which is devoted to the
"autobiography" of its author as formerly unhappy lover, the second to the
intended audience of his book. I do not think it is accidental that these two
parts are of equal length, each being allotted seven periods, or sentences.
What follows is a reductive paraphrase of this matter.

2. It is humane to be compassionate to those who suffer pain; those
who have been so comforted, as I have been, owe a special debt
to others less fortunate than they.

3. From my earliest youth until now I have been unhappily in love
with a noble lady.

4. I was perhaps saved from death by the good advice and
consolation of a friend.

5. It pleased God, who is infinite, to make my love finite when all
else failed to do so, so that all that is left of my passion is a better
regulated pleasure in loving, all unhappiness taken away.

6. My gratitude to them [now plural] will last until I die.

7–8. Now that I am free, I offer this book in exchange, if not to those
who are wise or lucky enough to have avoided love, then at least
to those who are in need of my comforting.

9–11. Do not women require such aid still more than men? Their
otiose, shut-in existence leaves them vulnerable to thoughts of
love unless they have access to the sort of advice that men do not
seem to require equally.

12. For men have many escapes: birding, hunting, fishing, riding,
gaming, or business.

13–14. Thus I have assembled these one hundred *novelle*, whether fables,
parables, or histories,[9] told by seven ladies and three men in time
of plague, along with the ladies' songs, stories concerning

---

8. See Hollander 1988.

9. For the descendance of these three terms from the traditional rhetorical triad *historia,
fabula, argumentum* see Stewart 1986; for their relationship to Dante see Hollander 1969,
256–58.

pleasing and harsh amorous incidents as well as other fortune-tossed events, so that the love-struck ladies may know what to flee and what to seek, thus abating their tribulation.

15.   If such should be the result—and may God grant that it be so—then let them give thanks to the god of love, who, by freeing me from his chains, has granted me the power to wait upon their pleasure.

Wending their way through both parts of the *Proemio* are a series of anti-thetically related pairs.[10] These may be described as falling into two groups, one of which contains words for the malady of love and its results, the second the medicine which may be applied to the patient in hopes of restoring her or him. The resulting chain of metaphorically related entities is arresting:

causes or symptoms of pain	**antidotal measures**
2. afflitti	compassione, conforto, piacere
3. amore, fatica, fuoco, appetito, noia	
4. noia, morto	rifrigerio, piacevoli ragionamenti, consolazioni
5. amore, faticoso, affanno	consiglio, piacere, dilettevole
6. pena, fatiche, morte	benefici ricevuti, benivolenza
7.	libero, alleggiamento
8.	sostentamento, conforto, utilità
9.	[sostentamento]
10. amorose fiamme	piaceri, pensieri allegri
11. malinconia, focoso disio, noia	ragionamenti
12. malinconia . . . afflige, noioso pensiero, noia	consolazione
13. quelle che amano, pestilenzioso tempo, mortalità	cento novelle
14. noia	diletto, sollazzevoli cose, utile consiglio
15.	liberandomi, piaceri

---

10. See Davis for some consideration of the binary structure of the work as a whole.

The connections and oppositions suggested by this list of some of the key words of the *Proemio* are, I think, worth close consideration. Reading "vertically" down through the first column of these concatenated terms, we note that the "afflicted" suffer from a varied roster of ailments, ranging from those that lead to physical death to those more usually thought of as pleasant activities: sexual relations. The word which rises from the *Proemio* as making its most representative statement is *noia,* which occurs half a dozen times. Morally and aesthetically it is the demon of the *Decameron.* Here it is associated with love, death, and plague. Our traditional "robust" reading of the *Decameron* has kept us from seeing the obvious parallels established in the text at its outset between sexuality and pestilence.[11] The word *noia* helps to make the implicit connections still more clear, as it moves from the pages of the *Proemio* to those of the *Introduzione* (2, 6, 67, 70, 77), into Panfilo's frame for the first tale (which echoes the first sentence of the *Proemio*—I.i.3), whence it makes its way into the first tale, where it is Cepparello's equivalent for the name of the mortal disease from which he suffers (I.i.32). *Noia,* one might begin to perceive, is something like the major preoccupation of the *Decameron,* one which runs the length of the text (the last time we encounter the word is in X.x.31, where it describes the anguish at heart felt by Griselda as she gives her baby daughter to her husband's servant to be killed—or so she thinks). Against the onslaught of sexual passion, plague, and death the text arrays a series of phonically related groups: compassione–conforto–consolazioni–consiglio; piacere–piacevoli ragionamenti–pensieri allegri; sostentamento–sollazzevoli cose. Many of these words are used twice or more and constitute a sort of *materia medica* to be used against the disease of love. We should have recognized by now whose voice we should be hearing in the background: the Ovid of the *Remedia amoris.*

The Ovidian persona of the *Ars amatoria* is that of the pornographic poet ("ego sum praeceptor Amoris" [I am Love's teacher]—1.17; "lascivi praeceptor Amoris" [instructor in lascivious love]—2.497; "nil nisi lascivi per me discuntur amores" [only lascivious loves are learned from me]—3.27). The first voice we hear, in the opening verses of the *Remedia,* claims to be that of an enemy of Cupid. What he in fact proposes as the purpose of his work is not the wars against Amor which the god himself is imagined as foreseeing ("bella mihi, video, bella parantur" [wars, I see, yes, wars being

---

11. But see the brief appreciations in Mazzotta 1972, 65; 1986, 30. For Boccaccio's interest in the tradition of *aegritudo amoris* see Ciavolella 1970 and 1976.

prepared against me]—1.2) but a police action on behalf of those lovers who are unhappy, while those who are joyful in their ardor are urged to continue in their pleasure (1.11–16). Those who, in the Middle Ages or today, take the title of the *Remedia* as indicating a sweeping indictment of the pleasures of the flesh are simply not readers of Ovid. The work has more in common with medical writings than with moral treatises. It is thus that he plays with his detractors, composing a treatise in verse which in fact is far more critical of them than it is of love (not that Ovid is ever uncritical of happy lovers, whom he rather presents as being brutish, trivial, and self-seeking).

Boccaccio's own pose in the *Proemio* is not very different. The resemblances between his first beginning and the *Remedia* are numerous. The following series of resemblances is given in brief compass (see the Addendum for the Latin and Italian texts):

1. Both narrators have been and continue to be lovers (if Boccaccio seems a less enthusiastic one than Ovid claims to be).
2. Both texts have as their "medical" purpose the saving from death those who suffer from unhappiness in love.
3. Both texts thus promise to liberate those who are in bondage.
4. In both texts *otium* is seen as a cause of unhappy amorous feelings.
5. Both texts suggest that activity will counteract that sickness, jointly specifying, among others, hunting, birding, and fishing.
6. Both texts offer instruction to those who would avoid the pains of love in what to flee and what to seek.
7. Both authors, having offered themselves as preceptors in how to learn the art of "unloving," conclude by referring to the gratitude that will be owed them by their auditors.

Even that rather skeletal series of resemblances will perhaps convince some readers who have not previously thought so that consultation of the *Remedia* is useful to an appreciation of Boccaccio's expressions of his intention in his *Proemio*. It may also suggest that we have at last discovered the identity of the unidentified "amico" whose "piacevoli ragionamenti" brought the author back from the brink of death in his unhappy love affair. He would rather seem to be the author of the *Remedia,* would rather seem to be the writer of a specific classical text, than an unnamed fourteenth-century giver of solace.

Ovid himself would return to these concerns in the *Heroides* (19.5–16). We hear the words of Hero, addressed to absent Leander.

urimur igne pari, sed sum tibi viribus inpar:
   fortius ingenium suspicor esse viris.
ut corpus, teneris ita mens infirma puellis—
   deficiam, parvi temporis adde moram!
Vos modo venando, modo rus geniale colendo
   ponitis in varia tempora longa mora.
aut fora vos retinent aut unctae dona palaestrae,
   flectitis aut freno colla sequacis equi;
nunc volucrem laqueo, nunc piscem ducitis hamo;
   diluitur posito serior hora mero.
his mihi summotae, vel si minus acriter urar,
   quod faciam, superest praeter amare nihil.

[We burn with equal fires, but I am not equal to you in strength; men, methinks, must have stronger natures. As the body, so is the soul of tender women frail—delay but a little longer, and I shall die! You men, now in the chase, and now husbanding the genial acres of the country, consume long hours in the varied tasks that keep you. Either the marketplace holds you, or the sports of the supple wrestling-ground, or you turn with bit the neck of the responsive steed; now you take the bird with the snare, now the fish with the hook; and the later hours you while away with the wine before you. For me who am denied these things, even were I less fiercely aflame, there is nothing left to do but love.] (trans. G. Showerman in Loeb Classics edition)

In recent years a number of commentators have had recourse to this passage in their discussions of the otiose ladies of the *Proemio*.[12] Since it is certainly well considered an auto-citation, one wonders why no attention has been given to its sources in the *Remedia*. A working hypothesis might hold that, while the apparent compassionate atmosphere of the *Heroides* would not seem inappropriate as a source for the apparently compassionate Boccaccio, the reader who resorts to this text would not be as happy to consider the likelihood that Boccaccio was in fact more interested in the evidently ironic and distanced formulations of the *Remedia*.

Consideration of the closeness of Boccaccio's language to that of Ovid's self-presentation in a similar role, as my Addendum suggests, is still more likely to convince us that the *Remedia*, more than any other work, is

---

12. Branca 1976, 979; Muscetta 1972, 158; Olson 1982, 209; Potter 1982, 126; Kirkham 1985b, 335 (also adverting to the *Remedia*, p. 337); Rossi 1993, 126–28.

the governing precedent text which Boccaccio's beginning invokes. Our initial sense of disbelief, based on an understanding of the *Remedia* which does not do justice to its complexity, may yield to a more sympathetic attitude once we consider that Boccaccio's view of himself as a remedial Ovid includes the awareness that Ovid himself was writing ironically and that the persona he knows he has apparently assumed is that of Dante, whose fifth canto is resolute in putting even the most sympathetic of carnal sinners into the pit.

If Boccaccio is Ovid, he is also Dante. Beginning with the *Decameron*'s subtitle, which has it that the *Decameron* is "cognominato Prencipe Galeotto," an evident gesture toward *Inferno* 5, Boccaccio makes it clear that no other literary text is as important to him as Dante's *Commedia*. This is not to forget how assiduously he perused—indeed copied out in his own hand—so much of the rest of the Dantean corpus but only to reflect his own sense of priority. Boccaccio's opening gesture toward Dante establishes a problematic textual connection rather than attempting to resolve a problem. It is my belief that a good deal of Boccaccio's traffic in the text of the *Commedia* has exactly such a task. And it seems to me that all of his moralizing readers, whether they hold that Boccaccio is a supporter of a conventional morality or the revolutionary proponent of a new one, make a similar mistake when they fail to account for the subversive and ironic relation between the author and his material, between the writer and his audience.[13] To read Boccaccio "straight" puts us at risk, the same risk we undergo if we attempt a similar reading of the amatory Ovid. In a recent article,[14] I have attempted to demonstrate that the very phrase in the *Proemio* which would seem to anchor the *Decameron*'s purpose to a Horatian and traditional literary moralism (the familiar binome *utile/dulcis* [useful/pleasing]), "diletto . . . utile consiglio" [delight . . . helpful advice], eventually undermines exactly such a conventional moral stance. In the world of the *Decameron*, that which is *utile* is, far more often than not, merely that which brings profit or pleasure (or the avoidance of pain). Thus, if the work begins as Horatian, it concludes by making the "useful" entirely dependent upon the human impulses of the user.

---

13. Luciano Rossi's recent revisionary study, "Ironia e parodia" (1989), with which I find myself in essential agreement and which does much to undermine some of the "certainties" in contemporary interpretation of the *Decameron*, offers welcome support to the ironic reading of the text proposed here. For an overview of the subject see Dilwyn Knox 1989. [And now see Delcorno, "Ironia/parodia," cited in my Introduction, n. 2.]

14. See Hollander 1985–86 [the preceding study in this collection].

Vittore Branca has opportunely reminded us that both the *Commedia* and the *Decameron* begin by referring to events or dates which mark the thirty-fifth year of the author's life.[15] The sense of an author-protagonist who has recently escaped from a life-threatening situation pervades both proemial passages. In both texts this situation is referred to as *noia* (*Proemio* 3, 4; *Inferno* 1.76: "Ma tu perché ritorni a tanta noia?" [but you, why are you turning back toward such great trouble?]). In their former difficulty each is aided by the counsel of a "friend": in Dante, this was Virgil, sent by Beatrice; in Boccaccio, as I have just proposed, the adviser is Ovid. The playfulness of this intertextual exchange may be still more sophisticated than even this much may suggest. In Dante, the appearance of Virgil to tell of Beatrice's *vita* in heaven is clearly reminiscent of the mournful passage in *Vita nuova* 23.6 in which "alcuno amico" [a certain friend of mine], one who is further described in the accompanying verse (23.24) as "omo . . . scolorito e fioco" [a man . . . pale and faint], comes to tell Dante that Beatrice is dead. This figure is nearly certainly in Dante's mind as he describes Virgil, bringing better news of Beatrice, in Inferno 1.[16] If Boccaccio drew a similar conclusion, his own "alcun amico" reflects both the salvific Virgil in the first canto of the *Commedia* and his antithetic model in the *Vita nuova*. As the Italian Ovid, one who leaves the role of Virgil to Dante, he is likely to have been pleased by exactly such a recondite reference. We might further speculate that it is in a neighboring passage in the *Vita nuova* that Dante, for the only time in his *opere,* refers to the *Remedia amoris* by name (25.9): Ovid too, he says, speaks of Love as though he were a person when he has him say, "Bella michi, video, bella parantur," in the book "c'ha nome Libro di Remedio d'Amore" [that is called the Book of the Remedy of Love]. Boccaccio's *Proemio,* which also shares two occurrences of hapax with the *Commedia* (*rifrigerio,* 4 and *Paradiso* 14.27; *faticoso,* 5 and *Inferno* 23.67), shares other elements in its vocabulary with its precursor (e.g., "come a Colui piacque" [as it pleased Another]—5; "ne' suoi più cupi pelaghi navigando" [sailing upon its deepest seas]—5),[17] in such a way as to indicate that, beginning with his subtitle, Boccaccio wanted his reader to entertain the possibility that the *Decameron* is to be read as Dantean moralization. It is my opinion that this gesture is made only to be withdrawn in favor of a more disconcerting and interesting

---

15. 1976, 981, remanding the reader to Branca 1970, 34f.

16. See Hollander 1983, 75–77.

17. The second resonance had been previously noted by Branca 1976, 977, and both are listed by Bettinzoli 1981–82, 269, 271.

claim, namely, that the *Decameron* is to be dealt with as a text descended from the playful and mocking book which calls itself Love's Remedy but which is in fact a work which examines love's problematic, which knows that, whatever else human life encompasses, its major premise is appetite. Correction of that appetite may be a desirable, if not an easily achieved, goal. Compassionate study of it is the aim of those who are themselves most human.

Addendum: The *Remedia amoris* and Boccaccio's *Proemio*

1. The narrators as past and present lovers:

> ego semper amavi,
> Et si, quid faciam nunc quoque, quaeris, amo.
>
> (7–8)

. . . dalla mia prima giovanezza infino a questo tempo oltre modo essendo acceso stato d'altissimo e nobile amore . . . ; mi fu egli di grandissima fatica a sofferire, certo non per crudeltà della donna amata, ma per soverchio fuoco nella mente concetto da poco regolato appetito. . . . il mio amore . . . si diminuì in guisa, che sol di se nella mente m'ha al presente lasciato quel piacere che egli è usato di porgere a chi troppo non si mette ne' suoi più cupi pelaghi navigando; per che, dove faticoso esser solea, ogni affanno togliendo via, dilettevole il sento esser rimaso. (3, 5)

2. Unhappy love as leading to death:

> At siquis male fert indignae regna puellae,
> Ne pereat, nostrae sentiat artis opem.
>
> (15–16)

> Qui, nisi desierit, misero periturus amore est,
> Desinat. . . .
>
> (21–22)

Nella qual noia tanto rifrigerio già mi porsero i piacevoli ragionamenti d'alcuno amico e le sue laudevoli consolazioni, che io porto fermissima opinione per quelle essere avenuto che io non sia morto. (4)

3. The need to be free of Love's sway:

> Publicus assertor dominis suppressa levabo
> Pectora: vindictae quisque favete suae.
>
> (73–74)

> Optimus ille sui vindex, laedentia pectus ,
> Vincula qui rupit, dedoluitque semel.
>
> (293–94)

> . . . ora che libero dir mi posso. . . . (7)

> . . . a Amore [le donne] ne rendano grazie, il quale liberandomi da'
> suoi legami m'ha conceduto il potere attendere a' lor piaceri. (15)

4. Otium as cause of unhappy love:

> . . . fugias otia prima. . . .
>
> (136)

> Otia si tollas, periere Cupidinis arcus. . . .
>
> (139)

> Tam Venus otia amat; qui finem quaeris amoris,
> Cedit amor rebus: res age, tutus eris.
>
> (143–44)

> Esse dentro a' dilicati petti, temendo e vergognando, tengono
> l'amorose fiamme nascose [cf. *Rem.* 105: "tacitae serpunt in viscera
> flammae"] . . . , e oltre a ciò . . . il più del tempo nel piccolo circuito
> delle loro camere racchiuse dimorano e quasi oziose sedendosi. . . .
> (10)

5. Activities which counteract lovesickness:

> Rura quoque oblectant animos . . .
> . . . tu venandi studium cole . . .
> Lenius est studium, studium tamen, alite capta
> Aut lino aut calamis praemia parva sequi,
> Vel, quae piscis edax avido male devoret ore,

Abdere suspensis aera recurva cibis.

$$(169, 199, 207-10)$$

[Gli uomini], se alcuna malinconia o gravezza di pensieri gli affligge, hanno molti modi da allaggiare o da passar quello . . . ; volendo essi, non manca l'andare a torno, udire e veder molte cose, uccellare, cacciare, pescare, cavalcare, giucare o mercatare. (12)

6. Author's advice in what to flee, what to seek:

. . . quos [cibos] fugias quosque sequare, dabo.

$$(796)$$

. . . parimente diletto della sollazzevoli cose in quelle [novelle] mostrate e utile consiglio potranno [le donne] pigliare, in quanto potranno cognoscere quello che sia da fuggire e che sia similmente da seguitare. (14)

7. Both authors conclude in a similar vein (the thanks due them from their auditors):

Postmodo reddetis sacro pia vota poetae,
  Carmine sanati femina virque meo

$$(813-14)$$

Il che [passamento di noia] se avviene, che voglia Idio che così sia, a Amore ne rendano grazie, il quale liberandomi da' suoi legami m'ha conceduto il potere attendere a' lor piaceri. (15)

Works Consulted

Works which refer specifically to the text of the *Proemio* are followed by a parenthesis, an asterisk preceding the indication of the pages that contain such reference.

Baratto, Mario. *Realtà e stile nel "Decameron."* 2d ed. Vicenza: Neri Pozza, 1974 [1970]. (*70, 72, 155, 280)
Barberi Squarotti, Giorgio. "La cornice del *Decameron* o il mito di Robin-

son." In *Il potere della parola: Studi sul "Decameron,"* 5–63. Naples: Federico & Ardia, 1983 [1970]. (*33–34)

Barolini, Teodolinda. "The Wheel of the *Decameron.*" *Romance Philology* 36, no. 4 (1983): 521–38. (*521–22)

Bernardo, Aldo S. "The Plague as Key to Meaning in Boccaccio's *Decameron.*" In *The Black Death: The Impact of the Fourteenth-Century Plague,* ed. D. Williman, 39–64. Binghamton, N.Y.: Medieval and Renaissance Texts and Studies, 1982. (*40–42)

Bettinzoli, Attilio. "Per una definizione delle presenze dantesche nel *Decameron.*" Parts 1, "I registri 'ideologici,' lirici, drammatici," and 2, "Ironizzazione e espressivismo antifrastico-deformatorio." *Studi sul Boccaccio* 13 (1981–82): 267–326; 14 (1983–84): 209–40.

Branca, Vittore. *Boccaccio medievale.* 3d ed. Florence: Sansoni, 1970 [1956].

———. *Note.* In *Tutte le opere di Giovanni Boccaccio,* vol. 4, *Decameron,* 976–1568. Milan: A. Mondadori, 1976.

Cerisola, Pier Luigi. "La questione della cornice del *Decameron.*" *Aevum* 49 (1975): 137–56. (*148–51)

Cian, Vittorio. "L'organismo del *Decameron.*" In *Scritti minori,* 129–39. Turin: G. Gambino, 1936 [1913].

Ciavolella, Massimo. "La tradizione dell'*aegritudo amoris* nel *Decameron.*" *Giornale storico della letteratura italiana* 147 (1970): 496–517.

———. *La "malattia d'amore" dall'antichità al medioevo.* Rome: Bulzoni, 1976.

Cottino-Jones, Marga. *Order from Chaos: Social and Aesthetic Harmonies in Boccaccio's "Decameron."* Washington, D.C.: University Press of America, 1982. (*4, 5, 6, 8–9, 18)

Davis, Walter R. "Boccaccio's *Decameron:* The Implications of Binary Form." *Modern Language Quarterly* 42 (1981): 3–20.

Delcorno, Carlo. "Note sui dantismi nell'*Elegia di madonna Fiammetta.*" *Studi sul Boccaccio* 11 (1979): 251–94.

De Michelis, Cesare. *Contraddizioni nel "Decameron."* Milan: Guanda, 1983. (*18–19, 28, 34–36)

Di Pino, Guido. "Il 'proemio' e l'introduzione alla quarta 'giornata.'" In *La polemica del Boccaccio,* 209–20. Florence: Vallecchi, 1953. (*209–20).

Gelli, Giovan Battista. *Commento edito e inedito sopra la "Divina Commedia."* Ed. C. Negroni. Florence: Bocca, 1887 [1553].

Getto, Giovanni. "La cornice e le componenti espressive del *Decameron.*"

In *Vita di forme e forme di vita nel "Decameron,"* 1–33. Turin: Petrini, 1958. (*1–9)

Gibaldi, Joseph. "The *Decameron* Cornice and the Responses to the Disintegration of Civilization." *Kentucky Romance Quarterly* 24 (1977): 349–57.

Hexter, Ralph J. *Ovid and Medieval Schooling: Studies in Medieval School Commentaries.* Munich: Arbeo-Gesellschaft, 1986.

Hollander, Robert. *Allegory in Dante's "Commedia."* Princeton: Princeton University Press, 1969.

———. *Boccaccio's Two Venuses.* New York: Columbia University Press, 1977. (*102–7)

———. *Il Virgilio dantesco.* Florence: Olschki, 1983.

———. *"Utilità* in Boccaccio's *Decameron." Studi sul Boccaccio* 15 (1985–86): 215–33. (*215–20)

———. *Boccaccio's Last Fiction: Il "Corbaccio."* Philadelphia: University of Pennsylvania Press, 1988. (*6, 29, 36, 39, 43, 46, 49, 51, 56, 57, 78–79)

Kirkham, Victoria. "An Allegorically Tempered *Decameron." Italica* 62, no. 1 (1985a): 1–23. [Reprinted in *The Sign of Reason in Boccaccio's Fiction* (Florence: Olschki, 1993), 131–71.]

———. "Boccaccio's Dedication to Women in Love." In *Renaissance Studies in Honor of Craig Hugh Smyth,* vol. 1. Florence: C/E Giunti & G. Barbèra, 1985b. (*333–43) [Reprinted in *The Sign of Reason in Boccaccio's Fiction* (Florence: Olschki, 1993), 117–29.]

Knox, Dilwyn. *Ironia: Medieval and Renaissance Ideas on Irony.* Leiden: Brill, 1989.

Marcus, Millicent Joy. *An Allegory of Form: Literary Self-Consciousness in the "Decameron."* Saratoga, Calif.: Anma Libri, 1979. (*84, 113–14, 119, 125)

Marino, Lucia. *The "Decameron" Cornice: Allusion, Allegory, and Iconology.* Ravenna: Longo, 1979. (*12, 28, 38–39)

Mazzotta, Giuseppe. "The *Decameron:* The Marginality of Literature." *University of Toronto Quarterly* 42, no. 1 (1972): 64–81. (*13n, 30 and n., 38, 57, 245–47)

———. *The World at Play in Boccaccio's "Decameron."* Princeton: Princeton University Press, 1986.

Muscetta, Carlo. "I modelli, il Proemio, l'Introduzione, I novellatori." In *Giovanni Boccaccio,* 156–60. Bari: Laterza, 1972. (*157–58)

Olson, Glending. *Literature as Recreation in the Later Middle Ages.* Ithaca and London: Cornell University Press, 1982. (*208–15)

Padoan, Giorgio. "Sulla genesi e la pubblicazione del *Decameròn.*" In *Il Boccaccio, le muse, il Parnaso e l'Arno,* 93–121. Florence: Olschki, 1978.

Potter, Joy H. *Five Frames for the "Decameron": Communication and Social Systems in the "Cornice."* Princeton: Princeton University Press, 1982. (*31, 41, 70–73, 83, 91, 93, 105, 120, 124–26, 135)

Prete, Antonio. "Ritmo esterno e tempi spirituali nella cornice del *Decameron.*" *Aevum* 28 (1964): 33–61. (*34–37)

Rossi, Luciano. "Ironia e parodia nel *Decameron:* Da Ciappelletto a Griselda." In *La novella italiana,* Atti del Convegno di Caprarola, 365–405. Rome: Salerno Editrice, 1989.

———. "Presenze ovidiane nel *Decameron.*" *Studi sul Boccaccio* 21 (1993): 125–37.

Russo, Luigi. "Proemio alle donne." In *Letture critiche del "Decameron,"* 9–15. Bari: Laterza, 1967 [1938]. (*9–15).

Scaglione, Aldo D. *Nature and Love in the Late Middle Ages.* Berkeley and Los Angeles: University of California Press, 1963.

Seung, T. K., "The Sovereign Individual in the *Decameron.*" In *Cultural Thematics: The Formation of the Faustian Ethos,* 207–16. New Haven and London: Yale University Press, 1976.

Singleton, Charles S. "On Meaning in the *Decameron.*" *Italica* 21 (1944): 117–24.

Smarr, Janet L. "Symmetry and Balance in the *Decameron.*" *Mediaevalia* 2 (1976): 159–87.

———. *Boccaccio and Fiammetta: The Narrator as Lover.* Urbana and Chicago: University of Illinois Press, 1986. (*165–74)

———. "Ovid and Boccaccio: A Note on Self-Defense." *Mediaevalia* 13 (1987): 247–55. (*252–53)

Stewart, Pamela D. "Boccaccio e la tradizione retorica: La definizione della novella come genere letterario." In *Retorica e mimica nel "Decameron" e nella commedia del Cinquecento,* 7–18. Florence: Olschki, 1986 [1979].

Day Ten of the *Decameron:*
The Myth of Order

with Courtney Cahill (1996)

In an essay published ten years ago Victoria Kirkham reminded Boccaccio's readers how much of the *Decameron* has simply escaped understanding.[1] While it is clearly a text that allows the reader to feel comfortable in the belief that its general tone and sense are accessible, it is noteworthy that there is so much disagreement about its essential strategies and puzzlement over so many of its details. Recently one of us attempted to formulate a revisionist reading of the work's often-understudied *Proemio.*[2] In the present study, we turn to its ending. We do so without polemic, offering our reading of the Tenth Day in a spirit of inquiry and hoping that it will be read as openly as it is written. This is to say not that we are unconvinced by our arguments but that we are aware that others may not immediately (or perhaps ever) accept them, that there are issues here that resist simple solutions and readers who will find it difficult to leave behind a paradigm that seems both pleasing and sensible.

In the reception of the *Decameron* during the last forty years, the work has usually been treated as a "comedy," in whatever sense. Surely the most influential modern statements in this vein have been made by probably the most capable and influential student of Boccaccio who has ever lived, Vittore Branca. His view, no doubt an attractive one, has become, if not uni-

---

1. "An Allegorically Tempered *Decameron,*" *Italica* 62 (1985), cited from *The Sign of Reason in Boccaccio's Fiction,* 131. All subsequent references to Kirkham's essays will be to their printings in this volume. [For agreement with these opening observations in Kirkham's essay, see p. 90 in the present book.] The reader will find bibliographical information in the list at the conclusion of this study.

2. See Hollander, "The Proem of the *Decameron,*" in this book.

versally accepted, nonetheless dominant. In *Boccaccio medievale* he describes the work in the following terms.

> Dalla prima all'ultima giornata . . . si svolge un ideale itinerario che va dalla riprensione aspra ed amara dei vizi dei grandi nella prima giornata allo splendido ed architettato elogio della magnanimità e della virtù della decima giornata . . . ; dall'iniziale riprensione dei vizi umani . . . si giunge nella X giornata all'epilogo magnifico e fiabesco, al giardino favolosamente fiorito delle più alte virtù. Ed ecco lo splendido crescendo dell'ultima giornata sembra voler fissare in una solenne atmosfera encomiastica i più alti motivi, le più grandi idee-forza che avevano regolato lo svolgersi della grandiosa ed eterna commedia umana. (15–17)[3]

> [From the first to the last Day . . . there advances a conceptual itinerary that moves from harsh and bitter rebuke of the vices of the great in Day One to the splendidly constructed praise of magnanimity and virtue in Day Ten . . . ; from the initial rebuke of human vice . . . one arrives, in the Tenth Day, at the magnificent fairy-tale conclusion, that garden in fabulous flower with the loftiest virtues. And now we find that the splendid crescendo of the last Day seems to want to fix in a solemn atmosphere of praise the loftiest motives, the most important of the key ideas that had governed the development of this majestic and eternal human comedy.]

While many of Boccaccio's critics agree that Day Ten represents, in Branca's words, a "splendido crescendo,"[4] some recent readers tend to question such a formulation.[5] In this study we will offer a different per-

---

3. For the by-now-familiar schema advanced by Branca that the *Decameron* moves from tragic to comic, from worst to best, beginning with Cepparello-Judas and ending triumphantly with Griselda-Mary, see *Boccaccio medievale*, 94–101.

4. There is strong support for Branca's position—for example, that of Joan Ferrante in her article "The Frame Characters."

5. However, S. Bernard Chandler offered a challenge to Branca's formulation as long ago as 1960. Chandler's rejoinder begins as follows: "When Branca applied the terms 'fiabesco' and 'favolosamente' to Day X, he was in fact isolating its distinguishing quality. An unreality pervades it, because Boccaccio could not contemplate magnanimous actions in the same light as other actions, could not imagine them as occurring in the everyday world." See "Man, Emotion, and Intellect," 409–10. As opposed to Chandler, who sees the problems with Day Ten in terms of Boccaccio's limitations as a writer, we find these "problems" to be part of his essential strategy.

spective on Day Ten, challenging the notion that the *Decameron* concludes as a comedy[6] and at its moral and aesthetic high point.[7] It is, we think, to Chandler's credit that he, some time ago, and despite the fact that he did not develop his insight as tellingly as he might have,[8] found Day Ten problematic, along with the comedic and celebrative interpretation that Branca and others have urged for it. Our attempt to understand the essential strategies that shape Boccaccio's last Day asks its readers to start afresh in their interpretations of these ten *novelle,* paying attention to the indications (and we think there are many such) that make a eupeptic reading difficult.[9] While we are aware that we are here dealing with matters of interpretation, and thus of things that ultimately lie beyond proof, we also believe that it is the eventual responsibility of any reader of a text to develop such an interpretive response. It is not enough to content oneself with saying that Boccaccio is a challenging writer, leaving to one side consideration of his authorial strategy as being beyond confirmation.

The idea that the *Decameron* never reaches the spiritual heightening

---

6. For a partial, if fairly vigorous, dissent from Branca's basic interpretation of the "comic" ascent of the *Decameron,* see Francesco Bruni, *Boccaccio,* 273: "Ora, è evidente che con la decima giornata Boccaccio ha voluto rialzare la materia, ispirata ai valori della liberalità e della magnificenza: ma questo schema ascensionale sembra riguardare la decima giornata rispetto alle prime nove, e non un innalzamento condotto progressivamente dalla prima giornata all'ultima" [Now, it is clear that with the Tenth Day Boccaccio wanted to elevate his matter, making it resonate with the values of generosity and splendor; but this ascendant schema seems to regard Day Ten in relation to the first nine rather than as a movement progressively upward from the First Day to the last].

7. For a similar view see Luciano Rossi's "Ironia e parodia"; with particular regard to Griselda, see his previous study, "Das *Dekameron.*" The reader will find in this essay a number of references to the work of Millicent Marcus and Giuseppe Mazzotta, who also have recorded views of the Tenth Day that question the more usual interpretation of its significance.

8. He lays the blame for the dissonance that he hears in the text to Boccaccio's inability to conceive of truly noble behavior: "That Boccaccio *intended* to portray liberality and magnanimity is undoubted since he says so in the heading to Day X: the trouble lies in his inability to envisage really noble gestures. His are motivated by self-interest (desire for praise and a fine reputation) or represent the avoidance of immorality rather than positive virtue" ("Man, Emotion, and Intellect," 411).

9. For two of the most optimistic readings of Day Ten available see Giorgio Cavallini, *La decima giornata,* and Marga Cottino-Jones, *Order from Chaos,* 170–90. Luciano Rossi, "Ironia e parodia," 397, responds to Cavallini's observations as follows: "Se si esaminano globalmente i racconti di quest'ultima decade, quel che sorprende è il sapore orientaleggiante della maggior parte di essi, insieme al tono distaccato e quasi di favola, scelto dall'autore; un tono che non è mai disgiunto da una superiore quanto sfumata ironia" [If we take the global view of the stories in this final ten, what is surprising is the orientalizing flavor of most of them, along with the detached and almost fairy-tale tone taken by the author, a tone that is never disjoined from an irony that is as arch as it is delicately shaded].

present in its great vernacular precursor and model, Dante's *Commedia,* continues to trouble critics who would like to read Boccaccio's vernacular *magnum opus* in somewhat similar terms.[10] Those who, like Marga Cottino-Jones and Victoria Kirkham, have insisted that Boccaccio offers his readers an upbeat conclusion advance as confirming evidence Day Ten's glorious idealism and, in particular, Griselda's moral triumph (X.x). By interpreting Griselda as a *figura* (or, to speak more precisely, as a Christian antitype), Cottino-Jones attempts to validate an allegorical reading of the story, one in which "Griselda stands out as a sacrificial character, a *pharmakos,* a *figura Christi* who is called on to offer herself . . . to restore her surrounding community to the harmony and happiness emblematic of a Golden Age. . . ."[11] By doing so, she affirms that the *Decameron* ends with a moral and spiritual heightening similar to that found at the conclusion of Dante's *Commedia* and of Petrarch's *Canzoniere.* In a similar key, Kirkham attempts to convince us that there is an uplifting conclusion to the *Decameron* by demonstrating that the moral triumphs exemplified in the stories of Day Ten "mark a progression to a nobler esthetic and ethical plane."[12] In particular, she focuses on the Griselda story to show that it is the triumph of this martyr-like figure that "crowns the idealistic plane of the *Decameron*'s concluding day" ("Last Tale in the *Decameron,*" 261).[13]

Our interpretation takes issue with such readings as those of Cottino-Jones and Kirkham, since we do not agree that the scope of Boccaccio's *Decameron* is somehow equivalent to that of Dante's *Commedia;* in our opinion, the work should not be read as an allegory that conforms to

---

10. For a similar observation see Luciano Rossi, "Ironia e parodia," 396. A careful statement of an opposing view is given by Joan Ferrante, "The Frame Characters," 214, who states that Boccaccio does not "give as broad or transcendent a purpose to his work as does Dante, but he suggests that it is meant to be edifying in a more modest way." Our own view more closely corresponds to that of Teodolinda Barolini, "Wheel of the *Decameron,*" 521: "From its first clause, indeed from its first word, the *Decameron* signals its non-transcendence: 'Umana cosa è aver compassione degli afflitti . . . ,' begins the author, locating us in a rigorously secular context and defining its parameters."

11. Marga Cottino-Jones, "*Fabula* vs. *Figura,*" 41.

12. Victoria Kirkham, "Last Tale in the *Decameron,*" 264.

13. Even Teodolinda Barolini, whose reading of the *Decameron* stays close to the literal (as opposed to an allegorical) sense of the text, programmatically interprets Day Ten (including X.x) as showing "men and women practicing generosity and renunciation, the very social virtues required for the *brigata*'s reintegration into society." Barolini argues that Day Ten signals a return to order wherein "the positive aspects of repression are stressed" ("Wheel of the *Decameron,*" 534). While Barolini therefore avoids what we would call the allegorical trap into which some others fall, she nonetheless argues for a progressive circular movement that inevitably leads to the view that the *Decameron* concludes at a higher moral level than the one at which it began.

Christian exegetical norms. We will argue that neither Griselda's story nor Day Ten as a whole should be read as triumphant endings in any sense, whether they be considered culminations of an upward movement similar to Dante's spiritual progression or completions of an evolution in what Teodolinda Barolini calls the "wheel of the *Decameron.*" Rather, it seems clear to us that Day Ten—and especially X.x—dramatizes several problematic issues previously raised by the *brigata.* For instance, questions of legality and contractual obligation that have remained unanswered during the entire sojourn confront us again in Day Ten. Tito's and Gisippo's ostensibly good-natured and disinterested relationship, for example, has an interesting and indeed disturbing parallel in the story of Cimone (V.i). As we shall propose, Gisippo, Tito, and Cimone are all students of philosophical learning who nonetheless succumb to irrational and, in many ways, bestial behaviors. In the same way, Griselda's obedience and tenacious *costanzia* are not so laudable if we reconsider her "martyr-like" behavior in terms of the similarly fanatical, if vengeful, acts so frequently portrayed in Day Eight and, still more pointedly, in Day Nine. Indeed, the entire Day can be read as an inverse companion piece to Day Nine. For just as the characters in Day Nine returned "an eye for an eye, a tooth for a tooth" in the name of a fitting revenge, many of the central figures of Day Ten exhibit a mentality based on a sort of inverted version of the *lex talionis* in their insistence on proving their own munificence in the face of challenge or rivalry.[14] Now, instead of getting only what one deserves, one gets far more than one should hope for, as, for example, in the service of establishing a superior's munificence.

We propose to consider Day Ten as an interrogation of the myth of order. Our use of the word *myth* here and elsewhere reflects the term as it is found in Frank Kermode's *The Sense of an Ending.*

We have to distinguish between myths and fictions. Fictions can degenerate into myths whenever they are not consciously held to be fictive. . . . Myth operates within the diagrams of ritual, which presupposes total and adequate explanations of things as they are and were; it is a sequence of radically unchangeable gestures. Fictions are for finding things out, and they change as the needs of sense-making change. Myths are the agents of stability, fictions the agents of change. Myths call for absolute, fictions for conditional assent. (39)

---

14. See the following, related discussion (pp. 152–54) of the rivalry among the tellers themselves that marks so surprising and significant a change in the behavior of the *brigata* during this Day.

It is our view that too many of Boccaccio's readers tend to turn his fictions into "myths" and thus fail to take into full account precisely his ability, as fiction-maker, to irradiate the apparently contradictory yet utterly normal patterns in the behavior of humankind. It is the power of the satirist, prepared by instinct and experience to avenge himself upon mythmakers, that we find at the core of Boccaccio's magnificent achievement in the *Decameron*. (We shall return to the subject of satire in our concluding remarks, pp. 159–63.)

We will argue that Day Ten continues to probe, rather than resolve, the issue represented by posited law, an issue that has remained problematic ever since the story of Martellino (II.i), in which we first encounter institutional "law"—in the form of a judge who will hang a suspect simply because he happened to have a grudge against Florentines: ". . . il giudice niuna cosa in sua scusa voleva udire; anzi, *per avventura* avendo alcuno odio ne' fiorentini, del tutto era disposto a volerlo fare impiccar per la gola. . . ."[15] [. . . the judge wished to hear no extenuating evidence in (Martellino's) behalf; rather, having *by chance* a certain hatred for the inhabitants of Florence, he was thoroughly disposed to having him strung up by the neck . . .] (II.i.31 [our italics]). We agree with both Barolini's and Mazzotta's argument that in the *Decameron,* the "law," as the institutional expression of order, is more often than not questioned as an effective communal force.[16] Although Mazzotta and Barolini both point out the negative aspects of law in the *Decameron,* neither of them specifically treats Day Ten as a critical examination of the myth of order and thus, in political terms, of the myth of law. What we witness in Day Ten are the destructive consequences that may result from upholding the law, particularly the rigid terms of contractual agreements.

---

15. All quotations are from Giovanni Boccaccio, *Decameron,* ed. Vittore Branca (Turin: Einaudi, 1984).

16. For instance, in his chapter "The Law and Its Transgressions" in *World at Play,* Mazzotta shows that posited law and judicial practice are both implicit and explicit concerns throughout the *Decameron.* By citing the numerous "courtroom scenes" in the *Decameron,* those legal as well as theatrical moments in which the truth is both revealed and concealed, Mazzotta discusses what he sees as one of the fundamental themes of the *Decameron:* the fact that both art and law are "worlds . . . drawn within the make-believe of appearances" (239). Barolini, too, calls attention to the precarious role that the law often plays in the stories. She believes that, with the exception of Day Ten (the only Day that, in her view, emphasizes the positive aspects of repression) the *novelle* "have encouraged following one's instincts and have exposed the pathology of repression—as, for instance, in Tancredi's incestuous relationship with his daughter in IV i" ("Wheel of the *Decameron,*" 533–34).

Outdoing and Rivalry: The Underside of Magnanimity

No one would deny that magnanimity is a noble subject. What we suggest is that the tales Boccaccio tells in its name reveal all too often what Michel de Montaigne, in the last of his *Essais,* referred to as "supercelestial thoughts [in conjunction with] subterranean conduct." In our view, most readers, promised the subject that would make the *Decameron* a triumphant comedy (in celebration of whatever value[s] the particular reader holds dear), have failed to see that the magnanimity exhibited in Day Ten is always problematic and never of the sort that Boccaccio himself describes in the *Esposizioni.* In his commentary on *Inferno* 2.43–45, citing Aristotle's *Ethics,* he describes "l'anima di Virgilio, il quale [Dante] cognomina *magnanimo,* e meritamente, per ciò che . . . colui è da dire 'magnanimo,' il quale si fa degno d'imprendere e d'adoperare le gran cose"[17] [the soul of Virgil, to whom Dante lends the term *magnanimous,* and justly so, because . . . he is to be called 'magnanimous' who makes himself worthy of initiating and carrying through great enterprises]. There is no hedging in this definition; it is clear that magnanimity is an unalloyed "good thing." And if we turn to Boccaccio's use of the words *magnifico* and *magnificenza* in the *Esposizioni* we find a similar result. Almost all who are associated with these terms are seen as unproblematically worthy beings: we hear of "le magnificenze" of the emperors of Tartary (ad *Inferno* 1.101–11); Virgil's "magnifiche opere in onore di Ottaviano Cesare" [magnificent works in honor of Augustus] (ad 2.43–45); "le magnifiche opere di Scipione Africano" (ad 2.59), who had acted on behalf of the Republic "magnificamente . . . contro a Cartagine" (ad 2.60) [magnificently . . . against Carthage]; fame is nothing other than discourse about the "magnifiche opere" of worthy folk like Pompey, Julius Caesar, and Alexander the Great (ad 2.60); the *limbicoli* are "magnifichi" (4.Int.; ad 4.103–5), and their lives on earth were marked by being "di grande animo e furono nelle loro operazioni magnifichi" [of noble mind and they were in their deeds magnificent] (ad 4.119–20); Saladin "fu in donare magnifico, e delle sue magnificenze se ne racontano assai" [was in giving magnificent, and of his magnificence much is related] (ad 4.129; no one will begrudge Boccaccio for saying so, since he himself had offered similar praise of Saladin in X.ix). Boccaccio's subsequent discussion of Alexander is, however, more complex.

---

17. These and the following citations from the *Esposizioni* are from Giorgio Padoan's edition as found in the database known as the Dartmouth Dante Project.

Fu costui, quantunque vittorioso e magnifico signore [for a possible source of the phrase see the salutation of the *Epistle to Cangrande,* "Magnifico atque victorioso domino"], come assai apare *[sic]* nelle sue opere, occupatore non solamente delle piccole fortune degli uomini ma de' regni e delle libertà degli uomini violentissimo e, oltre a ciò, crudelissimo ucciditore non solamente de' nemici, ma ancora degli amici, de' quali, già caldo di vino e di vivanda, ne' conviti e altrove, molti fece uccidere. (ad 12.107)

[[Alexander], no matter that he was a victorious and magnificent lord, as is readily apparent from his deeds, intervened most violently not only in the unimportant fates of individuals but in those of kingdoms and the very liberty of men; beyond that, he most cruelly put to death not only his enemies but his friends, of whom, when he was still warm with wine and food, at banquets and elsewhere, he had many killed.]

The ambiguity of the behavior of Alexander as described in the *Esposizioni* may have a good deal to tell us about Boccaccio's understanding of the inner motives of the "magnificent" characters of Day Ten. One of his glosses to *Inferno* 1 is perhaps even more suggestive. He is discussing the lion of Dante's three beasts in relation to pride, manifest in the man who overrates his own capacities.

In questo l'uomo superbo è simigliante al leone, per ciò che il disiderio del superbo è tanto di parer quello che egli non è, che cosa non è alcuna sì grave che egli non presumma *[sic]* di fare, quantunque a lui non si convenga, solo che egli creda per quello essere reputato magnanimo; e questa cechità *[sic]* ha già messo in distruzione molti regni, molte province e molte genti. (ad *Inferno* 1.31–60)

[In this respect the proud man is like the lion; because his desire is to appear to be what he is not, which is something so important that he would not presume to attempt it unless he believed that by doing it, however little it conform to his character, he might make himself appear magnanimous; and such blind behavior has already destroyed many kingdoms, provinces, and peoples.]

Boccaccio's words in the *Esposizioni* seem almost deliberately and parodically reminiscent of Nathan's strange justification of murder in the service of self-glorification (*Decameron* X.iii.32):

Né ti vergognare d'avermi voluto uccidere per divenir famoso, né credere che io me ne maravigli. I sommi imperadori e i grandissimi re non hanno quasi con altra arte che d'uccidere, non uno uomo come tu volevi fare ma infiniti, e ardere paesi e abbattere le città, li loro regni ampliati, e per conseguente la fama loro: per che, se tu per più farti famoso me solo uccider volevi, non maravigliosa cosa né nuova facevi ma molto usata.

[Neither be ashamed because you wanted to kill me in order to become famous, nor believe that I am surprised at this. The greatest emperors and kings have, with hardly any other craft than murder—not one man alone as you wished to do, but multitudes, burning fields and leveling cities—magnified their kingdoms and, in consequence, their own fame. Therefore, if you wanted to kill me alone in order to make yourself more famous, you sought to accomplish no marvel or novelty, but a thing often done.]

Even a cursory glance at the behaviors of those who are portrayed as "magnanimous" in Day Ten might give us some sense that these characters should be the objects of greater (and more analytical) scrutiny than they have been. In what follows we will touch briefly upon the tales that we will not consider more closely later in this essay.

X.i: Neifile relates how the king of Spain fails to reward a Florentine courtier for his military accomplishments. Ruggieri de' Figiovanni has come to his court for no other reason than recognition of his valor. Envious of the other courtiers whom the king does reward, he sets out, disappointed, to return to Italy, not aware that his companion, one of the king's retainers, has been sent along by his lord to spy upon him. When his mule urinates in the river instead of in the place the mules had been led to for this purpose, Ruggieri compares him to his negligent benefactor. Brought back to Spain in accord with the king's order, he tells Alfonso that the mule is like him in that he gives gifts when he should not and withholds them when he should give, just as his mule urinated where he should not have and did not where he should have. It is this envy-driven complaint that moves the king to his great act of "munificence." Even after Ruggieri picks the wrong chest, the king corrects Fortune (according to him the source of Ruggieri's discomfiture, not his own niggardliness) by giving him the royal scepter and other ornaments and jewels, the contents of the chest not chosen. Surely Ruggieri, from anything we hear, is not one deserving of such reward. And what is the motive of Alfonso's liberality? It is nothing other than Ruggieri's complaint and, we imagine, the king's need to show himself as munificent in the eyes of one who had insulted him. The utter venality of Ruggieri and the crass motives of the king seem to us to sketch a burlesque of "real" munificence rather than to represent qualities that might reasonably be considered "liberal." The totally unacceptable notion that a king would give over the very signs and instruments of his kingship joins with the intrinsic comparison of all such giving to mule piss[18] in such a way as to make the reader draw conclusions that the *brigata* avoids.

X.ii: Elissa's tale of the outlaw Ghino di Tacco and the abbot of Cluny is even stranger in its skewing of our moral and aesthetic expectations on this Day supposedly dedicated to generosity. For here a cleric,[19] held captive by a brigand and cured by him of a bad stomach, intervenes with Pope Boniface VIII on his behalf and secures him a living as a forgiven knight of the Church. Ghino, a consummate con-man, causes the munificence of his captive. There is nothing gratuitous about the abbot's act. If this is the stuff of which the soldiery of the Church is built, are we surprised at the behav-

---

18. Grace as excrement is a familiar image to readers of *Inferno* 15 and Benvenuto's commentary thereto (Dartmouth Dante Project, to vv. 110–14): Andrea de' Mozzi is accredited with the scabrous remark that "gratia Dei erat sicut stercus caprarum, quod cadens ab alto ruit in diversas partes dispersum" [the grace of God was as the shit of goats, because, falling from on high, it was variously dispersed].

19. We may consider that, with possibly a single exception in the case of the archbishop of Rouen, briefly if positively referred to in II.viii.88, the abbot of Cluny is the only cleric portrayed favorably in the entire *Decameron,* here and in I.vii, Filostrato's tale about Cangrande della Scala. In the subplot of a story that is much like X.i, Primasso finally breaks down the hesitant abbot, who is described in terms that fit well with the thematic concerns of Day Ten: "[Primasso] udì ragionare d'uno abate di Clignì, il quale si crede che sia il più ricco prelato di sue entrate che abbia la Chiesa di Dio dal Papa in fuori; e di lui udì dire *maravigliose e magnifiche cose* in tener sempre corte e non esser mai a alcuno, che andasse là dove egli fosse, negato né mangiar né bere, solo che quando l'abate mangiasse il domandasse" [Primasso heard speak of an abbot of Cluny, who, because of the rents he received, was believed to be the richest prelate in the Church of God from the Pope on down; and he heard wonderful and magnificent things said of him with regard to how he always held court and how to eat and to drink were never denied anyone who went there where he was, if that person begged for his portion only when the abbot was himself at table] (I.vii.12 [our italics]). It is as though Boccaccio were asked to name a good cleric. "Well," he replies, "there's the abbot of Cluny. . . ." In Day One the stories we hear told in the last Day would probably have had very different interpretations from their tellers and auditors. Joan Ferrante, "Narrative Patterns," argues that the fact that both Saladin and the abbot are referred to in the first and last Days reflects the ascent of virtue celebrated in the work: "On the first day they were caught out in small faults, on the tenth they demonstrate big virtues" (604). One might draw a different conclusion, believing instead that we are meant to remember the "real" versions of their behaviors from the vantage point of this Day of a suppositious magnanimity that appears to cancel reality, but only for a moment.

ior of a clergy that is consistently portrayed as despicable across the pages of the *Decameron*?

X.iii is considered, at some length, later in this essay. X.iv and X.v will receive some consideration as part of our discussion of X.x.

X.vi and vii: These complementary tales of two kings, Fiammetta's of Carlo and Pampinea's of Pietro, are both meant to show the munificence of royal males who turn their lust for attractive young women into more orderly affections. What strikes us in each case is that, at a crucial moment, the king's lust is forestalled not by his own moral imperative but by a quite different sort of consideration. Seduced by the company of two lovely young women, Carlo is at first determined to take both of them away from their father for his own sexual pleasure. It is only the counsel of Guy de Monfort that convinces him that such an act would be foolish and unworthy (X.vi.29): "Questo non è atto di re magnanimo anzi d'un pusillanimo giovinetto" [This is not the act of a magnanimous king, but of a cowardly youth]. To be sure, Carlo does do the right thing in the end; we only argue that the sexual tone of the story tends to undercut the munificence proposed for the lecherous king, particularly since, as Branca's notes to the tale make plain, in his time he was widely portrayed as an amorous adventurer. And Guy's advice is based much on *ragioni di stato* (he warns of the instability of the political situation in the kingdom of Naples—X.vi.28) and a sense of shame ("you have defeated Manfred; if you imitate his sexual improprieties, which opened the kingdom to you, you too will be disgraced"—X.vi.30–32). Similarly, Pietro gives over his lust for the lovely and love-struck Lisa, daughter of an apothecary, after experiencing the following anagnorisis (X.vii.35): "Solo il re intendeva il coperto parlare [see *Inferno* 4.51] della giovane e da più ogn'ora la reputava, e più volte seco stesso maladisse la fortuna che di tale uomo [a mere apothecary] l'aveva fatta figliuola" [The king alone understood the girl's covert speech and esteemed her more each passing hour, often to himself cursing the fortune that had made her the daughter of such a man]. Had Bernardo Puccini been not rich but of minor nobility, would Lisa have escaped the king's embrace?

We do not deny that these several stories (i, ii, vi, and vii) can be read as illustrating a magnanimity of sorts. We would hope only to have shown that their protagonists are so deeply flawed in their motives for generosity that the purported significance of these *novelle* is at least made problematic by the insights that we are allowed into the reasons for their behavior.

X.viii and X.x will be discussed later in this essay.[20]

X.ix: Panfilo's tale of Saladin and Torello seems to come the closest to fulfilling the conditions for genuine magnanimity put forward by the king of the day in his prolegomenon at the conclusion of the Ninth Day.[21] One almost drowns in all that magnanimity. While the tale is meant to celebrate the liberality of Saladin, we are first privy to the dogged hospitality of the noble Torello. As we attempt to discern what motivates his nearly out-of-control insistence on entertaining these disguised Saracens, we might ponder the first detail that we are given (X.ix.8): "Li quali come messer Torel vide, avvisò che gentili uomini e stranier fossero e disiderò d'onorargli" [When Torello saw them, he realized that they were noble and that they were foreigners, and wanted to do them honor]. And honor them he does. We are not suggesting that Torello has consciously set out to win over rich and noble strangers in order to abet his ultimate gain, only that his egotism in hosting is incited by a desire to be of service to those whom he perceives to be above him.[22] He is Cisti *fornaio* (VI.ii) on a grander scale.[23] Saladin's ultimate reward does, in fact, become the subject of Panfilo's tale. Yet one finds oneself spending a great deal of time contemplating the frenetic hostmanship of Torello. X.ix may offer us an example of double munificence. It also asks us to believe in flying carpets in order to do so.[24]

---

20. We note that those interpretations advanced in Howard Needler's article ("Song of a Ravished Nightingale," 510–13) with which our approach has much in common are limited to these two tales. The other eight tales of Day Ten Needler considers "fabulous instances of courtesy and generosity that override all passions" (512).

21. A few critics have harbored the idea that X.ix (and not X.x) is the highest moment of magnanimity achieved in the *giornata* (and, indeed, in the *Decameron*). See Francesco Bruni, *Boccaccio,* 273: "Ogni novella della decima giornata narra azioni superiori a quelle narrate nella precedente, e questa tensione giunge al massimo in Griselda e quasi si spezza" [Every *novella* of the Tenth Day narrates actions that are superior to those narrated in the preceding tale, and this tension reaches its height in Griselda and nearly breaks]. We do not agree, obviously, with the first premise of this observation. For a similar view of the shape of Day Ten, a moral crescendo in i–ix and a falling away in X.x, see Luigi Surdich, *La cornice,* 276–83. See also Laura White, *La scena conviviale,* 63, referring to "questa esemplare parabola di cortesia" [this exemplary parable of courtliness] that is X.ix.

22. Fido would not agree. According to him ("Il sorriso di messer Torello," 17), "Torello intuisce in loro qualità eccezionali" [Torello intuits that they have exceptional qualities]; Fido also refers to (20) "l'intuizione da parte di Torello di una nobiltà eccezionale sotto l'abito mercantile dei suoi ospiti" [Torello's intuition of an exceptional nobility hidden beneath the merchant costume of his guests]. In such a view Torello's actions are not to be considered self-serving. But what he notes in the foreigners is not their quality as individuals but their superior rank.

23. See Fido, "Il sorriso di messer Torello," 20–21.

24. Thomas Greene puts the matter delicately: "Thus the art of necromancy, which has heretofore served as an instrument to beguile the gullible (8.7, 8.9) is now presented as a legit-

The Law of the *piccolo popolo*

Before looking more closely at Day Ten we should first attempt to see how the very concept of law informs the *Decameron*'s outermost frame, with particular attention to the law imposed upon itself by the *brigata*. For it is here that we first see the formation of a legal paradigm that describes the law's function in an ideal situation, removed from the plague in a provisional community. The *brigata* structures itself as a *piccolo popolo,* or miniature nation. Each member is either the *re* or *reina* for a day, under whose *reggimento* the *brigata* will proceed. We can see that the *brigata* appropriates a language of monarchy and imposes it on its own "nation." For, in the wake of the widespread lawlessness caused by the plague, it is the aim of this mini-state to reconstruct its own order. Indeed, the reconstruction of order is one of the *brigata*'s primary motivations for embarking on their secular retreat, since, as Pampinea says (I.Int.95): "le cose che sono senza modo non possono lungamente durare" [things that are without measure are not capable of lasting for long]. Furthermore, Pampinea warns the ladies that they must preserve their lives (she refers to [I.Int.54] "la conservazione della nostra vita" [the preservation of our lives]) against the dissolute lawlessness of those who have given themselves over to *proponimento bestiale*. Thus, it is the aim of the *brigata* not only to distance themselves from death but also to prevent themselves from succumbing to bestial—or irrational and lawless—behavior.

Contingent upon the re-creation of order, however, is the prospect of playful and pleasurable recreation. As Pampinea later says (I.Int.65): "ce ne andassimo a stare, e quivi quella festa, quella allegrezza, quello piacere che noi potessimo, senza trapassare in alcuno atto il segno della ragione, prendessimo" [let us go (to our country houses) and there let us take whatever holiday, merriment, and pleasure that we can, without going beyond the bounds of reason in anything we do]. It is clear that, according to Pampinea, storytelling should and will be a rational endeavor, a logical combination of reason and creativity that defies the bestial and irrational lawlessness pervading the city. Thus the art of storytelling depends equally on pleasing and reasoning; it exists exclusively within the bounds of neither, but rather at their intersection. Pampinea describes her role as moral leader, after being made queen for Day One (I.Int.98): "Acciò che io prima essemplo dea a tutti voi, per lo quale di bene in meglio [see *Paradiso* 10.38]

---

imate art (10.4, 10.9) which helps to effect the happy conclusion. Some readers may gather that they can believe in magnanimity when they believe in necromancy" ("Forms of Accommodation," 309).

procedendo la nostra compagnia con ordine e con piacere e senza alcuna vergogna viva . . ." [So that I first may present an example for you all by which our company may live, proceeding from good to better, with order and with pleasure, and with no touch of shame . . .]. Since the *brigata* will experience *piacere* in a reasonable or ordered way, there is no reason why it should feel the shame of sin.

The strictness of the *brigata*'s legislation, then, is tempered by an aware-ness that the *piccolo popolo* must experience pleasure while obeying its own laws. Consequently, we should not be too shocked if and when the "law" is treated with a certain looseness, or casualness. Dioneo's privileged lawless-ness is perhaps the best example we have of the law's flexibility. Dissatisfied with Filomena's suggestion at the conclusion of Day One to restrict *(ristrignere)* the storytelling within some fixed limit (*alcun termine*— I.Conc.10), Dioneo says that he does not wish to be constrained by this law but rather prefers to remain free to tell whatever tale he likes whenever he chooses to tell it (I.Conc.12–13). Dioneo thus challenges the *brigata*'s law by requesting the exclusive privilege of being both the last speaker on each Day and the only one able to tell whatever story he wishes, even should it fail to accord with the monarch's rubrical guidance. If anyone, it is Dioneo who recognizes the larger sense of storytelling in its fullest expression, yielding pleasure as well as recognition of the claims of truth.[25] He cer-tainly does not abuse his special privilege of freedom from the Day's theme; rather than telling purely senseless or nonsensical tales, he almost invariably transgresses with a clear purpose. Although Dioneo exercises a certain artistic license in reciting his tales, they almost invariably respond to—albeit at times in a scabrous and humorously sexual way—the Day's prescribed theme. Indeed, we argue that Dioneo functions as a principle of order as much as, if not more than, a principle of disorder. Not only is he the storyteller who more than anyone else allows for a return to the *piacere* missing from so many of the stories; he is also the one who in fact reim-poses order when the tellers have strayed from the rubric. For example,

25. E. H. Wilkins, "Pampinea and Abrotonia," 141, writes: "It is generally recognized that Fiammetta represents Maria and that Dioneo represents Boccaccio." Wilkins's restatement of a nineteenth-century "biographical" reading of the relation between the odd-man-out of the book and his author is not, in our opinion, to be rejected so much as it is to be re-under-stood. In what way "is" Dioneo Boccaccio? We believe that he, more than any other member of the *brigata* (including Panfilo), represents the instinct toward recognition of what things truly are. He is less the voice of libidinous behavior than that of the consciousness of our actual sensibility. His task, as we believe Boccaccio formulated it, is to bring the uncomfort-able realization of our actual nature to consciousness. That task seems to us coextensive with his author's. For an examination of the ways in which Dioneo's tales are never too far from the topic of the Day see Alessandro Duranti's "Le novelle di Dioneo," esp. 16–17, 37.

even though Day Nine is a "free day," a motif of *vendetta* and *gastigamento* gradually develops in the skein of the narratives. Dioneo, in his tale (IX.x) of the "wife who became a mare," manages to respond to IX.ix by taking Solomon's advice (or, rather, Giosefo's interpretation of that advice) to treat wives like beasts and going one step further, as if to suggest that one might simply make one's wife a beast. Arguably, the Barlettan priest is a parodic conflation of Giosefo and Melisso, as he combines Melisso's munificence with Giosefo's bestial behavior. Dioneo thus both responds to other tales and enables a return to humor and to the *piacere* missing from IX.vii, IX.viii, and IX.ix.[26]

Still more important is the fact that the *brigata* is willing to treat the law as something that accepts change, rather than as a monolithic and undeviating institution. Although Pampinea outlines the law for the *brigata*'s storytelling, she is immediately willing to accede to Dioneo's request for "licensed license." We should take this resilient attitude toward the law and its ramifications into account when looking at Day Ten. Indeed, the *brigata* treats both law, or legal restrictions, and restrictions on creativity with a similar flexibility. What interests us most, and what is most pertinent to our argument, however, is that most—if not all—of the stories in Day Ten do not allow for such flexibility. As we will see, in Day Ten, the law, as it manifests itself in differing forms, is heeded with a stringency that is uncharacteristic of the *brigata*'s own paradigm of order. Although the letter of the law is usually maintained, the net result is irrational behavior that erupts because of a contractual agreement. As we will see, the tendency toward order in Day Ten is ultimately challenged by an equal pull in the opposite direction. This tendency culminates in X.x, where we see the behavior of a figure of institutional order, the marquis, implicitly compared to the behavior of the lawless Florentines in time of plague, for both exhibit a similarly destructive *bestialità*. Is it possible that Boccaccio is asking us to make a comparison between the lawlessness of the plague and the destructive consequences of a law that refuses compromise?

The Myth of Order Interrogated: X.iii, X.viii, X.x

It is interesting that Franco Fido's aesthetic evaluation of Day Ten finds exactly these three stories (iii, viii, x) "alcune delle novelle più fredde del

---

26. For the related theme of denuding, as it is common to IX.x and X.x, see Giorgio Barberi Squarotti, "Gli ammaestramenti di Dioneo," 185. See, as well, Emma Grimaldi, *Il privilegio,* 400.

libro" [among the colder *novelle* of the book] ("Il sorriso di messer Torello," 27).[27] If they were indeed written in praise of magnanimity, one would be tempted to agree with Fido; if, however, they all involve close scrutiny of the actual motives of supposedly "magnanimous" benefactors, as we believe, their "freddezza" has interesting implications.[28] We turn now to the story of Nathan (X.iii), since it interrogates not only the myth of generosity but also the myth of order through a travesty of arguably the greatest myth of (Christian) order: Christ's death as the redemptive corrective to postlapsarian disorder. To be sure, we can approach X.iii as a perversion of the biblical narratives that deal with the miracles of Christ. For not only is Nathan's act described, at least three times in the tale, as a *maravigliosa cosa,* but the relationship that develops between Nathan and Mithridanes recalls the bond shared between Christ and his disciples; that is, Nathan addresses Mithridanes as *Figliuol mio* (X.iii.13), and Mithridanes responds in kind by holding his benefactor in *reverenzia come padre* (X.iii.17). Moreover, Mithridanes undergoes something like a revelation upon discovering Nathan's true identity and refers to Nathan as *carissimo padre,* marvelling that Nathan has come to him so beneficently (X.iii.28): "con quanta cautela venuto siate per darmi il vostro spirito" [with how much care have you come to lend me your spirit]. Given the immediacy of Mithridanes' epiphany, the reader can hardly help but think of similar biblical moments in which an unbeliever undergoes sudden enlightenment and transformation. Indeed, Mithridanes is immediately transformed, for he not only addresses Nathan with reverence (substituting the honorific *voi* for the less formal *tu*) but also recognizes that he has sinned and consequently begs forgiveness (X.iii.29): ". . . tanto più mi cognosco debito alla penitenzia del mio errore: prendete adunque di me quella vendetta che convenevole estimate al mio peccato" [. . . so much more do I own myself obliged to do penance for my error: take, therefore, whatever revenge on me you deem fitting for my sin]. Perhaps the most striking appropriation of

---

27. According to Bergin, *Boccaccio,* these same three tales "transcend the limits of belief; their protagonists have moved from self-conscious altruism to exhibitionism" (323). In a similar vein, see Padoan, "Mondo aristocratico" (167–68): "l'esemplarità delle novelle della decima Giornata, che devono accendere gli animi alla fama lodevole (IX, Conclus. 5), rimane nel complesso alquanto astratta e fredda, ritenendo troppo della letterarietà delle 'Questioni' del *Filocolo*" [the exemplarity of the tales of the Tenth Day, which are supposed to warm their minds to thoughts of praiseworthy fame (IX.Conc.5), remains, in the end, somewhat abstract and cool, retaining too much of the literariness of the "Questions" of the *Filocolo*].

28. For a similar argument with regard to the *Corbaccio* see Hollander, *Boccaccio's Last Fiction.*

biblical language, however, is found in the *brigata*'s response (or rather in the narrator's interpretation of the *brigata*'s response) to the story, as the narrator says (X.iv.2): "Maravigliosa cosa parve a tutti che alcuno del proprio sangue fosse liberale" [It seems a wondrous thing to everyone that a man could be generous of his own blood]. What could be more *liberale* (or, for that matter, *maravigliosa*) than Christ's offering of his own blood for humanity's redemption? Interestingly, it seems that it is at this point in the Day that the *brigata* realizes that no other non-sexual action can surpass Nathan's deed, and so the *brigata* turns to recount the deeds of lovers. It is as though none of the members of the *brigata* desired to contribute another intrinsic challenge to Christ's unsurpassed munificence, although the queen's rubric for the Day implied that love stories would be its staple—perhaps excuse enough for the change of subject to Boccaccio's stock-in-trade.

The correspondence between Christ and Nathan,[29] however, loses its potentially positive force once we look at the real motives behind Nathan's miraculous act. First, the primary motive fueling Nathan's generosity is his desire for fame and recognition as a superlatively generous figure. As Mazzotta points out, the word *fama* recurs throughout X.iii, revealing that Nathan is primarily concerned with his legendary status as "the richest and most generous man who ever lived."[30] Surely he builds his palace "vicino ad una strada" [near a road] so that anyone who "wanted to go from west to east or from east to come west" (X.iii.5) could not fail to recognize his wealth. Furthermore, we know from the beginning that Nathan's primary concern, in what may be at least a generic parody of such biblical utterances as Matthew 7:16, "a fructibus eorum cognoscetis eos" [by their fruits shall ye know them], is to be known by his works: "disideroso che fosse per opera conosciuto" (X.iii.5).[31] Most significant, however, is the fact that

---

29. For discussion of the typological relevance of Nathan for Dante (reflections that may also help shed light on Boccaccio's choice of the name of his character) see Gian Roberto Sarolli, *Prolegomena*, 233–46.

30. We quote Mazzotta's words: " . . . let me stress how the importance of the name finds a thematic extension in Nathan's concern with 'fama,' a word that punctuates the narrative and which is to be taken in its full etymological sense from *fari*, that which is spoken of. Nathan wants to translate his life into a legend" (*World at Play*, 249). We would add that the words *fama* and *famoso* occur a total of nine times in X.iii; the closest "challenger" is IV.iv, with five occurrences. Here and elsewhere such statistics are based on *Concordanze del "Decameron,"* ed. Alfredo Barbina (Florence: C/E Giunti & G. Barbèra, 1969).

31. We have argued that one may interpret Torello's magnanimity in a similar light, since he goes out of his way to provide for Saladin essentially because he recognizes noble lineage in him and his companions (X.ix.8—see discussion prior to n. 22).

Nathan does not allow Mithridanes to go home without first making sure that his "convert" believes him to be the "richest and most generous man who ever lived." The tale concludes (X.iii.44): "E volendosi Mitridanes con la sua compagnia ritornare a casa, avendogli Natan assai ben fatto conoscere che mai di liberalità nol potrebbe avanzare, il licenziò" [And when Mithridanes wanted to return home with his companions, having made him take close cognizance that he never could surpass him in munificence, Nathan bid him go].

Interestingly, this is the first time that Filostrato uses the language of competition—*avanzare*—in reference to Nathan's desire to be incomparably munificent. We have certainly come a long way from Christ's disinterested *caritas*. Moreover, as Mazzotta points out, Nathan offers his domain to Mithridanes only under the condition that Mithridanes will not reveal his own name and, instead, assume Nathan's. In so doing, Nathan never abjures his narcissistic concerns. Nathan's self-aggrandizing and, we would argue, contentious motives thus undermine the liberality that he claims for himself. It seems clear to us that this story functions as a travesty or perversion of Christian teaching, with Nathan's behavior signifying a perversion of *caritas*. One might, in this light, do well to adduce Thomas Aquinas's condemnation of ostentation in almsgiving as not being charitable but vainglorious.[32]

What is perhaps not so clear on a first reading, however, is that the *novella* can also function as questioning a myth of order or myth of law. We can interpret Nathan's generosity in terms of the law by showing that his magnanimous deed both depends on and creates the need for a contractual agreement; that is, Nathan's liberality does not so much reside in a disinterested desire to give to others as it does in making others agree that he is the most munificent of men (in other words, he is one who "propter defectum caritatis . . . praefert inanem gloriam utilitati proximi," in Thomas's phrasing). Indeed, Nathan goes to such extremes to prove his unrivalled and incontestable generosity that he becomes eager even to have himself killed.[33] Nathan seems to believe that he would not be the most

---

32. See *Summa theologica* ii–ii, q. 132, a. 5, ad 3: "Ad tertium dicendum quod inanis gloria vituperatur circa eleemosynam propter defectum caritatis, qui videtur esse in eo qui praefert inanem gloriam utilitati proximi, dum hoc propter illud facit" [In answer to the third (objection), it must be said that vainglory in almsgiving is blameworthy because it constitutes a defect in charity, apparent in one who prefers vainglory to the good of his neighbor, seeing that he does the latter for the sake of the former].

33. We here recall Boccaccio's association of murder and "magnanimity" with reference both to Alexander the Great and Dante's lion of pride, to which we have earlier referred (see p. 116).

generous man in the world if he should fail to force Mithridanes to agree that he is the most generous man in the world. Nathan's "generous" behavior is therefore dependent on an implicit contract that requires Mithridanes' approval to obtain legitimacy, thus explaining why Nathan refuses to let Mithridanes return home until the latter agrees that no one could ever surpass *(avanzare)* his *liberalità*.

More important still is the explicit contract that Nathan in effect forces Mithridanes to accept. Immediately after Nathan reveals his identity to his potential murderer, Mithridanes attests that he is under obligation to him: "mi cognosco debito alla penitenzia del mio errore" [I own myself obliged to do penance for my error]. Moreover, as we have already seen, Mithridanes demands that Nathan punish him according to the severity of his sin: "prendete adunque di me quella vendetta che convenevole estimate al mio peccato" [take, therefore, whatever revenge on me you deem fitting for my sin] (X.iii.29). Here the language of punishment and indebtedness both recalls *novelle* told in Days Eight and Nine and anticipates stories yet to come in Day Ten. For when Mithridanes mentions the word *vendetta,* we probably remember the motif of *vendetta* as it was presented in Days Eight and, more violently, in Day Nine. What is perhaps most disturbing about this connection, however, is the fact that Days Eight and Nine were primarily concerned with retributive justice, the "eye for an eye, tooth for a tooth" mentality that allowed for such irrational behavior as the scholar's relentless *gastigamento* of the widow in VIII.vii.[34] Moreover, if in Day Ten magnanimity is supposed to represent a "socializing force," a return to the positive communal values so tellingly absent from the previous Days, then it would seem as though the very foundation of that community were precarious at best. The fact that Nathan rationalizes Mithridanes' attempt on his life by justifying regicide as a common historical event challenges the idea of order that many critics see at work in Day Ten. As he says to Mithridanes: ". . . per che, se tu per più farti famoso me solo uccider volevi, non maravigliosa cosa né nuova facevi ma molto usata" [. . . therefore, if you wanted to kill me alone in order to make yourself more famous, you sought to accomplish no marvel or novelty, but a thing often done] (X.iii.32). Not only is Nathan willing to be put to death in order to maintain his superlative status, but he also justifies a disordering act that defies posited as well as natural law. The very words with which he offers to forgive Mithridanes his trespass ("Né ti vergognare d'avermi voluto uccidere per divenir famoso" [be not ashamed because you wanted to kill me in

---

34. See Hollander, *Boccaccio's Last Fiction,* 21–23.

order to become famous]—X.iii.32) are, when examined from any distance, so morally convoluted as to be preposterous. Surely this sort of rationalization tells us far more about Nathan's unacceptable (even under a pagan sky) moral code than it says about his "magnanimity." This *novella* is so close to parody that it is surprising that it has so often been read as exemplary of true munificence.

In what may be the funniest moment in all of Day Ten, the words of the *vecchierella* should have revealed to a reader exactly the parodic tone that underlies the action of this particularly madhouse tale. After she comes to the thirteenth gate of Mithridanes' palace and he (understandably enough!) tries to send her packing, she rhapsodizes over Nathan's not recognizing her at any of his thirty-two gates, giving alms to her at each without revealing that he knew who she was, while this churl of a would-be Maecenas cancels her ticket after a mere thirteen (X.iii.10). Is the reader expected to respond "seriously" to any of these behaviors, taking them as earnest of magnanimity? And given the doubts one reasonably should have concerning Nathan's behavior after reading this story, can one really say that his self-sacrificial gesture exemplifies true magnanimity? Furthermore, can one also claim that the characters' actions accord well with the notion that the tales of Day Ten involve some sort of moral triumph? Its parodic disordering of perhaps the most sacred form of law—that is, the charity found in Christian Scripture—might have warned against a reading of X.iii as a positive representation of munificence.

In reference to the story of Tito and Gisippo (X.viii) we argue that the fulfillment of a different kind of contract—that of *amicizia*—can also lead to irrational and even bestial behavior.[35] In fact, one probably should read X.viii in light of the tale of bestial Cimone (V.i), Panfilo's parody of pastoral, in which Boccaccio interrogates the efficacy of formal education to nurture and thus to lead out from a state of boorishness and into a more civilized state of being. While we must be careful not to force a one-to-one

---

35. See Giovanni Getto, *Vita di forme,* 224: "[L'amicizia] diventa tuttavia principio essenziale della figurazione in una sola novella, che del resto è fra le meno vive, la novella di Tito e Gisippo, dove dà luogo ad una complicata casistica dei doveri dell'amicizia, la quale è così avvertita più su un piano di intellettualistica analisi che non di immediata affettività" [Friendship, moreover, becomes the formative principal of the narrative in only one *novella,* one that is, furthermore, among the least lively, that of Tito and Gisippo, where it gives occasion to complicated casuistry concerning the friends' duties toward one another; this is thus put forward on a plane of intellectualizing analysis rather than on one of touching immediacy].

correspondence upon certain characteristics of the two stories, the similarities between them are nonetheless striking, especially in terms of our discussion of Day Ten as a debunking of the myth of order.

First, both stories take place in or in the vicinity of Greece, the traditional locus of philosophy and reasoned choice. Second, the main characters of each story are involved in the study of philosophy. In V.i, for example, Panfilo explains that Cimone is literally transformed by philosophy
and by his interaction with it. As he says (V.i.18): "in assai brieve spazio di
tempo non solamente le prime lettere apparò ma valorosissimo tra' filoso-
fanti divenne" [in the briefest while not only did he master the rudiments of
literacy, but he became most capacitous among those who philosophized].
In the same way, Tito and Gisippo dedicate themselves (X.viii.8) "alla glo-
riosa altezza della filosofia" [to the glorious heights of philosophy]. Third,
the name Aristippus occurs in both stories. Although in V.i the name is that
of Cimone's father and may, it is surely arguable, only indirectly reflect
Boccaccio's interest in its original holder, in X.viii it is ascribed to the
actual Aristippus (fifth century B.C.), founder of the Cyrenaic school of
practical ethics.[36] As Mazzotta says, Aristippus stood as an emblem for an
ethical hedonism, "for the belief, that is, that only practical ethics offers a
reliable pathway to the pursuit of a life of happiness and that happiness is
dependent on pleasure" (*World at Play,* 255).[37] Not only does each story,
whatever its sources, therefore evoke a sense of philosophical wisdom
through its Grecian setting, but each also dramatizes ethical concerns in a
pre-Christian value system.[38] What is one to make of the fact that each of
these figures uses (or rather abuses) his rational learning in highly irrational ways?

---

36. In his commentary to (the literal sense of) *Inf.* 4.137 Boccaccio mentions Aristippus as
being insulted by Diogenes for advising a course of flattery (of the tyrant of Syracuse, Dionysius) to the philosopher. How much Boccaccio knew about Aristippus's role as the actual
founder of the doctrines (mortality of the soul, pleasure as the highest principle) attributed to
Epicurus is difficult to say.

37. For an earlier perception of the importance of Aristippus's teaching to an appreciation of the strategies of X.viii see Needler, "Song of a Ravished Nightingale," 503.

38. Louis Sorieri, *Boccaccio's Story of "Tito e Gisippo,"* 21, finds the main source for X.viii
in *Athis et Prophilias,* an early thirteenth-century work by Alexandre de Bernay in 20,732
verses. Salvatore Battaglia, "La novella di Tito e Gisippo," believed that the essential source
for X.viii was the narrative found in the *Disciplina clericalis* called "Exemplum de integro
amico." Branca, *Boccaccio medievale,* 10, says that X.viii "non è che un'ornata trascrizione da
una delle più acclamate opere di quella età, la *Disciplina clericalis,* arricchita di elementi
derivati da un poemetto di Alessandro di Bernay" [is but an ornate transcription of one of the
most celebrated works of the era, the *Disciplina clericalis,* enriched by elements derived from
a minor poem of Alexandre de Bernay].

It is in this context that the identity of the historical Aristippus becomes significant. Although the characters of these stories are educated in philosophy, it is a philosophy based on ethical hedonism. Mazzotta cites Cicero's *De finibus* and Augustine's *De civitate Dei* to show that Aristippus's ethics are both similar to Epicurean ethics and the very opposite of those of Antisthenes. As Augustine explains, Antisthenes assigns the *summum bonum* to virtue, whereas Aristippus (as well as Epicurus) assigns it to pleasures of the body, *in voluptate corporis* (Mazzotta, *World at Play*, 256).[39] Thus Cimone and Tito share another common bond based precisely on an Aristippean ethics based *in voluptate corporis;* that is, both men succumb to carnal desire *(amor voluptatis)* and the irrational behavior it often effects. In fact, the scenes that depict Cimone and Tito first beholding their respective objects of amorous desire are similar in their erotic style. For instance, when Cimone first sees Efigenia, the narrator explains that the love-struck *bestia* visually anatomizes the body of his beloved. He says (V.i.9): "E quinci cominciò a distinguer le parti di lei, lodando i capelli, li quali d'oro estimava, la fronte, il naso e la bocca, la gola e le braccia e sommamente il petto, poco ancora rilevato" [And then he began to study the various parts of her, admiring her hair, which he esteemed to be gold, her forehead, her nose and mouth, her throat, her arms, and most of all her breasts, as yet only slightly raised]. In the same way, Tito pays particular attention to the individual parts of Sofronia upon first beholding her (X.viii.11) : "la cominciò attentissimamente a riguardare; e ogni parte di lei smisuratamente piacendogli . . . di lei s'accese. . . ." [he began to gaze at her most attentively; and every part of her pleasing him beyond measure . . . he fell in love with her]. The aggressive ocular behavior of these two men has a parallel in the behavior of the scholar of VIII.vii, another man of some standing as a "philosopher" (with his much-touted Parisian training), who, when he momentarily succumbs to carnal desire, dissects the widow's body with his gaze (VIII.vii.66): ". . . veggendo lei con la bianchezza del suo corpo vincere le tenebre della notte e appresso riguardandole il petto e l'altre parti del corpo . . ." [. . . seeing her, the whiteness of her body conquering the shad-

---

39. See Victoria Kirkham, "The Classical Bond of Friendship," 246–48, who makes a good deal of the etymologies of some of the classical names in X.viii, opposing Mazzotta's reading of the historical significance of Aristippus's name, preferring to link it with Greek *ariston* in the tradition of Fulgentius's "philological" allegorization of Aristaeus as "the best" in his pursuit of Eurydice. We do not think that in this particular, either, the claims of history should yield to those of (rather fanciful) allegorizing.

ows of night, and then gazing at her breasts and the other parts of her body . . .]. Each of these scenes depicts a moment in which a male gaze anatomizes a female body. The seeming difference between Cimone and Tito, however, lies in the fact that they apparently undergo opposite transformations. Cimone's transformation from beast *(montone)* to man is supposedly the result of love (V.i.23): "Aristippo, considerando che Amor l'avesse di montone fatto tornare un uomo . . . il confortava" [Aristippus, in the belief that Love had made him turn from a ram into a man . . . lent him his support]. His moment of carnal excitation therefore occurs prior to his transformation from *montone* to *uomo*. Tito, however, is educated *before* he experiences his moment of carnal desire. The two men move in opposite directions: Cimone starts off as a beast, whereas Tito in effect becomes one. Of course, we must take it into account that, after Cimone's transformation, he exhibits even more bestial behavior by carrying off Efigenia.[40] In any case, what is most important to understand is that both these men act irrationally despite the fact that they have been educated in *filosofia*.

Furthermore, we would argue that when Tito progressively contradicts his own arguments, he exhibits irrational behavior; that is, after he first sees Gisippo's Sofronia, he undergoes an internal debate with himself over his newfound passion. At this point Tito affirms the hegemonic force of *Amor*, the laws, or *leggi*, which are actually *legami* that hold the lover in bondage. In his words:

Le leggi d'amore sono di maggior potenzia che alcune altre: elle rompono, non che quelle della amistà ma le divine. Quante volte ha già il padre la figliuola amata, il fratello la sorella, la matrigna il figliastro? . . . Oltre a questo io son giovane, e la giovanezza è tutta sottoposto all'amorose leggi. (X.viii.16–17)

---

40. But see Alfred Bonadeo, "Marriage and Adultery," insisting that critics "overlook the real determinant of the marriage, Cimone's irrational and brutish pursuit. At the end of the novella Efigenia is said to begin a long blissful existence with her husband, but as a victim of her lover's doings she may not be as happy as Boccaccio pictures here" (289). Bonadeo's point could have been made even more tellingly, for the conclusion of V.i never tells us that Efigenia (or Cassandrea) is happy, only that (V.i.71) "Cimone con Efigenia lieto si tornò in Cipri e Lisimaco similmente con Cassandrea ritornò in Rodi, *e ciascun lietamente con la sua visse lungamente contento nella sua terra*" [Cimone, with Efigenia, joyfully returned to Cyprus and Lisimaco similarly, with Cassandrea, returned to Rhodes; *and each lived a long and happy life in his own country with his woman*] (our italics). The point of view of the traduced women is hidden from us; we have no reason to believe that either of them is happily married.

[Love's laws are stronger than any other and break not only those of friendship but those of God. How often has a father fallen in love with his daughter, a brother with his sister, a stepmother with her stepson? . . . Beyond all this, I am young, and the ranks of youth are marshalled under the laws of Love.]

Tito's immediate response to his desires clearly reveals his allegiance to *Amor*. For, according to him, not only are the laws of love more potent than divine laws, but they also at least partially justify such an unthinkable act as incest.[41] Later, however, when Tito must defend himself publicly against the charge of having offended the Athenians—not to mention his deceptive entrapment of Sofronia—he entirely reverses his claims for the superiority of love by affirming the absolute superiority of friendship. In Tito's opinion, "le sante leggi della amicizia" create a bond more powerful than even that of consanguinity (X.viii.62): "il legame della amistà troppo più stringa che quel del sangue o del parentado" [the bond of friendship is even more binding than that of blood or family]. As Mazzotta points out, we can assume that Tito's earlier argument in behalf of love is the governing one, since it was debated in private, whereas the later argument in behalf of friendship is untruthful, since it was purposefully constructed for an audience (*World at Play*, 258). What is more important to keep in mind, however, is that what matters is not only the argument itself—that is, the argument for love over friendship or the one for friendship over love—but also Tito's presentation of it. Having been schooled in the arts of rhetoric and ratiocination, Tito can exploit his craft by devising cogent arguments that will allow him to satisfy his personal desires. Boccaccio thus reveals not only an ironic view of this version of the myth of friendship but also an ironic sense of rhetorical persuasion. For, if anything, what we see in X.viii is the delusory potential of "rhetorical" language—as well as the logical process of reasoning behind rhetoric—since it allows one to say convincingly what one does not truly mean. What is more, for all the comment on the length of Tito's "oration to the Greeks,"[42] there is small notice of its flaws.[43] While there are many, we will

---

41. Tito has obviously not read the tragic story of Tancredi and Ghismonda (IV.i), where a case of a father's unnatural affection for his daughter leads to her death.

42. See Kirkham, "The Classical Bond of Friendship," 238 and n., citing earlier observations that this is the longest speech in the *Decameron*.

43. Kirkham thinks more highly of Tito as rhetor than we do: "Tito delivers an eloquent oration, successfully defending the ruse" ("The Classical Bond of Friendship," 237); she considers Tito's self-defense "a tour-de-force of epideictic oratory" (246).

indicate only four.[44] First, he tells an untruth when he claims (X.viii.65) that Gisippo did not love Sofronia; can we forget that we had earlier been told that he did (X.viii.24)? Second, even though Tito himself admits that he will violate the rules of epideictic rhetoric in praising himself (X.viii.60), the fact that he does so in such flagrantly jingoistic and crass terms (the Athenians gave Sofronia to a Greek, Gisippo to a Roman; the Athenians gave her to a noble man, Gisippo to a nobler one; the Athenians gave her to a rich man, Gisippo to a much richer one [X.viii.65]) should surely have caused more uncomfortable notice than it has. Third, he indulges in casuistry that is totally and self-evidently indefensible: since he had married Sofronia with all the correct verbal and annulate forms ("e con le debite parole e con l'anello l'ebbi sposata"—suppressed is the far more significant fact that he did so as a falsifier of persona, as Dante had described this sin in *Inferno* 29), if she feels herself deceived (X.viii.80), he says, "non io ne son da riprendere, ma ella, che me non domandò chi io fossi" [I am not to blame for it, but she, who did not ask me who I was]. It is hard to imagine a less convincing argument or a less honest one.[45] Fourth, what is finally understood about Tito's rhetoric is that, not unlike some of the rhetorical set pieces in Thucydides, unknown to Boccaccio, in which Athenians crush their adversaries, seemingly by force of words, but actually by force of threatened force, it eventually relies on the power of threat. If the Athenians oppose his will, he will go off to Rome with Gisippo (whose friendship, taken utterly for granted, as though the Athenian were a mere appurtenance of his Roman "friend," is now a bartering chip in a vulgar argument) and return to take Sofronia away from them by force (X.viii.86): "e quanto lo sdegno de' romani animi possa, sempre nimicandovi, vi farò per esperienza conoscere" [and how great the wrath of Roman minds can be, ever holding you as enemies, I will make you know from experience].[46] Boccaccio shows the Athenians' consent to

---

44. Salvatore Battaglia, "La novella di Tito e Gisippo," is also skeptical about the seriousness of the speech: "Basterebbero i primi periodi di preambolo a denunziare l'atteggiamento presuntuosa [*sic*] e mirabolante di cui Tito s'investe e che comunica all'intero racconto un'intonazione semiseria, piuttosto da imbonitore" [The first sentences of its preamble are enough to unmask the presumptuous and falsely admiring attitude struck by Tito that lends to his entire speech an only half-serious intonation, indeed one of self-congratulation] (515).

45. It is clear that we do not share Kirkham's opinion that Tito and Gisippo should be understood "not as miscreants in a morally repugnant situation, but as exemplars of the most noble classical virtue, friendship" ("The Classical Bond of Friendship," 240).

46. This moment of disconcealment of the naked face of power has much in common with the similar moment in which Mithridanes thinks he can now kill Nathan with impunity. "Vegliardo, tu se' morto!" [Old guy, you're a dead man!] are his only words (X.iii.25).

be the result of a combination of their foolishness, in that some of them are convinced by his arguments, and of their fear of force (X.viii.88): ". . . e in parte spaventati dall'ultime sue parole . . ." [. . . and in part frightened by the last of his words. . .]. We ask, is Tito's the voice of friendship?

Boccaccio could have written X.viii in such a way as to avoid all these many contradictory pieces of evidence. He did not do so not because he was incapable of such writing but because he wanted to portray something other than munificence, something that masquerades as munificence but is better understood as self-love. Tito is a rogue, Gisippo a very special kind of fool, a stock figure, the "patsy," one that we know well enough from life as well as from fiction, whose will is so weak that he surrenders even those things dearest to him at the whim of the stronger. Gisippo, we think, is in fact the most interesting creation in this tale, a fictional creature whose ability to disturb is covered over by weak readings of the tale that contains him. If one were to take away the ending of X.viii, finishing the narrative with Gisippo, scorned indeed by his "friend" in Rome,[47] and finally about to be crucified for the murder he did not commit,[48] no one would or could read this *novella* as a tale that celebrates munificence.[49] It would rather be a tale of deception and victimization (until the conventional "happy ending" [the last sentence of the narrative—110—has the two couples happily sharing a household], we never hear a single word that indicates that Sofronia is content with her lot, not one; the same may be said, with still more force, of Efigenia in V.i, similarly taken off by the violence of a "husband"). This ending, like that of, for instance, II.i, overrules the laws of experience with

---

47. The scene is interesting. When Gisippo goes to Tito's house to see if the Roman still recognized his now miserable Athenian friend, Tito passes him by, and "a Gisippo parendo che egli veduto l'avesse e schifatolo, ricordandosi di ciò che già per lui fatto avea, sdegnoso e disperato si dipartì" [since it seemed to him that Tito had seen and shunned him, recalling all that he had done for him, Gisippo went away indignant and without hope] (X.viii.92). The scene is gratuitous unless Boccaccio wanted to raise this suspicion (or reconfirm it) in us. Needler's observations ("Song of a Ravished Nightingale," 508) are much to the point.

48. Kirkham reads the detail *in bono:* "This is, in other words, not just a Roman setting. To be more precise, it is a pre-Christian setting. Octavian, the crucifixion to which Gisippo is sentenced, and his rescue by a man called Tito all point forward to the Christian era— Christ's Coming, his sacrifice on the Cross, and the avenging of the Emperor Titus" ("The Classical Bond of Friendship," 247). That is a possible reading, but not one to which we are drawn.

49. Sorieri points out (*Boccaccio's Story of "Tito e Gisippo,"* 22) that in Alexandre de Bernay's poem it is Athis, the Athenian, who is the one who gives the speech arguing that Cardiones (the wife) should go to Rome with Prophilias (the Roman). Boccaccio's version, whether it consciously departs from this model or not, goes out of its way to make Tito the champion of his own self-serving cause.

those of romance.[50] We expect, on the basis of our experience, that Martellino will be put to death, and that Gisippo will be too. Boccaccio's two friends enjoy the sort of imposed ending that Berthold Brecht employed to such devastating effect in his version of the *Threepenny Opera*. All who believe that the royal messenger really rides in to save the Macks of this world from the gallows are invited to dissent.

We are not saying that Boccaccio is employing this particular friendship to debunk the myth of friendship in general. However, readers of the *Decameron* cannot claim that "friendship" is represented in a positive way in many of its stories.[51] With only such partial exceptions as are represented by the amicable relations found in I.ii (Abraam giudeo and Giannotto), VII.x (Tingoccio and Meuccio), VIII.viii (a friendship preserved by wife-swapping in Siena), X.ix (Saladino and Torello), we hardly ever encounter characters who even might be considered meaningfully joined by the bond of friendship.[52] We witness instead many a collaboration (often to a nefarious or self-serving end), hardly ever the shared and gratuitous affection of friendship. Filomena's peroration (X.viii.111–19), "Santissima cosa adunque è l'amistà . . ." [A most holy thing, then, is friendship . . .], one of the longest and most rhetorically loaded introductions or conclusions found in any *novella,* reminds us that friendship would indeed be a solution to most of the problems, a remedy to most of the ills, encountered in the pages of the *Decameron.* Its presence here both puts into sharp relief the absence of this human relationship in almost all of the tales and, in our opinion, is set forth in such a way as to call its nominal role into question even in the tale that seems most dedicated to its praise.

In our view, then, X.viii is another story in Day Ten that both interrogates the law and challenges the myth of order. Just as X.iii dramatizes the virtue of magnanimity in terms of a contractual agreement, X.viii dramatizes the virtue of friendship in terms of what comes to be seen as surprisingly similar to a contractual agreement: the bond of *amicizia.* Indeed,

---

50. James Zito, dead long before his time, who taught for many years at Columbia University and Sarah Lawrence College and who hardly ever set down in writing thoughts that were well worth having, liked to define romance as "the imposition of the will upon experience."

51. See discussion in Getto, *Vita di forme,* 224–25. For Boccaccio's own effusive (and countervailing) praise of friendship in his epistles see Ginetta Auzzas, "'Quid amicitia dulcius?'"

52. Words for "friend," "friendly," and "friendship" fairly explode from the pages of X.viii. It includes 5 of the 7 uses of the word *amicizia* in the entire *Decameron,* 9 of the 28 of *amistà,* and 27 of the 148 of the various forms of *amico*—a total of 41 uses (out of 183 in all) of these three words.

those critics who maintain that Day Ten represents a return to higher ethical values would perhaps change their mind about the authenticity of
Tito's and Gisippo's *amicizia* upon more closely considering Tito's descriptions of it. Although we get a sense from the narrator's presentation of the
boys' pre-adult years that they grew up as equals, side-by-side, in mutual
friendship, Tito destabilizes that equilibrium when, in his speech, he speaks
of himself as being superior, whether in riches or in lineage, to Gisippo.
Far from restoring harmony, Tito disrupts, as we have seen, social symmetry by calling attention to his own individual superiority.

What was supposedly a harmonious relationship thus becomes an emulous one, as exemplified by the way in which Tito and Gisippo try to outdo
each other's munificence in an effort to raise the power of one's *amicizia*
over that of the other. Further, how can we say that Day Ten represents law
and order in a positive light when what we ultimately witness in X.viii is a
disruption of the law? After Tito and Gisippo have argued over who will
accept punishment, the civil authority—represented by no less a personage
than Octavian, the emperor-to-be—allows the actual murderer to go free.
Thus, what results from the need to maintain one order—namely, the contract of friendship—is a disruption of a higher institutional order: the
order of the court and, by extension, of society.[53] Certainly we cannot say
that this is good for the community or insist that X.viii is a story that represents a return to order and social harmony. Rather, the fabric of society
is rent in many ways: a murderer is set free, a woman is tricked and coerced,
and friendship is exposed as subject to logic—something that can be
proved and disproved as easily as mathematical formulae or philosophical
theories.

The last story that we will consider in terms of the myth of order and the
dangers of contractual obligation is X.x, the *novella* dedicated to Gualtieri
and Griselda, arguably the most problematic in the *Decameron*.[54] A critical

---

53. It is worth noting here that in another story of Day Ten, X.ii, another "undesirable"
is allowed to go free, now because of the magnanimity of his victim. We refer to Ghino di
Tacco, the man famous "per la sua fierezza e per le sue ruberie" [for his fierceness and his
thievery] (X.ii.5) who is given his freedom simply because the abbot felt sorry for him and
admired the way in which Ghino allowed him to choose what items would be stolen from
him.

54. See Michel Olsen, "Griselda, *fabula* e ricezione," 253–64, for a review of the debate
over the significance of the relationship between Griselda and her husband. And for recent
work on the *fortuna* of the Griselda story see the several entries under Morabito in our bibliography and that for Luca Carlo Rossi. This is not to forget the still valuable appendix to
Boccaccio medievale, in which Branca discusses the "Origini e fortuna europea della
Griselda" (388–93).

consideration of this last story is essential to a better understanding of the *Decameron* for two reasons: first, because it is the last story and thus demands our attention as its end piece;[55] and second, because Dioneo tells it with an explicitly anti-exemplary intent, and thus in a way opposed to the majority of "moral tales with moral readings" of the Day.[56] Indeed, given the explicitly contextual organization of the *Decameron,* we would not be doing the story justice if we did not take Dioneo's explicative remarks into account, not to mention the essential fact that it is Dioneo who is telling the story.[57] Kirkham rejects the notion that Dioneo tells the tale in a purely ironic way, and she disagrees with the argument that Griselda "is so ridiculously exaggerated that her story almost has to undercut sardonically any pretended movement toward perfection on the *Decameron*'s concluding day" ("Last Tale in the *Decameron,*" 264). This is, however, very much the attitude of Attilio Momigliano. His notes to the *novella* (in his edition of forty-nine tales from the *Decameron*) fairly bristle with complaints against Boccaccio's fictive malfeasance. We offer only a sampling.

X.x.3: Dioneo's ascription of "matta bestialità" to Gualtieri:
Il giudizio sulle azioni del marchese di Saluzzo è assennato: ma tutta la novella è falsa, e non solo nella rappresentazione di

---

55. Kirkham points out that "by the precepts of Ciceronian rhetoric, which Boccaccio knew well and practiced, the end is always reserved for what is most important, since that is the part that we best remember [*Ad Herennium* 3.10.18]. . . . Dante had stated the rule in *Convivio* II 8, 2: 'sempre quello che massimamente dire intende lo dicitore sì dee riservare di dietro; però che quello che ultimamente si dice, più rimane ne l'animo de lo uditore'" [always that which the speaker cares most to communicate should be held in reserve; for that which is spoken last is what remains most vivid in the mind of the listener] ("Last Tale in the *Decameron,*" 264). Although we agree with Kirkham that the "end is always reserved for what is most important," while also believing that beginnings share this role, we do not agree with her that what Boccaccio intended to emphasize at the end was Griselda's moral triumph. By not fully recognizing the importance of the context of the tale—i.e., the fact that Dioneo tells it with a clear anti-exemplary intent—in our opinion Kirkham allows herself to impose a far too stringent allegorical reading, overestimating the redemptive power of this and of the other tales told in Day Ten.

56. Actually, Dioneo challenges Panfilo's directive at the end of Day Nine (IX.Conc.5) to recite exemplary, didactic tales—"Queste cose e dicendo e udendo senza dubbio niuno gli animi vostri ben disposti a valorosamente adoperare accenderà" [Telling and hearing these stories will, without any doubt, enkindle your minds, already well disposed to such purpose, toward virtuous conduct]—by reciting a tale in which the actions of the characters should not be imitated: ". . . la quale io non consiglio alcun che segua . . ." [. . . which I do not advise anyone to follow . . .].

57. Here we disagree with Itala Rutter, "The Function of Dioneo's Perspective," who argues that "the exemplary purpose of Gualtieri's explanation [X.x.61–63] escapes Dioneo, who here operates only on the human level and is clearly not Boccaccio's mouthpiece" (38). She considers Dioneo's various interpretive remarks "superficial" (39).

Griselda. Quelle bestialità sono ben giudicate, ma ritratte in un modo che disorienta; non hanno un fondamento saldo nell'indole del marchese. (Momigliano, *Il "Decameron,"* 479)

[His judgment on the actions of the marquis of Saluzzo is sensible; but the *novella* itself is utterly false, and not only for its representation of Griselda. [The marquis's] brutish behavior is well castigated, but portrayed in a manner that is disorienting and without foundation in his character.]

X.x.34: Gualtieri's reaction to the birth of his son:
La condotta di Gualtieri si comprenderebbe solo se egli fosse un pazzo: e non è. (ibid., 486)

[The conduct of Gualtieri could be understood only if he were a madman; and he is not.]

X.x.44–45: Griselda's piteous entreaty of Gualtieri:
Essa è idiota nel contegno, aristocratica nel discorso; Gualtieri è ad un tempo uno spietato bestione e un uomo assennato: la novella è senza costrutto. (ibid., 488)

[She is idiotic in her behavior, aristocratic in her discourse; Gualtieri is at once a pitiless brute and a man of good sense: the *novella* is poorly constructed.]

Instead of interpreting Gualtieri's *matta bestialità* (as described by Dioneo) as an innate character flaw, Kirkham attributes the marquis's stupidity to a behavioral flaw, a "short-sighted absorption in hunting and fowling[58] [that] shuts out any thought of marriage and children" ("Last Tale in the *Decameron*," 261–62).[59] Perhaps "allegorically-minded"

---

58. It is amusing to consider that Gualtieri's activities are specifically among those urged by Ovid in the *Remedia* and by the author in his *Proemio* to forestall the prick of lust. See Hollander, "The Proem of the *Decameron*," in this book, pp. 95, 98, 103–4. It is as though, in Boccaccio's eyes, Gualtieri were *too* successful at avoiding the snares of love.

59. But see Francesco Tateo, "La novella di Gualtieri?" for a reading of the tale that tends to side with Dioneo's view of Gualtieri's insufficiencies as leader and husband. Similar points had been made by Pernicone, "La novella del Marchese di Saluzzo," 219, seconded by Baratto, *Realtà e stile*, 342n, and by Grimaldi, *Il privilegio*, 401–2: "Gualtieri è il reale protagonista" [Gualtieri is the true protagonist]. One learns a great deal about a given reader's

critics[60] are overly influenced by *De insigni obedientia et fide uxoria,* Petrarch's Latin retelling of Boccaccio's Griselda story that explicitly calls attention to an exemplary intent. As Petrarch says at the end of the tale:

> Hanc historiam stilo nunc alio retexere visum fuit, non tam ideo ut matronas nostri temporis ad imitandum huius uxoris patientiam, que michi vix imitabilis videtur, quam ut legentes ad imitandam saltem femine constantiam excitarem, ut quod hec viro suo prestitit, hoc prestare Deo nostro audeant.[61]

> [It seemed to me a good idea to retrace this story with a different pen, to exhort not so much the matrons of our age to imitate the patience of this wife, which seems to me inimitable, as much as my readers, that they take as exemplary the constancy of this woman, so that they may have the strength to give to our God what she gave to her husband.]

However, Dioneo's ironic aside (X.x.68), "Chi avrebbe, altri che Griselda, potuto col viso non solamente asciutto ma lieto sofferir le rigide e mai più non udite prove da Gualtieri fatte?" [Who, besides Griselda, would have been able, with visage not only dry but joyful, to suffer the stern and unheard-of trials engineered by Gualtieri?], and his explicit negation of didactic intent (X.x.3), "la quale io non consiglio alcun che segua" [which I do not advise anyone to follow], clearly establish a narratorial stance that warns against our reading the tale as the *exemplum* that Petrarch interprets it to be. We may choose to follow Petrarch but must surely offer good reasons for doing so.

   More important still is the fact that these same readers (beginning with Petrarch) fail to answer the essential question: why would Boccaccio suddenly lapse into an allegorical and religious mode when his entire text has

approach from whether or not he or she believes that X.x is the "novella di Gualtieri" or the "novella di Griselda." We hope that it is apparent that, for us, it is the "novella di Gualtieri e Griselda."

   60. According to Joan Ferrante, "The Frame Characters," 223, X.x "makes sense only as an allegory of perfect devotion to God, despite apparently undeserved affliction." Janet Smarr, *Boccaccio and Fiammetta,* 273 n. 58, while aware that the Petrarchan allegorizing of the *novella* raises serious issues that are difficult to resolve, tries to accommodate that basic interpretation as follows: "What we can say, nonetheless, is that Griselda's relationship to Gualtieri, based on her willful determination to adhere to the rules established at the time of their marriage, represents the ideal relation of the human soul to God."

   61. Cited from Luca Carlo Rossi, *Giovanni Boccaccio, Francesco Petrarca, Griselda,* 61, 63.

remained insistently literal and secular? As Marcus says, regarding theolo-
gized readings: "Though convincing in themselves, none of these typological readings accounts for Boccaccio's sudden introduction of a figural
mode into a text which has been secular up to this point."[62] We agree with
Marcus's assertion that we must place the tale in its context in order to
understand more clearly the irony and anti-didacticism—or what she
might call the "secularity"—that lie behind it.[63] Critics who would like to
read X.x as Boccaccio's apotheosis of both Griselda and the *Decameron* as
a whole would do well to consider the tale in the context of other tales, like
X.iii, X.iv, X.v, and X.viii, where the need to fulfill a contractual obligation
leads to irrational, and even bestial, behavior.[64]

We should like to double back in our pursuit of the themes of this Day
in order to consider some points in two of the *novelle* that we have not yet
touched on. If we look at X.iv (Messer Gentile) and, to some degree, X.v
(Dianora, Gilberto, and Ansaldo the necromancer), we can find interesting
parallels to X.x that may help to clarify the dynamics of Griselda's and
Gualtieri's relationship. In both of these stories, women are obliged to men
by means of a contractual agreement. In X.iv, Niccoluccio's wife affirms
that she is *obbligata* to Gentile, the spurned lover who paradoxically "saved
her life" as a result of his necrophiliac exploitation of her.[65] Consequently,
she agrees to remain hidden until Gentile can present her to her husband in
a public forum. The contract or obligation that binds them, however, is
ultimately beneficial only to Gentile, who is able to parade as the hero of
the moment both by aggrandizing himself and by belittling Niccoluccio
publicly for his hasty and careless declaration of his wife's death. As Gentile says to Niccoluccio and the other "gentili uomini" who have gathered
to hear his speech:

> Egli è alcuna persona la quale ha in casa un suo buono e fedelissimo
> servidore, il quale inferma gravemente; questo cotale, senza attendere il

---

62. Millicent Joy Marcus, "The Marchioness and the Donkey Skull: The Tale of the
Patient Griselda," in *Allegory of Form*, 98.

63. In her words: "The metaliterary importance of this tale does not emerge from a study
of content alone. . . . Only by considering its formal context, i.e., the teller's commentary, the
various internal publics, and the terminal position of the tale in the sequence of stories, can
we begin to do justice to its meaning" (Marcus, *Allegory of Form*, 108).

64. For instance, and as Charles Haines notes ("Patient Griselda," 237), Griselda's giving
her children over to be put to death.

65. On the filiation of this tale from its previous version in the *Filocolo* see the discussion
in White, *La scena conviviale*, 139–60.

fine del servo infermo, il fa portare nel mezzo della strada né più ha cura di lui; viene uno strano e mosso a compassione dello infermo e' sel reca a casa e con gran sollicitudine e con ispesa il torna nella prima sanità. Vorrei io ora sapere se, tenendolsi e usando i suoi servigi, il primo signore si può a buona equità dolere o ramaricare del secondo, se egli raddomandandolo rendere nol volesse. (X.iv.26–27)

[Imagine someone having in his household a good and faithful servant who falls gravely ill; this fellow, without waiting until his sick servant actually dies, has him carried out into the street and has no further use for him. A stranger comes along and, moved to compassion by the sight of the sick man, takes him back to his house, where, with great care and considerable expense, he brings him back to health. Now I would like to know whether, if the second master keeps the servant and makes use of his services, the first has any right to lament or complain? And should the second, if asked, have to give him back when he does not want to?]

It is obvious who are the "real-life" counterparts to Gentile's provocative and self-aggrandizing anecdote of the person who did not care (Niccoluccio), of the sick "servidore" (his wife), and of the "strano" who did care (Gentile). What Gentile fails to include in his little story of the hero who saves the day, however, is the fact that the "stranger's" motives were activated not by disinterested generosity but rather by an initially uncontrolled sexual urge. The text itself calls attention to Gentile's quite un-*gentile* behavior when he puts his hand on what he thinks to be a dead woman's breast, only to discover after the fact that she is still alive. Surprisingly, critics forgive Gentile his necrophiliac thrills, praising him for renouncing his sexual desire and for his eventual generosity.[66] Or, as Barolini puts her case:

---

66. For example, Mario Baratto, *Realtà e stile,* 147: "solo questo Gentile, che coglie i suoi unici baci nella sepoltura dell'amata, in una raffinata originalità di omaggio e di passione, può essere capace della sottigliezza generosa del finale, quando vuole fare 'un caro e solenne dono' al marito di Catarina, ma 'in presenza de' migliori cittadini' (X.iv.20) che soli potranno apprezzare la finezza del gesto, la peregrinità della passione e del sacrificio" [only this man Gentile, who gleans his only harvest of kisses from his beloved's tomb with an unheard-of refinement confected of equal parts of homage and arousal, would be capable of the generous subtlety of his final gesture, when he desires to give "a pleasing and solemn gift" to Catarina's husband, but only "before the eyes of the best of our fellow Bolognesi," who alone will be able to appreciate both the style of the gesture and the rare quality of his desire and of his sacrifice]; Thomas Bergin, *Boccaccio,* 322: "the generosity of Gentile . . . , who restores to life and to her family a woman he loves—and asks nothing in return"; Laura White, *La scena*

And what must the *brigata* seek to incorporate into their lives? From the fourth novella, in which Messer Gentile returns the lady he has raised from the dead to her husband, to the eighth, in which Gisippo gives Sofronia to Tito, all the stories of Day X are concerned with sexual renunciation; thus, the central portion of the Day presents generosity in a particularly aggravated form. ("Wheel of the *Decameron,*" 532)

Given Gentile's sexual transgression, however, it is clear that the story is not finally "concerned with sexual renunciation." Gentile does not raise his lady from the dead because of his noble deed; rather, the fact that she happens to be alive is merely a fluke or coincidence, the same sort of fortuitous circumstance highly characteristic of the *Decameron*'s fictions. Nor can we imagine that he would have stopped at breast-fondling had his neighbor's wife not shown signs of life. Gentile's contract is therefore predicated not only on sexual transgression but also on lies. Bernard Chandler had some time ago reacted to the tale in ways that seem to us much closer to its point.

In fact, Gentile's so-called chivalrous action consisted solely in doing what morality and duty required of him, as the narrator, Lauretta, admits at the conclusion. It is as though Boccaccio is ill at ease because he cannot make a character behave "naturally." Gentile scarcely deserved to be "con somme lode tolto infino al cielo" [praised to the skies] by each member of the company. ("Man, Emotion, and Intellect," 411)

Had Chandler considered that perhaps the values of the *brigata* are what is called in question, rather than the ability of Boccaccio as writer, he might have made some of our work unnecessary.[67]

---

conviviale, 152: Gentile's incomparable joy is "indice del superamento umano della egoistica passione e del godimento anticipato della propria generosità" [evidence of his human conquest of self-centered ardor and of his anticipation of his happiness in his own generosity].

67. There are relations in certain details of this story both to elements in VIII.vii (the scholar and the widow) and in other stories of Day Ten (in particular, X.viii and X.x). In all of these stories, women are both denuded and deluded by men who either seek revenge on them (VIII.vii), want to trick them into doing something (X.viii), or want to test their fidelity (X.x). In each case, the contractual agreement is both predicated on and results in transgression and deceit. Gentile's behavior with a corpse reveals the desires that he had previously kept hidden and that are given expression only in the presence of death and in darkness.

The story of Madonna Dianora and Messer Ansaldo (X.v) is even more straightforward in what we would call its hortatory intent, one which likewise warns of the potential dangers of contractual obligation. This story of the magical March garden dramatizes the familiar topos of "men who will perform unheard-of deeds in order to gain the love of a woman," with Dianora acting the role of the teasing female we have seen in such figures as the widow of VIII.vii and Francesca in IX.i. We would argue that the primary focus of the story, however, is not Ansaldo's successful performance of his magical deed but rather the agreement that is enacted between Ansaldo and Dianora. It is in this story that the verb form of the noun *patto*—*pattovire*—twice occurs (it elsewhere only appears in V.i.25, where the ill-starred "pattovite nozze di Efigenia" [Efigenia's marriage contract] with Pasimunda are referred to). In fact, the verb occurs when Gilberto, Dianora's husband, refers to the irrevocability of the pact by which Dianora is *obbligata* to Ansaldo. As he says:

> Dianora, egli non è atto di savia né d'onesta donna d'ascoltare alcuna ambasciata delle così fatte, né di *pattovire* sotto alcuna condizione con alcuno la sua castità. Le parole per gli orrecchi dal cuore ricevute hanno maggiore forza che molti non stimano, e quasi ogni cosa diviene agli amanti possibile. Male adunque facesti prima ad ascoltare e poscia a *pattovire*. (X.v.14–15 [our italics])

> [Dianora, it is not a wise or a chaste woman's doing to pay heed to such messages as those, nor to come to terms under any condition or with any one at all regarding her chastity. Words that reach the heart through the ears have more power than many believe, and almost any task becomes possible for those who are in love. You did poorly, then, first when you listened and then when you came to terms.]

Unfortunately, Dianora misinterprets Gilberto's command, itself probably unnecessarily respectful of laws that should not be heeded, when she tells Ansaldo that it was not the promise she had made that led her back to him but rather her husband's orders. For it is precisely because of her "word of honor" that Gilberto commands Dianora to return to Ansaldo: the binding nature of the pact, in his view, prevents one from breaking it. Moreover, Dianora further misinterprets her husband's speech on the dangers of contractual agreement when she vows a second time her eternal obligation to Ansaldo after he releases her from the pact (X.v.23): ". . . di che io vi sarò sempre obligata" [. . . for which I shall always be under obligation to you]. Obviously, the fact that she was caught in the bondage of a binding agreement the first time is not enough to prevent Dianora from entering into a second bond, a second bondage. We can see, then, that the binding nature of a pact can ultimately lead to an undoing of order; in the case of Dianora and Gilberto, the result is an undoing of marital order. As Gilberto says, Dianora's bargain with Ansaldo could have led her to compromise not only her own marital vow to Gilberto but also her chastity ("né di pattovire sotto alcuna condizione con alcuno la sua castità"). Once again, then, Boccaccio seems to be making an implicit connection between the lawlessness of the plague and the destructive consequences (e.g., the loss of chastity) of a contract or law that refuses compromise.

After witnessing the binding power of the *promessa* as it affects women in stories X.iv and X.v, we do not think we can exempt from similar consideration Griselda's own *promessa* to Gualtieri in X.x, one which certainly places Griselda in a position of bondage. Many readers of X.x apply an allegorical interpretation to the story, one whereby Gualtieri is the godly figure who puts his Job-like subservient on trial in order to test her absolute belief in him.[68] Indeed, we can understand why these critics want to read Griselda as a "figure" of Job or of Christ, for the trials she undergoes are certainly of a similar magnitude as those of Job, and her humility and successive transformations (that is, she is first "ignuda," then transformed, then denuded again) recall Christ's own *humilitas* and transformation. Even a faithful literalist like Mazzotta to some degree reads the characters allegorically, as the text at least seems to invite us to do, although he concludes his study by arguing that the story itself ultimately questions the possibility of pure, "un-ironic" allegory.[69]

Considering the tale's Dionean—that is to say, unallegorical and anti-

---

68. For instance, Kirkham sees Griselda as being Christ-like, Marian, and Job-like. As she puts her case: "The long-suffering wife's likeness to Job, Christ, and Mary implies a common denominator. It is her Humility, of which all three biblical persons are types, as Passavanti's guidebook recognizes" ("Last Tale in the *Decameron,*" 257). Kirkham discusses at some length Griselda's biblical precedents. See also Janet Smarr, *Boccaccio and Fiammetta,* 191: "Griselda is a Job figure and as such appropriately placed to prepare the brigata for their return to Florence." If that is so, then Gualtieri must represent God. For Smarr's hesitant attempt to resolve the problem see our n. 60.

69. Mazzotta considers Gualtieri's double role as a figure of God and of Satan. As he says, "Precisely to the extent that Gualtieri arrogates to himself literally what is God's unique lordship over human events, he ends by playing the role that in Job's tragedy is that of the tempter" (*World at Play,* 125).

didactic—context, however, we should be careful not to impose an unwarranted allegorical reading on either the characters or the story itself. Perhaps a key to the tale's irreducible literalness is found in Griselda's behavior. Although most critics have commented on Gualtieri's *matta bestialità*, as it is described by Dioneo,[70] we would argue that Griselda's behavior is equally open to critical interrogation and even, perhaps, disapprobation. To be sure, given her tenacious silence and resistance to dialogue, we can assume that the *brigata* itself does not espouse what many critics consider to be Griselda's exemplary behavior. The *brigata*'s storytelling involves an active exchange of reason and creativity that encourages—indeed, necessitates—dialogue and debate.[71] Griselda, however, shuns dialogue and debate. Boccaccio (or Dioneo) constructs her response to Gualtieri's demand that she obey him in such a way as to emphasize her almost painful obedience. Gualtieri, as the text tells us:

. . . domandolla se ella sempre, togliendola egli per moglie, s'ingegnerebbe di compiacergli e di niuna cosa che egli dicesse o facesse non turbarsi, e s'ella sarebbe obediente e simili altre cose assai, delle quali ella a tutte rispose di sí. (X.x.18)

---

70. See, for example, Robin Kirkpatrick, "The Griselda Story," 233: "As the teller of the tale insists in his introduction, the Marquis is guilty of 'matta bestialitade.' This is a striking beginning; for the theme of the day is the virtue of magnanimity and yet Boccaccio has, it seems, set himself to demonstrate that the apparent greatness of purpose on which the Marquis prides himself is nothing but a cloak for cruel whimsicality." At 248n. Kirkpatrick adds: "Compare the self-deceit of Mitridanes . . . who contemplates murder in order to safeguard a reputation for magnanimity." See also Luciano Rossi, "Das *Dekameron*," 32: "Das Publikum zog den beunruhigenden parodistischen Spielen des Originalwerks das lineare *exemplum* der von Petrarca gebotenen ehelichen Gefügigkeit vor. Tatsache ist, dass in der lateinischen Neubearbeitung eine kritische Verschleierung des feudalen Despotismus höchstens durchschimmert. Im *Dekameron* hingegen betrifft die Kritik der *matta bestialità* auch das männliche Verhalten in der Beziehung zu den liebenden Frauen" [The reading public preferred the linear *exemplum* of spousal accommodation, offered by Petrarch, to the disturbing, parodistic playfulness of the original work. The truth is, there is evident in the Latin reworking a critical veiling of feudal despotism. In the *Decameron*, on the other hand, the critique of 'mad bestiality' is also directed against male behavior toward loving women].

71. It is clear that, while Griselda as a character might resist debate, interpreters of her conduct certainly do not. After Dioneo finishes his story, for instance, the narrator points out how heatedly members of the *brigata* (and specifically "le donne") respond to it (X.Conc.1): "e assai le donne, chi d'una parte e chi d'altra tirando, chi biasimando una cosa, chi un'altra intorno ad essa lodandone, n'avevan favellato . . ." [and the ladies had discussed it at some length, some taking one side, others another, some finding fault with one thing, others praising yet another . . .]. The very language here expresses a rhetoric of debate absent from Gualtieri's and Griselda's uncompromising contract.

[. . . asked her whether she, if he took her to be his wife, would strive to please him ever after, allowing nothing that he might say or do to bother her, and whether she would be obedient, and other similar things, to all of which her response was "yes."]

Here, the syntax labors along in a succession of if-clauses (indeed, *se* is used three times) and conjunctions ("e . . . e . . . e . . . e . . .") in order to call attention to the terse and dramatic "di sí" with which the sentence, exhausted, ends. It is almost as if we could hear Gualtieri's bold and overbearing commands suffocating Griselda's pathetically tiny affirmative.

That almost silent affirmative, however, has bold and overpowering consequences of its own, especially since Griselda does in fact keep her word by virtually repeating this same "yes" to each of Gualtieri's monstrous commands. On one hand, we could say that Griselda's refusal to break her contract with Gualtieri reveals a certain ignorance on her part, an ignorance similar to that of Dianora, who also became entrapped in contractual bondage. On the other hand, we could also say that her "refusal to refuse" reveals Griselda's rigid mentality in proving her absolute obedience. In this way, she exhibits a behavior similar to that of Nathan, someone who also was willing to go to the extreme of death in order to prove his absolute munificence. For Griselda is willing to subject her children to murder in order to remain true to her word. Indeed, just as we have argued that Nathan's *caritas* is a perversion of Christ's true *caritas,* we would argue that Griselda's *humilitas* is a perversion of its typological counterpart. Christ did not die on the Cross so that women should give their innocent children to be murdered.

More important, however, is the spirit of revenge inherent in Griselda's most "martyr-like" actions. Indeed, there are subtle indications within the story that might point to Griselda's vengeful behavior. For instance, critics like Mazzotta and Marcus have called attention to the fact that Dioneo uses the obscene phrases "scuotere il pelliccione" [jiggle your fur] and "coda ritta" [erect tail] both before and after telling his story, to suggest an alternative ending, perhaps one with a more verbally and sexually assertive heroine.[72] Mazzotta interprets the first phrase as hearkening back to IV.x, the tale about a surgeon from Salerno, Mazzeo della Montagna, who, like so many of the *Decameron*'s inadequate husbands, is a victim of cuckoldry.

---

72. Teodolinda Barolini's recent study of the relation of words and sexual acts in the *Decameron* became available too late for us to do more than observe its usefulness in pursuing this line of inquiry. See "'Le parole son femmine e i fatti sono maschi': Toward a Sexual Poetics of the *Decameron* (*Decameron* II 10)," *Studi sul Boccaccio* 21 (1993): 175–97.

For Mazzotta, the allusion to IV.x calls the reader back to a world of romance, or at least of romantic comedy (*World at Play,* 129). Marcus alludes to an occurrence of the second phrase in a different story, VII.i, the story of Gianni Lotteringhi, his lustful wife, and the volatile donkey skull. She interprets both of Dioneo's bawdy references as gestures toward interpretive open-endedness, especially since VII.i is (according to her) explicitly concerned with narrative discourse and interpretation (Marcus, *Allegory of Form,* 103). What neither Mazzotta nor Marcus does call attention to, however, is the fact that the phrase "scuotere il pelliccione" is also used in VIII.vii.[73] There the scholar reprimands the widow for preferring young to old men simply because the young ones are better love-makers (VIII.vii.103): "Certo io confesso che essi con maggior forza scuotano i pelliccioni . . ." [Naturally I admit that they jiggle your fur more energetically . . .]. While we must be careful not to push the connection too far, it is interesting to consider X.x in light of some of the same issues presented in VIII.vii—namely, those of revenge and punishment. Just as Mazzotta thinks that the phrase *(scuotere il pelliccione)* plunges us back into "the heart of the *Decameron*'s comedy" (*World at Play,* 129), we would argue that the associations with that story (VIII.vii) take us back into a world of *vendetta* and *gastigamento,* whether reflected in Gualtieri's punishing behavior or the vengeance that Griselda might with justice have taken on such a husband.

Furthermore, although critics have acknowledged Dioneo's explicit condemnation of Gualtieri's *matta bestialità,* they have often failed to acknowledge his ironic jab at Griselda's behavior as well, for he says (as we have noted) in concluding (X.x.68): "chi avrebbe, altri che Griselda, potuto col viso non solamente asciutto ma lieto sofferir le rigide e mai più non udite prove da Gualtier fatte?" [Who, besides Griselda, would have been able, with visage not only dry but joyful, to suffer the stern and unheard-of trials engineered by Gualtieri?]. Considering that the tale-teller himself is dubious (to say the very least) about his female character, we would argue that it is crucial to recognize that Griselda's behavior is worthy of a certain condemnation.[74] Indeed, she and Gualtieri are very well matched: for each

---

73. This last occurrence is noted by Grimaldi, *Il privilegio,* 407n.

74. Beginning at least with Momigliano there has been a strong minority view that castigates her behavior. To Bergin, Griselda is "the pathological wife of Walter" (*Boccaccio,* 325), an opinion essentially shared by Bonadeo ("Marriage and Adultery," 291). Duranti, studying the tales of Dioneo, does not share this view. While he considers the behavior of Gualtieri as exemplifying "ferocia sadica" [sadistic ferocity], he believes that Griselda is "un personaggio sublime autentico" [an authentically sublime character] ("Le novelle di Dioneo," 27).

is, if in widely divergent ways, narcissistic and, in these different ways, equally uncompromising.

Perhaps as much as any other story in the *Decameron,* then, this final *novella* explodes the myth of order. Given what we have seen of the monstrous extremes to which Griselda will go in order to keep her contractual obligation, we do not think that we can say, as Kirkham does, that her story "crowns the idealistic plane of the *Decameron*'s concluding day" ("Last Tale in the *Decameron,*" 261). A far cry from ideality (also claimed for Griselda by Cottino-Jones: "an idealized embodiment of perfection" ["*Fabula* vs. *Figura,*" 39]), what we are shown in Day Ten (and in X.x in particular) are the extremes to which humans will go in order to maintain the law—in Griselda's case, it is the maintenance of the conjugal contract.

What has not heretofore been discussed, as far as we have been able to ascertain, is a possible source for Dioneo's harsh words for Gualtieri: those of Dante's presentation of Filippo Argenti (*Inferno* 8.46–51) and, in particular, Virgil's dispraise of all those, like Filippo, who pridefully (and wrongfully) consider themselves great (vv. 49–51).

> Quanti si tegnon or là sù gran regi
> che qui staranno come porci in brago,
> di sé lasciando orribili dispregi!

[How many up there consider themselves great kings who here will lie like pigs in mud, leaving behind them terrible contempt!]

Dioneo's words of dispraise for Gualtieri, in which he is compared to those found in "[*case*] *reali* . . . che sarien più degni di guardar *porci* che d'avere sopra uomini signoria" [royal houses . . . who would be more worthy of keeping pigs than of having sovereignty over men] (X.x.68 [our italics]), similarly connect bad rulers and swine. Boccaccio's gloss in the *Esposizioni* to this passage follows: "il 're' è dinominato da *rego-regis,* il quale sta per 'reggere' e per 'governare.' Di questi cotali, quantunque di molti sieno le lor teste ornate di corona, non son però tutti da dovere essere reputati re; e però dice l'autore ben *si tengono:* ma, perché essi si tengano, essi non sono . . ." ["king" is derived from *rego-regis,* which signifies "to rule" and "to govern." Of such as these, however many have their heads adorned with crowns, not all are to be reputed kings; and thus well does the author say "they consider themselves"; although they may so consider themselves, they are not . . .]. Boccaccio then cites a passage in a similar vein from Seneca's *Thyestes*. He concludes: "Dalle quali parole possiam comprendere quanti sieno oggi quegli li quali degnamente si possano tenere re. Non sono adunque re questi cotali che re si tengono, anzi sono tiranni" [From which words we are able to understand how many are those today who may justly consider themselves kings. Such as these who so consider themselves are not kings but rather tyrants].[75] The marchese of Saluzzo proves himself less a *re* than a *tiranno*. He is, at least intrinsically, thus juxtaposed against the king in X.vii, Pietro d'Aragona, who, according to Pampinea, the narrator of his story, is a king worthy of emulation: "Così adunque operando si pigliano gli animi de' subgetti, dassi altrui materia di bene operare e le fame eterne s'acquistano: alla qual cosa oggi pochi o niuno ha l'arco teso dello 'ntelletto, *essendo li più de' signori divenuti crudeli e tiranni*" [And it is in so acting that one wins over the minds of one's subjects, offers to others a model for good conduct, and achieves eternal fame; in our time, few or none have drawn the bow of their intellect toward such ends, *since most rulers have become cruel and tyrannical*] (X.vii.49 [our italics]). Pampinea, the most optimistic of the members of the *brigata,* as perhaps only befits their leader, tells the one story of the Day which at least seems most closely to carry out the mission announced by Panfilo (IX.Conc.4): "di ragionare sopra questo, cioè: di chi liberalmente o vero magnificamente alcuna operasse intorno a' fatti d'amore o d'altra cosa" [to tell a tale on this subject, namely, of one who did something generous or indeed splendid, whether in the matter of love or something else]. The rest of the Day's so-called "munificent" rulers are examined in the harsher light of reality. We come to see them for what they are, and Pietro, as we have argued, is not exempt from such examination.

Gualtieri is a name well known to Boccaccio and to his fellow Florentines. Can there be any doubt but that the marquis of Saluzzo, sharing his name, shares his quality as tyrant? The "Duke of Athens," Gualtieri di Bri-

---

75. For a similar remark, see his commentary to *Inf.* 12.108, where he details the crimes of the two tyrants of Syracuse, Dionysius I and II, concluding with the following: "Per le quali malvagità e violenze, così nel sangue come nell'aver del prossimo, o del padre e del figliuolo che intender vogliamo, e per ciò che *non come re ma come tiranni signoreggiarono,* meritamente l'autore qui nel sangue bogliente tra la prima spezie de' violenti nel dimostra" [On account of these evil and violent deeds, either of blood or against the possessions of one's neighbor—whether we think of the father or the son—and because they *held lordship not like kings but like tyrants,* justly does the author reveal their place here in the boiling blood, among the first classification of the violent] (our italics).

enne, was asked to serve as *podestà* in 1342. The experiment in government
was a clamorous failure.[76] For Dioneo (and Boccaccio) to have chosen his
name for the "hero" of the last *novella* of the *Decameron* was surely not an
innocent decision. The "magnanimity" of such a ruler must be understood
in a darker light.

If the tale actually "represents the radical rupture between the allegory
of order and its human, literal counterpart" (Mazzotta, *World at Play*,
126—and we would agree that it does), then it seems clear that we cannot
and indeed should not read it allegorically, especially since we have already
seen that a one-to-one correspondence between what could be a typological relation (e.g., Griselda and Job) breaks down when we consider its
"human, literal counterpart." Unlike the other members of the *brigata*
who at least thought that they were obeying Panfilo's directive to recite
moral, didactic narratives, Dioneo "reasserts the integrity of the text by
separating it off, once and for all, from the tradition of the *exemplum*"
(Marcus, *Allegory of Form*, 101–2). As Marcus continues:

> In his refusal to be didactic at this point in the text, Boccaccio's own
> special form of didacticism emerges. Unlike Dante, whose teachings are
> univocal and direct, residing in the content of the work, Boccaccio
> makes his points through subtle manipulations of form, leaving it up to
> the readers to discern his moral lesson. (108)

By subverting the form of his own potential allegory, Dioneo challenges
what for the *brigata* is a return to law on Day Ten, following the rubrical
freedom of Day Nine. In this way, he challenges the myth of order that
many critics see at work in Day Ten: for if the last Day does represent a
return to order, what do we make of the fact that the last story of that Day
challenges the concept of order on both a thematic and stylistic level?

After thinking about this question at length, we are still not sure that

---

76. For the details, mainly economic, of Gualtieri's disastrous fourteen months of dictatorship in Florence and his overthrow by the *magnati* in July 1343 see Marvin B. Becker, *Florence in Transition*, 1:148–72. And see the brief notice in Joy H. Potter, *Five Frames*, 15. Neither of these writers considers the problem or draws the conclusion that we do, namely, that
Boccaccio's Gualtieri is meant to recall Florence's, not only by his name, but in his tyrannical behavior. As far as we know, the only other critic to have made this essential point, if in
passing, is David Wallace, *Giovanni Boccaccio*, 105 (see also his similar remark in "'Whan
She Translated Was,'" 190; he has not observed Hollander's previous suggestion to the same
effect: see *"Utilità"* in the present book, p. 80). In a spirit of speculation we add that the
"tredici anni o più" [thirteen years or more] (X.x.47) of Griselda's travail may be meant to
reflect the fourteen months of the dictatorship.

there is a straightforward answer to it. The very fact that there are so many interpretations of X.x would seem to imply that perhaps there is no single answer, rather that Boccaccio left the story deliberately obscure and thus open to multiple interpretation, as his *brigata*'s divided response surely seems to indicate.[77] Indeed, it would be a difficult, if not impossible, task to reduce any story—or, for that matter, any Day—of the *Decameron* to a single, governing theme. We have tried to approach Day Ten in terms of the theme of law and its attendant form of expression, the contractual agreement, in an effort to challenge critics who see an ascending movement in the *Decameron*. As we hope we have shown, the stories of Day Ten do not represent a return to positive communal values; nor do they leave us with a feeling of harmony, the feeling that we have progressed from a depraved, plague-ridden world to an ideal, lawful, and rational community. We agree with Barolini that the movement of the *Decameron* is that of a circle, one that increasingly tends toward Florentine reality and that eventually ends where it began. However, we are not as positive as she is concerning the text's circular movement: whereas she understands it as a progressive revolution, to us it seems more likely that there is no progress. To be sure, the *brigata* must prepare itself in the later Days to re-enter the world of the plague—lawless and death-bearing. In fact, if we approach Day Ten as the Day that anticipates the *brigata*'s re-entry into the world,[78] then we can detect an increasing anxiety in the minds of the storytellers, one that manifests itself in the overbearing emphasis on the "law" that we have seen at work in the final Day. Indeed, at the beginning of several consecutive stories that follow the first, its teller asserts that she or he will tell a tale that outdoes the praise of the magnanimous act that has just been celebrated.[79]

---

77. While we do not go as far as he does in arguing for a "polyvalent" tale of Gualtieri and Griselda, we find that in this remark we are echoing Guido Almansi, *The Writer as Liar*, 133–34 (his initial statement has IV.i as its subject): "This wide variety of conclusions should initially dispose us to investigate the possibility that there are several different narrative levels co-existing in the *novella*, and perhaps to suspect that this is an intentional plurality of meaning and interpretation on Boccaccio's part, one which he was inclined to introduce in other major stories. In this connection it is enough to think of the *novella* of Griselda . . . where the polyvalence of the text suggests that it is a deliberate, one might even say malicious, product of Boccaccio's authorial strategy."

78. What are we to make of the fact, however, that although we know it is the last Day, the *brigata* does not? It is only after Dioneo finishes his tale of Griselda that Panfilo suggests that the *brigata* return to Florence.

79. As Branca observes in his note at X.ii.3: "Si imposta fin dalla seconda novella il ritmo ascensionale, quasi di gara nel presentare esempi sempre più straordinari, che caratterizza la X giornata" [From the second story on one senses the insistence of a rising rhythm, almost of

It has thus not gone unnoticed that the Tenth Day ushers in a new attitude among the members of the *brigata,* namely, one of rivalry.[80] If those who perceive a "darkening" that occurs in the second half of the *Decameron* are right in that perception, what we are suggesting about the last Day puts it into proximity with the previous four.[81] It is clear, even before the outburst of the Ghibelline lady, that the relations among the storytellers have

---

rivalry, in the presentation of examples ever more extraordinary, which characterizes the Tenth Day]. See Emma Grimaldi, *Il privilegio,* 354, in the same vein. But see, in a harsher light, the remarks of Millicent Marcus, *Allegory of Form,* 96: "The members of the story-telling team are vying with each other in their tales of magnificence as many of the narrators include claims of victory over previous 'contenders' and implicit challenges to subsequent tellers to equal or surpass each example. Such a competitive mode subverts the very theme of magnificence, for this virtue suggests the disinterested outpouring of wealth in Dante's sense of celestial economics, where giving increases rather than decreases the donor's assets" [see *Purgatorio* 15.52–57]. See also Luciano Rossi, "Ironia e parodia," 397, who writes that the tellers "fanno a gara per rivendicare alla loro storia il 'primato' su tutte le altre" [vie with one another in order to claim for their own story the "prize" over all the others].

80. Moving from Getto's point in *Vita di forme,* 281, that these interruptions give a flavor of "realism" amidst growing "unreality," Brian Richardson, in "The 'Ghibelline' Narrator," makes a fairly strong case for Emilia as being the Ghibelline lady who brings political discord into the Day. But now see the stronger case made for its being Elissa by Michael Paden, "Elissa: La ghibellina."

81. For a series of remarks about the parodic nature of the Tenth Day with which we are in general agreement see Luciano Rossi, "Ironia e parodia," esp. 396–405. Rossi more or less summarizes his position as follows (398): "Se proviamo a leggere le novelle della decima giornata in questa nuova prospettiva, ci accorgeremo che in tutte, anche se in modi diversi, la presunta liberalità segue un atto di debolezza, se non addirittura un impulso spregevole" [If we experiment with reading the *novelle* of the Tenth Day from this new perspective, we become aware that in all of them, if in different ways, presumed generosity follows upon an act of weakness, if not indeed a contemptible impulse]. For a strong statement in intrinsic opposition see Joan Ferrante, "The Frame Characters": "The stories on the last day describe generosity and virtue in its *[sic]* highest forms. They are arranged in an increasing degree of selflessness from the first, in which a knight commits great deeds to increase his own fame and is disappointed when he receives no tangible reward, to the ninth, Panfilo's, where generosity is properly practiced for its own sake, with no thought of possible requital. The day ends with Griselda's perfect patience and devoted love in the face of all afflictions" (226). For the most recent expression of this point of view see Michelangelo Picone, "Autore/narratori," in Bragantini and Forni, *Lessico critico decameroniano,* 59, who concludes his essay as follows: ". . . [l]'itinerario che conduce da Ciappelletto (I 1) che si serve della parola falsa per trasformare la sua vita di pessimo uomo in quella di un santo, che 'inventa' quindi il racconto della sua vita, a Griselda (X 10) che usa invece la parola vera, e più spesso il silenzio, per evidenziare l'esemplarità della sua condotta esistenziale, e quindi per significare l'identità di vita e racconto" [. . . the road that leads from Cepparello, who employs false speech to transform his life as the worst of men into that of a saint, who thus "invents" the story of his life, to Griselda, who, on the other hand, employs truthful speech and, more often, silence, to give evidence of the exemplarity of her actual conduct, and thus to signify the identity of life and its narrative].

become, for the first time, essentially emulous.[82] And it is not so much that
each hopes to be associated with the higher qualities of her or his hero-
ically munificent protagonist but that each wishes to have produced the
best story. Nathan and Mithridanes become, in some sense, the avatars of
the narrators, each trying to outdo the others in narrating *magnificenzia,*
and thus each utterly losing track of the moral basis of munificence in the
first place. This is close to the point made by Fiammetta, preparing to tell
her tale, as she reflects upon the debate caused by the tale of Dianora,
Gilberto, and Ansaldo. Such debates are more suited to scholars than to
ladies, she says, and she claims that she is putting aside a tale that might
have led to more such debate in favor of one that records the chivalrous
behavior of a king (X.vi.3–4). Her very tactic, however, serves first to tend
to glamorize her King Carlo, and then to set off a dispute among the members of the *brigata* when the Ghibelline lady refuses to praise a Guelph
ruler (X.vii.2). This pattern is repeated at the end of Pampinea's tale, when
the Ghibelline outdoes the rest in praising a Ghibelline king (Piero).
Filomena, at the end of her tale of Tito and Gisippo, praises friendship in
such a way as to render less important the other virtues lauded so enthusi-
astically; it is "madre di magnificenzia e d'onestà" [mother of munificence
and gracious comportment] (X.viii.111) and thus, we are left to conclude,
higher even than the virtue that is the subject of the Day's praising. It is
only momentarily, with Panfilo, that rivalry ceases. His introductory
remarks, a foil to those that have preceded them in this Day, are in complete agreement with Filomena's encomium of friendship. All that may
leave a reader a bit disconcerted in his remarks is his formulation of the
results of friendship: "se pienamente l'amicizia d'alcuno non si può per li
nostri vizii acquistare, almeno diletto prendiamo del servire, *sperando che
quando che sia di ciò merito ci debba seguire*" [if our vices make it impossible for us to gain another's friendship completely, at least let us take pleasure in service, *in the hope that one day or another our reward may follow*]
(X.ix.4 [our italics]). Had the italicized phrase been omitted, Panfilo's purposes would have been "orthodox." It is not, and it reintroduces the desire
to serve oneself well that, if accurate enough in describing actual human

---

82. Bergin, *Boccaccio,* sounding a bit like Chandler in blaming our author for failing to
achieve what he never intended to (see our n. 5), responds to the atmosphere of rivalry among
the fabulists as follows: "Although the tenth day contains some good stories the reader senses
that the new climate is not quite suited to Boccaccio's Muse; the storytellers seem less at ease;
there is a perceptible feeling of tension as they vie with each other to see who can portray the
noblest subject" (322).

behavior,[83] sounds a bit "off" in this elevated and elevating context. And, as we have seen, this is exactly the tone of the moment in the text that undercuts the behavior of Torello, who pursues Saladino (as Betto and his *brigata* pursue Guido Cavalcanti in VI.ix) because he senses there may be something to be had from the companionship of so obviously lofty a fellow.

Of Dioneo's deflating effect we have already spoken. On no Day does his abruptness show more markedly than here, first in his debunking of the story of Torello (X.x.2), where another husband who fared less well than Torello, Gianni Lotteringhi (VII.i), is imagined as being a far less enthusiastic audience for such drivel as flying beds that keep husbands from being cuckolded. (In a sense, Dioneo "pulls the rug out from under" Day Ten.) And his second gesture is to undermine completely the moral basis for the appreciation of his own protagonist, immediately scored off as a maddened beast. It is at least a little surprising that so many continue to read this *novella* as the tale of Griselda, and Gualtieri as a positive figure.

All of the rivalry among the members of the *brigata* here in Day Ten is certainly noteworthy, especially if we are meant to believe that the *Decameron*'s conclusion is a positive one. And we should probably keep in mind the compact that they all seemed to assent to in S. Maria Novella. The words are Pampinea's (I.Int.96): "E acciò che ciascun pruovi il peso della sollecitudine insieme col piacere della maggioranza e, per conseguente da una parte e d'altra tratti, non possa chi nol pruova invidia avere alcuna, dico che a ciascuno per un giorno s'attribuisca e il peso e l'onore" [And so that each may experience the burden of command along with its pleasure, and, as a result, become acquainted with both, so that no one may envy anyone else for not having known them, I say that to each one of us the burden and the honor shall be lent for a day]. Day Ten, by introducing invidious feelings and remarks among the now openly competitive members of the storytellers, has shown a breach in the decorum of the *brigata* that indicates that perhaps home, even plague-ridden, is the only place they have left to go.[84]

---

83. For an attempt to demythologize the Romantic view of human activity as depicted in the *Decameron* so often sponsored, particularly in the nineteenth and first half of the twentieth century, see the understanding that Boccaccio's intent is to display the self-seeking behavior of what is referred to as "the sovereign individual" by T. K. Seung, "The Sovereign Individual in the *Decameron*."

84. See Cesare De Michelis, *Contraddizioni,* 14: "Ora, contraddicendo i propositi iniziali, Panfilo suggerisce la via del ritorno senza che nessun indizio lasci neppur sperare che la terri-

While we have no final solutions to offer, or even interesting hypotheses that might nourish further thoughts about their eventual meaning and function, we do not want to leave unmentioned the ten *ballate* sung, in turn, by each member of the *brigata*. One day someone may develop a hypothesis to account for their role that commands consent. Without reviewing the work that has been done on a subject that is generally neglected, probably because it is so difficult, we would only observe that the significance of this prominent feature of the *Decameron* continues to elude its pursuers, including these pursuers. Yet we want to point out that the last song, sung by Fiammetta, favored in some way among the women of the *brigata* at least by her importance in Boccaccio's pseudo-autobiography, is one of jealousy, thus underlining the *rivalità* that is so prominent and disturbing a feature of the last Day, with its supposed upward movement to a higher plane of human behavior.

The law, as we find it represented in Day Ten, is more often than not revealed to be a precarious institution, something that allows robbers and murderers to go free and even forces women into abjuring their free will, "obligated" by binding pacts. Moreover, we have seen characters like Nathan, Tito, Gualtieri, and even Griselda go to irrational extremes in order to maintain a contractual agreement. In this way, the extreme legalism of Day Ten is reminiscent of the lawless extremism of the beginning of the text, when we saw men and women dying like beasts ("come bestie morieno"—I.Int.43) from the plague, as well as succumbing to bestial, irrational behavior in the absence of both natural and human law. Does it not seem, then, that Boccaccio might be showing that extreme concern for subjection to the law is, potentially, as destructive as extreme lawlessness? In both cases men and women abandon rational thought and give themselves over to rampant, even destructive desire. David Wallace is the only critic known to us who has made the connection between the plague and an extreme case of "law and order." As he says:

The effect of the Black Death on Florence is rather like the effect of tyranny on any city: it is a disease that runs out of control, feverishly devouring the body politic. . . . Boccaccio's Griselda is the faithful and enduring Christian subject, and while Walter is not to be compared to

---

bile epidemia stia finalmente venendo meno, né che l'ordine sociale sia stato almeno in parte restaurato" [Now, contradicting their initial intentions, Panfilo suggests the measure of returning home without a single indication that would allow even the hope that the terrible epidemic is finally abating or that the social order has been even in part restored].

God, he might be seen as God's agent. He might, as a tyrant, be compared to the Black Death.[85]

The very fact that the text points out that men of law (like Gualtieri) can exhibit the same *bestialità* as that of the lawless victims of the plague should force us to re-evaluate the ostensible idealism and moral rectitude that many critics find operative in Day Ten.[86] Also, the fact that, starting with X.iv, the word *noia* occurs in all the seven concluding tales of the Day,[87] that same word that the narrator of the *Decameron* used to describe both his love-sickness ("più di noia che bisogno non m'era spesse volte sentir mi facea" [it often made me experience greater pain than necessary]— *Proemio.* 3) and the insufferable conditions of the plague ("A questa brieve noia . . . seguirà prestamente la dolcezza e il piacere" [After this brief annoyance . . . will shortly follow sweetness and pleasure]—I.Int.6), should probably have caught the attention of those who read Day Ten as a comic triumph.[88] Gualtieri's own summation of his purpose in treating Griselda as he did should be enough to call such a judgment into question.

> Griselda, tempo è omai che tu senta frutto della tua lunga pazienzia, e che coloro li quali me hanno reputato crudele e iniquo e bestiale [Dioneo's opening words come back to mind] conoscano che ciò che io faceva a anteveduto fine operava, volendoti insegnar d'esser moglie e a loro di saperla tenere, e a me partorire perpetua quiete mentre teco a vivere avessi: il che, quando venni a prender moglie, gran paura ebbi che non m'intervenisse, e per ciò, per prova pigliarne, in quanti modi tu sai ti punsi e trafissi. E però che io mai non mi sono accorto che in parola né in fatto dal mio piacere partita tu sii, parendo a me aver di te quella consolazione che io disiderava, intendo di rendere a te a un'ora ciò che

---

85. David Wallace, "'Whan She Translated Was,'" 189–90.

86. As David Wallace puts the case, at least with respect to Gualtieri, "His final, theatrical act of public reconciliation, in which he reunites Griselda with the children he has himself stolen from her, is to be seen not as *magnificenzia* but as an obscene parody of it" ("'Whan She Translated Was,'" 105).

87. See X.iv.29, v.19, vi.10, vii.6, viii.54 and 84, ix.113, x.31. A precise English translation is difficult. "Tedium," "nuisance," "annoyance" are among modern ones; in Boccaccio, since it signifies, among other things, the plague itself, its meaning is sometimes considerably more harsh.

88. For a view of the centrality of the word *noia* to the *Proemio* of the *Decameron* see in the present book, "*Decameron:* The Sun Rises in Dante," p. 56, as well as "The Proem of the *Decameron,*" p. 97, where the word's importance to the work as a whole is emphasized.

io tra molte ti tolsi e con somma dolcezza le punture ristorare che io ti
diedi. (X.x.61–62)

[Griselda, it is now time that you should taste the fruit of your long
patience, and that those who have considered me cruel and unjust and
brutish recognize that what I did I did with an end in view; I wanted to
teach you how to be a wife, wanted them to know how to keep one; and
I wanted to give occasion to continual tranquillity for as long as I had
to spend with you. I was greatly fearful that, when I took a wife, I might
lose that tranquillity; for that reason, to put you to the test (in how
many ways you well know), did I pierce and run you through. Because I
have never become aware that you desisted from seeking my pleasure,
either in word or deed, and in the belief that I have had from you the
consolation that I desired, I intend to return to you in one hour what I
took from you in many and with the most soothing sweetness bind up
the wounds that I inflicted.]

While we do not want to put too much weight on this speculation, we
would like to suggest that one clue to this Gualtieri may be read in his
obverse, the Gualtieri d'Anversa of II.viii, the only other character in the
cento novelle to bear this name. He, in this like Gualtieri di Brienne, is
called to govern in place of another (II.viii.4) and tries to do so justly, until
the wife-of-Potiphar-like (and similarly unnamed) queen of France
attempts his virtue. This Gualtieri refuses to betray his absent lord and
flees the false accusations of the queen with every care for his two children,
his son Luigi and daughter Violante (who bears the name of Boccaccio's
favorite illegitimate child, born in 1349). The rest of the long tale records
his successful effort to succor these children. This wifeless courtier could
be seen as exemplary in his paternal affections. Dioneo's Gualtieri, in his
self-exoneration to his wife, uses the verb for parturition to indicate not the
children whom he feigned to have put to death, who are not even mentioned as part of the result of this most strange marriage, but the peace
that he has gained from his wife's subservience. II.viii, one might argue,
offers a far better *exemplum* of *liberalità* in a Gualtieri than does X.x.

That Petrarch chose to read X.x as an allegory starring Griselda as Job
and Gualtieri as God is an apparently reasonable response to Gualtieri's
view of the narrative that contains him. The reading of the Book of Job
sponsored by Gregory the Great in his *Moralia* is precisely the way to avoid
what elsewise becomes a crushing dilemma, with Gualtieri as *exemplum* of

matta bestialità and Griselda that of *folle pazienza*. Giorgio Barberi Squarotti is exactly right, in our opinion, in suggesting that a reading of this *novella* cannot escape from its undertone of religious language and concerns.[89] The question, however, remains. In our minds, do we allow Gualtieri to perform as God, thus soothing our otherwise disturbed sense of the utter inappropriateness of his conduct as husband in a work that continually shows us women who insist on being treated as fully developed human beings and not as chattel? Or do we judge him from Dioneo's more human perspective and find him wanting as a man? Before Panfilo suddenly brings the *Decameron* to a halt, turning the attention of the *brigata* away from past and present things and asking them to "*antiveder* le future" [foresee future ones] (X.Conc.2; his word picks up Gualtieri's "*antiveduto* fine";[90] these are the only two uses of the italicized word in the *Decameron,* thus intrinsically associating Gualtieri's cruel plan and Panfilo's desire to return to the world-in-plague of Florence),[91] they, like us, are caught between praise and blame as they consider the meaning of Dioneo's tale (X.Conc.1). Like the plague that initiated their departure from the city, which is described as being either the result of the turnings of the celestial spheres (and thus "natural"?) or of a just punishment sent from God (and thus supernatural?),[92] Gualtieri's actions may be considered as part of an

---

89. See "L'ambigua sociologia di Griselda," 203–4, pointing out that Petrarch's religious allegory is not altogether wrong; Barberi Squarotti speaks on 206 of the "fondo religioso delle prove di Griselda" [the religious underpinning of Griselda's ordeals], and on 207 he says that "Gualtieri ha in sé, come propria struttura, il fatto di essere controfigura di Dio" [Gualtieri has it in himself, as part of the way in which he is structured, the fact that he is a negative figure of God].

90. While her interpretation of this connection is different from ours, it is observed by Itala Rutter, "The Function of Dioneo's Perspective," 39.

91. For an examination of the question of the return to the city that is heedful of its complexity see Fido, "Il sorriso di messer Torello," 11–14. But see also the view that Panfilo's desire to return is at odds with the *brigata*'s original purpose (for example, Pampinea's notion that they should see what termination heaven reserves for the plague [I.Int.71]) as advanced by Cesare De Michelis, *Contraddizioni,* 14 (cited earlier at our n. 84). De Michelis elsewhere (32–33) takes issue with Fido's rather optimistic resolution of the contradictions of the work. See also Lucia Marino, *The Decameron "Cornice,"* 73–77.

92. ". . . nella egregia città di Fiorenza, oltre a ogn'altra italica bellissima, pervenne la mortifera pestilenza: la quale, per operazione de' corpi superiori *o* per le nostre inique opere da giusta ira di Dio a nostra correzione mandata sopra i mortali . . ." [in the famous city of Florence, more beautiful than any other on the Italian peninsula, arrived the death-bearing pestilence, which, whether because of the workings of the celestial bodies *or* because of our evil deeds, sent down upon mortal beings by the just wrath of God for our correction . . .] (I.Int.8 [our emphasis]). Had Boccaccio said *e* and not *o,* the ambiguity of the statement would not have been nearly so noticeable but would still have been present.

allegory of Christian redemption or as an *all-zu-menschlich* display of contemptible behavior, as its very teller considers it. While we accept Barberi Squarotti's precisions, we find that the discomfort that results from the two discordant formulations tends to tilt the balance toward Dioneo's view. For, if God's treatment of his creatures needs to be so singularly harsh, these same creatures (as we have seen them in ten days' worth of tales) will seek a less lofty understanding of the matters that motivate their behaviors, sexual pleasure, financial success, avoidance of blame and pain. Boccaccio knows that there is another way of judging the actions that he narrates; Dante had shown him that. And it is this that he insists on, somewhat defensively, proclaiming his lowness (as opposed to Dante's *altezza*) in the first and last *apologiae* that he gives us (IV.Int.; X.Conc.): ". . . le presenti novellette . . . , non solamente in fiorentin volgare e in prosa scritte per me . . . , ma ancora in istilo umilissimo e rimesso quanto il più si possono" [. . . the present little stories . . . , written by me not only in the Florentine vernacular and in prose . . . but also in the humblest and lowest possible style] (IV.Int.3). Such details in Boccaccio's self-presentation tend to make Dioneo's view the better one, we believe.[93]

Boccaccio the Satirist?

Since Boccaccio does not often speak of satire, some of his words on this subject may be of interest. In his eleven-page defense of poetry occasioned by the words "poeta fui" [I was a poet] (*Inferno* 1.73), he, in his *Esposizioni,* defends Plato from himself (for having wanted to banish poets from the republic) at his highest rhetorical pitch, familiar from any passage in which Boccaccio takes it upon himself to champion poetry: "Chi fia di sì folle sentimento che creda che Platone volesse che Omero fosse cacciato della città. . . . Chi crederrà *[sic]* ch'egli avesse cacciato Virgilio, chi Orazio o Giovenale, acerrimi riprenditori de' vizi?" [Who would be of so foolish an

---

93. For a very different view see Carlo Muscetta, *Giovanni Boccaccio,* 299, referring to X.Conc.5: "L'amarezza persistente di Dioneo, ritornato coerente al personaggio dopo la sua funzione di novellatore, la sua sferzata finale contro Gualtieri e i commenti della brigata non turberanno il sereno tramonto dell'ultima giornata, che con questo trionfo delle più pure idealità può ben concludersi nelle parole di Panfilo sulla temperie morale di quel soggiorno in villa" [The persistent bitterness of Dioneo, who has now returned to being his true character after functioning as storyteller, his final lashing out at Gualtieri, and the comments of the *brigata,* none of these disturbs the serene twilight of the last Day, which, with this triumph of the purest ideals, does well to conclude with the words of Panfilo on the fair moral climate of their sojourn at the villa].

opinion as to believe that Plato wanted Homer driven out of the city. . . .
Who would believe that he would have done the same to Virgil? Who
Horace or Juvenal, those implacable reprovers of vice?]. This first mention
of Horace in the *Esposizioni* associates him with Juvenal in ways that
clearly indicate that Boccaccio, unsurprisingly, considered him a satirist.
We later (gloss to *Inferno* 4.90) hear of "il satiro d'Orazio o di Persio o di
Giovenale" in the passage in which Boccaccio delimits the major genres,
"lo stilo eroico" (Homer and Virgil), "il tragedo" ("Seneca poeta"), "il
comico" (Plautus and Terence), and "il satiro" (Horace and Juvenal). In his
gloss to the previous verse (4.89: "Orazio satiro") Boccaccio had distinguished the various styles employed by Horace: "versi lirici" in his *Odes* (in
common, this style, with the Psalms); the *Ars poetica,* a treatise; and, in his
other works (the *Epistles* and the *Sermones* are specifically mentioned), "fu
accerrimo *[sic]* riprenditore de' vizi [repeating the formulation found in
the gloss to 1.73], per la qual cosa meritò di essere chiamato poeta satiro"
[he was implacable in his reproof of vice, for which he deserved to be
referred to as a satiric poet]. There is one other explicit linkage of Horace
to satire (ad 4.91–93): "Orazio scrisse ode e satire" [Horace wrote odes and
satires]. Perusal of Boccaccio's remarks in the *Esposizioni* reassures one
who would assert that he thought of Horatian and Juvenalian satire as
having as its subject the revelation of human failings. *Vizio,* a word found
in more than seventy passages in the *Esposizioni,* is not only the subject of
the *Inferno* but, in a less somber vein, that of the Roman satirists. It is also
tempting to think that Boccaccio held a similar view of Ovid's satirically
edged depictions of Roman "lovers" in his amatory works. And there is the
question of Roman comedy as its interests intersect with those of the
satirists. These are not questions that we here address in this brief attempt
to open a discussion of the nature of the *Decameron*'s genre.

However, it seems clear that Boccaccio is aware of the tradition that
held satire to have two natures, one "biting" (in the tradition of Juvenal),
the other "nibbling" (in the tradition of Horace).[94] With regard to Horace
and Juvenal, Elliott describes their respective satirical styles as follows.

Horatian satire seeks to displace the social mask by the flick of laughter; Juvenalian satire would cleanse a rotten society in the fire of its hate.
Juvenal's allegiance thus is to a more "primitive" satiric mode than that

---

94. For a modern discussion of the two kinds of satire that preserves this familiar distinction see Robert C. Elliott, *Power of Satire,* 100–129. For another recent restatement of this
commonplace see Anderson, *Essays on Roman Satire,* 3, referring to "Horatian wit" as
opposed to "Juvenalian indignation" as the poles of satirical tone and intent.

of Horace—to a mode the spirit and tone of which go back, in some respects, to the bitter wrath of Archilochus. (*Power of Satire*, 115)

Boccaccio's *brigata* seems to be rehearsing precisely this distinction when, in VI.iii, Lauretta distinguishes between two kinds of *motti*.[95] The subject is the result of the Day's rubric, proposed by Elissa (V.Conc.3) in terms that allow for a well-turned and biting *motto* to be used as a counterattack against one's own biters: "Noi abbiamo già molte volte udito [particularly in Day One] che con be' motti o con risposte pronte o con avvedimenti presti molti hanno già saputo con debito *morso* rintuzzare *gli altrui denti* o i sopravegnenti pericoli cacciar via" [We have heard many times that with clever sayings or ready answers or sudden shrewdness many have known how with a well-deserved *bite* to repel *the teeth of another* or to fend off danger before it overtakes them] (our italics). Lauretta's ensuing tale (VI.iii) of Nonna de' Pulci (her name coincidentally associates her with another kind of biter, fleas, and, even if Boccaccio did not know it, thus with the very carriers of the plague that killed her) is put forward as an example of a justifiably "biting" *motteggiare*. She reminds her companions that there are two kinds of *motti*.

> ... vi voglio ricordare essere la natura de' motti cotale, che essi, come *la pecora morde,* deono così *mordere* l'uditore e non come *'l cane:* per ciò che, se come *il cane mordesse* il motto, non sarebbe motto ma villania. La qual cosa ottimamente fecero e le parole di madonna Oretta e la risposta di Cisti [VI.i and VI.ii]. È il vero che, se per risposta si dice e il risponditore *morda come cane,* essendo come *da cane prima stato morso,* non par da riprender come, se ciò avvenuto non fosse, sarebbe: e per ciò è da guardare e come e quando e con cui e similmente dove si motteggia. Alle quali cose poco guardando già un nostro prelato, non minor *morso* ricevette che 'l desse: il che io in una piccola novella vi voglio mostrare. (VI.iii.3–4 [our italics])

[I would like to remind you that the nature of *motti* is such that they should bite the one who hears them as does the sheep and not the dog;

---

95. For Boccaccio's awareness of the tradition of "biting satire" in Ovid's *Ibis*, a work modelled on that of Callimachus, see Hollander, *Boccaccio's Two Venuses*, 139–40, where the "bird-song" that is the *Corbaccio* is related to Ovid's *Ibis*. For further details see Hollander, *Boccaccio's Last Fiction*, 34–35, 55 n. 77. [And now see Hollander, "Boccaccio, Ovid's *Ibis,* and the Satirical Tradition," forthcoming in the *Atti* of the Seminario internazionale, Gli Zibaldoni di Boccaccio: Memoria, scrittura, riscrittura (Firenze-Certaldo, 26–28 aprile 1996), ed. Michelangelo Picone (Florence: Cesati, 1997).]

for if a *motto* were to bite as does a dog, it would be not a *motto* but an insult. Madonna Oretta's words in reply and those of Cisti were excellent examples of how to do this well. It is nonetheless true that if a person has been first, as it were, bitten by a dog and responds in the same way, then it seems not fair to criticize that person as though there had not been provocation; as a result, one must pay attention as to how and when and with whom and even where one bandies words. Little sensitive to such niceties, one of our clergymen got back no less a bite than he gave—and in a little story, I would like to tell you about that.]

That Nonna's biting wit is permissible because it is a rejoinder to the insulting proposition made to her by the bishop of Florence serves to remind Lauretta's auditors—all of us—that the usual mode of *motti* is less savage.[96] (One might be tempted to claim that where the *Corbaccio* is meant to be perceived as an exercise in Juvenalian "biting satire," the *Decameron* is usually to be taken as exemplifying the milder and Horatian kind.)

It is also of interest that this introduction of the two subgenres of satire is accompanied by the first reference to the plague of 1348 since the Introduction, where Pampinea, in keeping with Dioneo's desire that they escape from the confines not only of the plague but of the thought if it, urged upon the *brigata* that "niuna novella altra che lieta ci rechi da fuori" [no news but good news be allowed to reach us from the outside world] (I.Int.101).[97] As Barolini points out ("Wheel of the *Decameron,*" 529), Dioneo's own reference to the plague, "la perversità di questa stagione" [the present unpleasantness] in the disordered city (VI.Conc.9), shows that the breaking of this "rule" in Day Six is not casual but marks the increasing pressure of a return to reality, to the world of death, in the second half of the *Decameron.* That the text, as it moves back toward reality, should associate itself with satire should not, perhaps, surprise us.[98]

---

96. The passage cited immediately above would itself suggest what turns out simply to be true, namely, that the verb *mordere* occurs more often in VI.iii than in any other tale of the *Decameron.* Its mere two pages contain eight uses of the verb (of the twenty-five in the work).

97. Barolini notes ("Wheel of the *Decameron,*" 529) that it is Lauretta, whom she sees as being more associated with an appreciation of the reality of things than most of her companions (536 and n.), who breaks the rule established by Dioneo (I.Int.93) that the cares of the *città tribolata* be left behind. We would like further to speculate that it is Lauretta who is given this role because her model, Petrarch's Laura, herself, at least according to Petrarch (and thus for his friend Boccaccio), died in the plague.

98. For a discussion of the medieval understanding of satire as closely connected to both praise and blame (and not blame alone), see Paul Miller, "John Gower, Satiric Poet," a study

It is our view that, leaving the matrix tragedy/comedy to one side, Boccaccio has rather joined his work to the tradition of Roman satire and
Roman comedy, works dedicated to the seeing of what is (rather than what
might or should be), that he sees himself and Dioneo, his fictive counterpart, in the tradition of Ovid, Terence, and Horace.[99] And what the members of the *brigata* emphasize from the start, amidst the fear of death and
the temptation to lawlessness, is order, form, compromise, and rational
behavior, even if the stories that they tell often depict chaos and irrationality, mirroring their own fears and their own temptations. Although a
reader's search for "level ground" among the ups and downs of the
Decameron may be doomed to failure, it is useful to remember that behind
the apparent chaos, all-too-believable irrationality, and self-serving behaviors lies both humor and, perhaps more important, the quality of compassionate self-recognition that the text emphasizes from its inception:
"Umana cosa è. . . ."[100]

---

that is relevant to Boccaccio as well. Miller offers a summary of a definition that, he claims,
would be accepted by the vast majority of medieval scholiasts: "Satire is that type of ethical
verse, ranging in tone between bitter indignation, mocking irony, and witty humour, which
in forthright, unadorned terms censures and corrects vices in society and advocates virtues,
eschewing slander of individuals but sparing no guilty party, not even the poet himself" (82).
Allow prose to this definition and it is not far from an adequate topographical description of
the *Decameron*. [Now see the two recent contributions by Suzanne Reynolds concerning
satire, with particular relevance to Dante, but of more general interest as well: "*Orazio satiro*
(*Inferno* IV,89): Dante, the Roman Satirists, and the Medieval Theory of Satire" and "Dante
and the Medieval Theory of Satire: A Collection of Texts," in the supplement to *Italianist* 15
(1995): 128–44, 145–57. The recent *Lessico critico decameroniano* not only has no main entry
for *satire* but is without an entry for the term in its *Indice analitico,* though in at least two passages the word does appear in its pages (171, 244–48), in the entries "Ironia/parodia," by
Carlo Delcorno, and "Memoria," by Giuseppe Velli. Hollander, *Boccaccio's Two Venuses,*
frequently alludes to Boccaccio's ironic strategies in the *opere minori in volgare* (there are
some twenty entries in its Index).]

99. For the suggestion that, given Boccaccio's other and perhaps more evident citations
of Horace's versified treatise on poetry, the opening word of the *Decameron, umana,* reflects
the first word of Horace's *Ars poetica, humano,* see Hollander, "*Utilità,*" in the present book,
n. 2. Michelangelo Picone, "Gioco," is also mindful of a potentially Horatian dimension to
the *Decameron,* noting that Horace's *Ars poetica* set into relief the problem of seriousness and
game for such work as Boccaccio's (105–6). [Giuseppe Velli has now argued (in Bragantini
and Forni, *Lessico critico decameroniano,* 229) that Boccaccio's *exordium* closely reflects
phrasing found in the *Historia destructionis Troiae* of Guido delle Colonne: "cum afflictis
compati humanitas suggerat" [since our humanity suggests we should have compassion on
those who are afflicted]. To agree with him does not require desertion of the argument for a
Horatian beginning, even if Velli, when he thinks of satire in relation to Boccaccio (see our n.
98), thinks only of Juvenal.]

100. Only after we had received the galleys of this article did we find and read three
articles that we should have considered in our discussion: Shirley S. Allen, "The Griselda Tale

Works Consulted

Almansi, Guido. *The Writer as Liar.* London: Routledge & Kegan Paul, 1975.

Anderson, William S. *Essays on Romen Satire.* Princeton: Princeton University Press, 1982.

Auzzas, Ginetta. "'Quid amicitia dulcius?'" In *Boccaccio e dintorni, Miscellanea di studi in onore di Vittore Branca,* 2:181–205. Florence: Olschki, 1983.

Baratto, Mario. *Realtà e stile nel "Decameron."* Rome: Riuniti, 1984 [1970].

Barberi Squarotti, Giorgio. "Gli ammaestramenti di Dioneo." In *Il potere della parola,* 174–92. Naples: Federico & Ardia, 1983 [1977].

———. "L'ambigua sociologia di Griselda." In *Il potere della parola,* 193–230. Naples: Federico & Ardia, 1983 [1977].

Barolini, Teodolinda. "The Wheel of the *Decameron.*" *Romance Philology* 36 (1983): 521–40.

Battaglia, Salvatore. "La novella di Tito e Gisippo." In *La coscienza letteraria del medioevo,* 509–25. Naples: Liguori, 1965.

Becker, Marvin B. *Florence in Transition.* 2 vols. Baltimore: Johns Hopkins Press, 1967.

---

and the Portrayal of Women in the *Decameron,*" *Philological Quarterly* 56 (1977): 1–13; Georges Barthouil, "Boccacce et Catherine de Sienne (la dixième journée du *Decameron:* noblesse ou subversion?)," *Italianistica* 11 (1982): 249–76; Giulio Savelli, "Struttura e valori nella novella di Griselda," *Studi sul Boccaccio* 14 (1983–84): 278–301. The review of changing critical attitudes toward Griselda offered by Savelli, even though we do not finally share his views (we are more in accord with the ironic reading of X.x proposed by Allen), is a helpful contribution. However, of these three studies, the one that is most significantly absent from our discussion, given our reading of the Tenth Day, is the venturesome article by Barthouil; he, as do we, proposes a "lecture subversive" (258) for these final ten tales. While with regard to particulars there are more disagreements than agreements between us, some of our agreements are striking, especially in our readings of X.iii (see his 251 and 260). We apologize to these three students of Boccaccio for this belated recognition of their work and to those others of whom we may have lost track in the *selva* of Boccaccian bibliography. We also want to mention the discussion by Reginald Hyatte of X.viii that is found in his book, published too late for us to have taken it into account, *The Arts of Friendship: The Idealization of Friendship in Medieval and Early Renaissance Literature* (Leiden, New York, and Cologne: E. J. Brill, 1994), 146–63. [Further spirit of recrimination now registers an earlier printing of Hyatte's essay, "Reconfiguring Ancient *amicitia perfecta* in the *Decameron* 10,8," *Italian Quarterly* 32 (1991): 27–37. Hyatte refers to still another relevant study, Barbara Blackbourn, "The Eighth Story of the Tenth Day of Boccaccio's *Decameron:* An Example of Rhetoric or a Rhetorical Example?" *Italian Quarterly* 27 (1986). And for X.x see Nella Giannetto, "Parody in the *Decameron:* A 'Contented Captive' (II.x) and Dioneo," *Italianist* 1 (1981): 17–18, calling attention to Dioneo's counterexemplary intent.]

Bergin, Thomas G. *Boccaccio.* New York: Viking, 1981.

Bonadeo, Alfred. "Marriage and Adultery in the *Decameron.*" *Philological Quarterly* 60 (1981): 287–303.

Bragantini, Renzo, and Pier Massimo Forni, eds. *Lessico critico decameroniano.* Turin: Bollati Boringhieri, 1995.

Branca, Vittore. *Boccaccio medievale e nuovi studi sul "Decamerone."* 6th ed. Florence: Sansoni, 1986 [1956].

Bruni, Francesco. *Boccaccio: L'invenzione della letteratura mezzana.* Bologna: Il Mulino, 1990.

Cavallini, Giorgio. *La decima giornata del "Decameron."* Rome: Bulzoni, 1980.

Chandler, S. Bernard. "Man, Emotion, and Intellect in the *Decameron.*" *Philological Quarterly* 39 (1960): 400–412.

Cottino-Jones, Marga. "*Fabula* vs. *Figura:* Another Interpretation of the Griselda Story." *Italica* 50 (1973): 38–52.

———. *Order from Chaos: Social and Aesthetic Harmonies in Boccaccio's "Decameron."* Washington, D.C.: University Press of America, 1982.

De Michelis, Cesare. *Contraddizioni nel "Decameron."* Milan: Guanda, 1983.

Duranti, Alessandro. "Le novelle di Dioneo." In *Studi di filologia e critica offerti dagli allievi a Lanfranco Caretti,* 1:1–38. Rome: Salerno, 1985.

Elliott, Robert C. *The Power of Satire.* Princeton: Princeton University Press, 1960.

Ferrante, Joan. "The Frame Characters of the *Decameron:* A Progression of Virtues." *Romance Philology* 19 (1965): 212–26.

———. "Narrative Patterns in the *Decameron.*" *Romance Philology* 31 (1978): 585–604.

Fido, Franco. "Il sorriso di messer Torello." In *Il regime delle simmetrie imperfette,* 11–35. Milan: Franco Angeli, 1988 [1977].

Getto, Giovanni. *Vita di forme e forme di vita nel "Decameron."* 4th ed. Turin: Petrini, 1986 [1958].

Greene, Thomas M. "Forms of Accommodation in the *Decameron.*" *Italica* 45 (1968): 297–313.

Grimaldi, Emma. *Il privilegio di Dioneo.* Salerno: Edizioni Scientifiche Italiane, 1987. (See esp. 349–407.)

Haines, Charles. "Patient Griselda and *matta bestialità.*" *Quaderni d'italianistica* 6, no. 2 (1985): 233–40.

Hollander, Robert. *Boccaccio's Two Venuses.* New York: Columbia University Press, 1977.

————. *Boccaccio's Last Fiction: "Il Corbaccio".* Philadelphia: University of Pennsylvania Press, 1988.

Kermode, Frank. *The Sense of an Ending.* New York: Oxford University Press, 1967.

Kirkham, Victoria. "An Allegorically Tempered *Decameron.*" In *The Sign of Reason in Boccaccio's Fiction,* 131–71. Florence: Olschki, 1993 [1985].

————. "The Last Tale in the *Decameron.*" In *The Sign of Reason in Boccaccio's Fiction,* 249–65. Florence: Olschki, 1993 [1989].

————. "The Classical Bond of Friendship in Boccaccio's Tito and Gisippo (*Decameron* X 8)." In *The Sign of Reason in Boccaccio's Fiction,* 237–48. Florence: Olschki, 1993 [1990].

Kirkpatrick, Robin. "The Griselda Story in Boccaccio, Petrarch, and Chaucer." In *Chaucer and the Italian Trecento,* ed. Piero Boitani, 231–48. Cambridge: Cambridge University Press, 1983.

Marcus, Millicent Joy. *An Allegory of Form: Literary Self-Consciousness in the "Decameron."* Saratoga, Calif.: Anma Libri, 1979.

Marino, Lucia. *The Decameron "Cornice": Allusion, Allegory, and Iconology.* Ravenna: Longo, 1979.

Mazzotta, Giuseppe. *The World at Play in Boccaccio's "Decameron."* Princeton: Princeton University Press, 1986.

Miller, Paul. "John Gower, Satiric Poet." In *Gower's "Confessio Amantis": Responses and Reassessments,* ed. A. J. Minnis, 79–105. Cambridge: D. S. Brewer, 1983.

Momigliano, Attilio. *Il "Decameron": 49 novelle commentate da Attilio Momigliano.* Milan: F. Vallardi, 1936 [1924].

Morabito, Raffaele, ed. *Griselda.* Vols. 1, *La circolazione dei temi e degli intrecci narrativi: Il caso Griselda,* and 2, *La storia di Griselda in Europa.* L'Aquila: Japadre, 1988–90.

————. "La diffusione della storia di Griselda dal XIV al XX secolo." *Studi sul Boccaccio* 17 (1989): 237–85.

————. *Cantari di Griselda.* L'Aquila: Japadre, 1990.

————. *Una sacra rappresentazione profana: Fortuna di Griselda nel Quattrocento italiano.* Tübingen: Max Niemeyer, 1993.

Muscetta, Carlo. *Giovanni Boccaccio.* Bari: Laterza, 1972. (See esp. 284–99.)

Needler, Howard. "Song of a Ravished Nightingale: Attitudes toward Antiquity in *Decameron* X, 8." *Literary Review* 23 (1980): 502–18.

Olsen, Michel. "Griselda, *fabula* e ricezione." In *Griselda,* vol. 2, *La storia di Griselda in Europa,* ed. Raffaele Morabito, 253–64. L'Aquila: Japadre, 1990.

Paden, Michael. "Elissa: La ghibellina del *Decameron.*" *Studi sul Boccaccio* 21 (1993): 139–50.

Padoan, Giorgio. "Mondo aristocratico e mondo comunale nell'ideologia e nell'arte di Giovanni Boccaccio." *Studi sul Boccaccio* 2 (1964): 81–216.

Pernicone, Vincenzo. "La novella del Marchese di Saluzzo." In *Studi danteschi e altri saggi,* ed. Matilde Dillon Wanke, 211–25. Genoa: Università degli Studi di Genova, Istituto di Letteratura Italiana, 1984 [1930].

Picone, Michelangelo. "Gioco e/o letteratura: Per una lettura ludica del *Decameron.*" In *Passare il tempo: La letteratura del gioco e dell'intrattenimento dal XII al XVI secolo (Atti del Convegno di Pienza, 10–14 settembre 1991),* 105–27. Rome: Salerno, 1993.

Potter, Joy H. *Five Frames for the "Decameron": Communication and Social Systems in the "Cornice."* Princeton: Princeton University Press, 1982.

Richardson, Brian. "The 'Ghibelline' Narrator in the *Decameron.*" *Italian Studies* 33 (1978): 20–28.

Rossi, Luca Carlo, ed. *Giovanni Boccaccio, Francesco Petrarca, Griselda.* Palermo: Sellerio, 1991.

Rossi, Luciano. "Das *Dekameron* und die romanische Tradition: Die ausserordentliche Geduld der Griselda." *Vox Romanica* 44 (1985): 16–32.

———. "Ironia e parodia nel *Decameron:* Da Ciappelletto a Griselda." In *La novella italiana: Atti del Convegno di Caprarola,* 365–405. Rome: Salerno, 1989.

Rutter, Itala Tania. "The Function of Dioneo's Perspective in the Griselda Story." *Comitatus* 5 (1974): 33–42.

Sarolli, Gian Roberto. *Prolegomena alla "Divina Commedia."* Florence: Olschki, 1971.

Seung, T. K. "The Sovereign Individual in the *Decameron.*" In *Cultural Thematics.* New Haven and London: Yale University Press, 1976. (See esp. 207–16.)

Smarr, Janet Levarie. *Boccaccio and Fiammetta: The Narrator as Lover.* Urbana and Chicago: University of Illinois Press, 1986.

Sorieri, Louis. *Boccaccio's Story of "Tito e Gisippo" in European Literature.* New York: Institute of French Studies, 1937.

Surdich, Luigi. *La cornice di amore.* Pisa: ETS, 1987.

Tateo, Francesco. "La novella di Gualtieri?" In *Griselda,* vol. 1, *La circolazione dei temi e degli intrecci narrativi: Il caso Griselda,* ed. Raffaele Morabito, 35–38. L'Aquila: Japadre, 1988.

Wallace, David. "'Whan She Translated Was': A Chaucerian Critique of the Petrarchan Academy." In *Literary Practice and Social Change in Britain, 1380–1530,* ed. Lee Patterson, 156–215. Berkeley: University of California Press, 1990.

———. *Giovanni Boccaccio: "Decameron."* Cambridge: Cambridge University Press, 1991.

White, Laura Sanguineti. *La scena conviviale e la sua funzione nel mondo del Boccaccio.* Florence: Olschki, 1983.

Wilkins, E. H. "Pampinea and Abrotonia." *Modern Language Notes* 23 (1908): 111–16, 137–42.

Appendix: *Hapax Legomenon* in Boccaccio's *Decameron* and Its Relation to Dante's *Commedia*

(1983 [unpublished])

The entries in this index are derived from the *Concordanze del "Decameron,"* ed. Alfredo Barbina, under the direction of Umberto Bosco, 2 vols. (Florence: C/E Giunti and G. Barbèra, 1969). These, based on the second Le Monnier edition (1960) of Vittore Branca, are necessarily at odds, on occasion (some fifty times, in fact), with the later text of the *Decameron* brought forth by Branca in the series under his general editorship: *Tutte le opere di Giovanni Boccaccio* (Milan: A. Mondadori, 1965–), vol. 4 (1976). I have been able to adjust my results by checking them against this later text. Nonetheless, it seems hardly a requirement to say that any compilation of this kind will perforce contain errors and inaccuracies. In addition to those attributable to the compiler's trembling hand, there are those that reside in the data themselves—given their profusion, the editorial developments since the *Concordanze* were published (and those to come), and the normal vagaries of fourteenth-century orthography. Yet, granted the philologist's understandable curiosity about words that, like shooting stars and not like comets, appear once only in a universe of some 275,000 written words, it seemed well worth the trouble to assemble this sequential index of them. Further, and in light of the still developing interest in Boccaccio's awareness and use of the text of Dante's *Commedia,* it also seemed reasonable to provide some systematic indication of the relation of single occurrences of words in the *Decameron* to the semantic field of the *Commedia.* Of the 1,822 occurrences of *hapax* in the *Decameron* listed here (not including several dialectical forms, words for numbers and place names [and their related adjectives], and most proper nouns), 496 are words also found in the *Commedia*. Further, there are some 227 instances of a *hapax* in the *Decameron* that is also a *hapax* in the *Commedia,* in which work there occur some 2,200 instances of *hapax* [see Robert Hollander, "An Index of *Hapax Legomena* in Dante's *Commedia,*" *Dante Studies* 106 (1988): 81–110]. While I can offer no tables of comparison on which to base this judgment, it does seem that these statistics support the notion that the text of the *Decameron* is simply suffused by the linguistic richness of the *Commedia*. Thus, that *hapax* is a common condition of so many Boccaccian and Dantean words is probably not the result of chance. Nor is it necessarily always the result of conscious appropriation. It seems most reasonable to believe that Dante's greatest fourteenth-century champion, the eventual first compensated Dante professor, was already deeply immersed in his single most fecund source.

The following presentation of *hapax* in the *Decameron* should be clear enough. I think I need explain only that words followed by the indication "[2]" are what I have called a "pseudo-*hapax*," as defined on p. 62; that boldface indicates a "double *hapax*" (a word that occurs only once in the *Decameron* and once in the *Commedia*); that the *siglum* "#" denotes the number of occurrences of a Boccaccian *hapax* in Dante when these are six or more. The user is asked to be aware that the computer program utilized did not permit the listing of more than five occurrences in Dante of a Boccaccian *hapax;* consultation of a concordance to the *Commedia* will satiate lingering hungers in this regard. The National Endowment for the Humanities supported the year of leave in which this project, along with several others, was completed. I am grateful to my fellow citizens for their largesse. I am also indebted to my research assistant at Princeton University, Timothy Hampton [now on the faculty at Berkeley], for his labors on behalf of this enterprise. The help of my son, Buzz Hollander, who [at the age of thirteen, mature for a programmer—indeed, as it turned out, he was already past his peak] developed the computer program that sorted this material, is acknowledged with gratitude and paternal affection.

Hanover, N.H.
23 August 1983

[It is my hope that others will find this assemblage of words to be of use in many ways, including ones that I cannot possibly foresee. Looking over the results after having revised them for I trust the last time (that task now

belongs to others), I do note some fairly striking things about the phenomenon of shared *hapax*. First, there is a fairly high incidence of this
when Boccaccio speaks in his own voice: in the *Proemio,* there are five
occurrences; in the *Introduzione,* eight; in IV.Int., three; in the *Conclusione,*
eight. Thus more than 10 percent of the instances of this phenomenon
occurs in something less than 5 percent of the text. And if we consider
Dioneo's tales, we find that it rarely occurs in them, in fact a total of six
times in eight of his tales. But in two of these, III.x and VI.x, it is very frequent: his tale of Cipolla, that Dante-imitating rogue, contains the densest
occurrence in the entire work (eleven times in fifty-six periods), while his
scabrous tale of Rustico and Alibech is equaled only by one other tale
(IX.9), each showing five in thirty-five periods. I am not sure exactly what
one learns from this, but I am intrigued by the possibilities and hope that
others will find a way to make use of these and other data.]

	DECAMERON			COMMEDIA
COGNOMINARE [2]	o	o	1	NOT PRESENT
PRENCIPE [2]	o	o	1	1.27.85; 3.6.45; 3.8.34; 3.11.35; 3.25.23
GALEOTTO [2]	**o**	**o**	**1**	**1.5.137**
RIFRIGERIO	**o**	**o**	**4**	**3.14.27**
INCOMMUTABILE	o	o	5	NOT PRESENT
CUPO	o	o	5	1.7.10; 1.18.109; 2.14.52; 2.20.12; 3.3.123
PELAGO	o	o	5	1.1.23; 2.14.52; 3.2.5; 3.19.82
FATICOSO	**o**	**o**	**5**	**1.23.67**
ABISOGNARE	o	o	7	NOT PRESENT
CIRCUITO	**o**	**o**	**10**	**2.28.103**
ALLEGGIARE	**o**	**o**	**12**	**1.22.22**
AGO	o	o	13	1.20.121; 2.32.133; 3.12.29
ARCOLAIO	o	o	13	NOT PRESENT
PARABOLA	o	o	13	NOT PRESENT
PISTELENZIOSO	o	o	13	NOT PRESENT
PASSAMENTO	o	o	14	NOT PRESENT
AUTORE	1	o	1	1.1.85; 3.26.40

IUDICIO	I	O	2	NOT PRESENT
RICORDAZIONE	I	O	2	NOT PRESENT
DANNOSO	I	O	2	1.6.53; 1.11.36
LAGRIMEVOLE	I	O	2	NOT PRESENT
ORRIDO	I	O	4	NOT PRESENT
ERTO	I	O	4	1.19.131; 1.24.63
INIZIO	I	O	6	2.7.39; 2.26.10
INCARNAZIONE	I	O	8	NOT PRESENT
FIORENZA	I	O	8	#FIFTEEN
CORREZIONE	I	O	8	NOT PRESENT
ORIENTALE	I	O	8	2.1.13; 2.30.23; 3.31.119
INUMERABILE	**I**	**O**	**8**	**3.18.101**
MISERABILMENTE	I	O	8	NOT PRESENT
EGREGIO	I	O	8	3.6.43; 3.19.137
IMMONDIZIA	I	O	9	NOT PRESENT
OFICIALE	**I**	**O**	**9**	**2.2.30**
SUPPLICAZIONE	I	O	9	NOT PRESENT
PROCESSIONE	I	O	9	NOT PRESENT
ORRIBILMENTE	**I**	**O**	**9**	**1.5.4**
INEVITABILE	I	O	10	NOT PRESENT
ANGUINAIA	**I**	**O**	**10**	**1.30.50**
ENFIATURA	I	O	10	NOT PRESENT
COMUNALE	I	O	10	NOT PRESENT
LIVIDO	I	O	11	1.3.98; 1.19.14; 1.25.84; 1.32.34; 2.13.9
MALORE	I	O	13	NOT PRESENT
MEDICANTE	I	O	13	NOT PRESENT
APPARIZIONE	I	O	13	NOT PRESENT
TOCCATORE	I	O	15	NOT PRESENT
FEDEDEGNO	I	O	16	NOT PRESENT
VISIBILMENTE	I	O	17	NOT PRESENT
GUANCIA	I	O	18	#TWELVE
AVVOLGIMENTO	I	O	18	NOT PRESENT
MODERATAMENTE	I	O	20	NOT PRESENT
SUPERFLUITÀ	I	O	20	NOT PRESENT
TEMPERATISSIMAMENTE	I	O	20	NOT PRESENT
DISSOLUZIONE	I	O	24	NOT PRESENT
SOFFICIENZA	I	O	24	NOT PRESENT
OPPRIMERE	**I**	**O**	**25**	**3.22.1**

VARIAMENTE	I	0	26	NOT PRESENT
OPPINANTE	I	0	26	NOT PRESENT
NIPOTE	I	0	27	NOT PRESENT
CREDIBILE	I	0	27	NOT PRESENT
SUBSIDIO	I	0	28	NOT PRESENT
SCARSITÀ	I	0	29	NOT PRESENT
STUPORE	I	0	30	#SEVEN
FUNERALE	I	0	32	NOT PRESENT
FEROCITÀ	I	0	33	NOT PRESENT
COMPAGNEVOLE	I	0	34	NOT PRESENT
POSTPORRE	I	0	34	3.12.129; 3.14.131; 3.29.89
BECCAMORTO	I	0	35	NOT PRESENT
PREZZOLATO	I	0	35	NOT PRESENT
FRETTOLOSO	I	0	35	NOT PRESENT
DISOCCUPATO	I	0	35	NOT PRESENT
REDENZIONE	I	0	36	3.7.57; 3.20.123
CORRUZIONE	**I**	**0**	**38**	**3.7.126 [2]**
SCORTO	I	0	41	NOT PRESENT
STIVATO	I	0	42	NOT PRESENT
SOMMO [n.]	I	0	42	#TEN
INIMICO	I	0	43	NOT PRESENT
PICCOLEZZA	I	0	43	NOT PRESENT
COLTO	I	0	43	3.5.72; 3.22.45
RAZIONALE	I	0	46	NOT PRESENT
CORREGGIMENTO	I	0	46	NOT PRESENT
SATOLLO	I	0	46	2.24.122; 3.2.12
MARZO	I	0	47	NOT PRESENT
MEMORABILE	I	0	48	NOT PRESENT
IPOCRATE	I	0	48	1.4.143; 2.29.137
ESCULAPIO	I	0	48	NOT PRESENT
ABITATORE	**I**	**0**	**49**	**2.14.41**
MARTEDÌ	I	0	49	NOT PRESENT
LUGUBRE	I	0	49	NOT PRESENT
ISCONCIO	I	0	50	NOT PRESENT
PARLARI	I	0	50	NOT PRESENT
CONFUSIONE	I	0	51	2.31.13; 3.16.67
ALTRETALE	I	0	58	NOT PRESENT
IMPAURIRE	I	0	59	NOT PRESENT

ISCHIFILTÀ	I	0	65	NOT PRESENT
VERDEGGIARE	I	0	66	NOT PRESENT
ONDEGGIARE	**I**	**0**	**66**	**3.4.115**
PROVEDENZA	I	0	74	#EIGHT
FAVOREGGIANTE	I	0	85	NOT PRESENT
CONCORDE	I	0	86	3.13.31; 3.15.9; 3.26.47
CONSANGUINITÀ	I	0	87	NOT PRESENT
FRATELLEVOLE	I	0	87	NOT PRESENT
MERCOLEDÌ	I	0	89	NOT PRESENT
COLMO	I	0	90	1.19.128; 1.21.3; 1.34.114; 3.18.98
CORTILE	I	0	90	NOT PRESENT
CURIOSO	I	0	90	NOT PRESENT
GIUNCO	I	0	91	2.1.95; 2.1.102
GIUNCATO	I	0	91	NOT PRESENT
FESTEVOLMENTE	I	0	94	NOT PRESENT
COMINCIATRICE	I	0	95	NOT PRESENT
APPARENTE	I	0	97	NOT PRESENT
SPENDITORE	I	0	99	NOT PRESENT
TESORIERE	I	0	99	NOT PRESENT
NETTEZZA	I	0	101	NOT PRESENT
SOMMARIAMENTE	I	0	102	NOT PRESENT
DRIZZARE	I	0	102	#FORTY-EIGHT
DILICATAMENTE	I	0	105	NOT PRESENT
LIUTO	I	0	106	NOT PRESENT
VAGHETTO	I	0	107	NOT PRESENT
DORMIRE [n.]	I	0	109	NOT PRESENT
TAVOLIERE	I	0	110	NOT PRESENT
SCACCHIERE	I	0	110	NOT PRESENT
DECLINARE	**I**	**0**	**112**	**3.31.120**
AMMIRABILE	I	I	2	NOT PRESENT
TRANSITORIO	I	I	3	NOT PRESENT
AUDACE	I	I	4	NOT PRESENT
ACUME	I	I	5	3.1.84; 3.28.18; 3.32.75; 3.33.76
MAESTÀ	I	I	5	NOT PRESENT
ISCACCIARE	I	I	5	1.18.81; 1.28.97
PROMOSSO [p.part.]	I	I	7	NOT PRESENT
INTRALCIATO	I	I	7	NOT PRESENT

STRALCIARE	I	I	7	NOT PRESENT
CREDITO	I	I	7	NOT PRESENT
RIOTTOSO	I	I	8	NOT PRESENT
MISLEALE	I	I	8	NOT PRESENT
ASSETTATUZZO	I	I	9	NOT PRESENT
GRANDEMENTE	I	I	10	NOT PRESENT
VOLONTEROSAMENTE	I	I	13	NOT PRESENT
BESTEMMIATORE	I	I	13	NOT PRESENT
IRACUNDO	I	I	13	NOT PRESENT
GIUCATORE	I	I	14	NOT PRESENT
METTITORE	I	I	14	NOT PRESENT
DADO	I	I	14	NOT PRESENT
SCIOPERATO	I	I	18	NOT PRESENT
PROCURA	I	I	19	NOT PRESENT
SANTÀ	I	I	20	NOT PRESENT
DISORDINATAMENTE	I	I	21	NOT PRESENT
ISCRITTURA	I	I	30	3.4.43; 3.19.83; 3.32.68
PUNTALMENTE	I	I	34	NOT PRESENT
VERGINE	I	I	39	#NINE
REGOLA	I	I	40	1.6.9; 3.22.74
INSALATUZZA	I	I	41	NOT PRESENT
NETTAMENTE	I	I	43	NOT PRESENT
RUGGINE	I	I	43	NOT PRESENT
SPERGIURARE	I	I	49	NOT PRESENT
PENSIERUZZO	I	I	51	NOT PRESENT
SCHERANO	I	I	51	NOT PRESENT
APPORTARE	I	I	77	1.10.104; 3.25.129; 3.27.138
TAVOLATO	I	I	78	NOT PRESENT
PERSUADERE	**I**	**I**	**83**	**2.33.47**
CAMISCIO	I	I	84	NOT PRESENT
PIEVALE	I	I	84	NOT PRESENT
FUSCELLO	I	I	85	NOT PRESENT
INFALLIBILE	I	2	3	1.29.56; 3.7.19
TRAFFICO	I	2	4	NOT PRESENT
DRAPPERIA	I	2	4	NOT PRESENT
DIRITTURA	I	2	5	NOT PRESENT
PROSPERARE	I	2	6	NOT PRESENT
GROSSAMENTE	I	2	8	NOT PRESENT

PERTINACE	I	2	10	NOT PRESENT
FINARE	I	2	10	NOT PRESENT
DICHIARIRE	**I**	**2**	**14**	**2.8.51**
DISONESTISSIMAMENTE	I	2	19	NOT PRESENT
SOGDOMITICO	I	2	19	NOT PRESENT
MERETRICE	**I**	**2**	**19**	**1.13.64**
SIMONIA	**I**	**2**	**21**	**1.11.59**
PROCURERIA	I	2	21	NOT PRESENT
SUBSTENTAZIONE	I	2	21	NOT PRESENT
SIGNIFICATO	I	2	21	NOT PRESENT
FUCINA	I	2	24	NOT PRESENT
DIABOLICO	I	2	24	NOT PRESENT
STROPICIO	I	4	8	NOT PRESENT
SALUTIFERO	I	4	9	NOT PRESENT
DIAMANTE	**I**	**4**	**18**	**2.9.105**
GRAVISSIMAMENTE	I	4	20	NOT PRESENT
PRONTISSIMAMENTE	I	4	21	NOT PRESENT
REPRIMERE	I	5	1	NOT PRESENT
GONFALONIERE	I	5	5	NOT PRESENT
COPPIA	I	5	6	NOT PRESENT
COPIOSAMENTE	I	5	14	NOT PRESENT
SALVAGGINA	I	5	14	NOT PRESENT
ERETICO	I	6	4	3.4.69; 3.12.100
PRAVITÀ	I	6	4	NOT PRESENT
IMPETUOSISSIMAMENTE	I	6	6	NOT PRESENT
ALLEVIAMENTO	I	6	6	NOT PRESENT
MISCREDENZA	I	6	6	NOT PRESENT
INQUISITO	I	6	6	NOT PRESENT
EMPIMENTO	I	6	6	NOT PRESENT
TAVERNIERE	I	6	8	NOT PRESENT
EPICURO	**I**	**6**	**9**	**1.10.14**
ETERNITÀ	**I**	**6**	**9**	**3.29.16**
SPAURIRE	I	6	9	NOT PRESENT
GRASCIA	I	6	9	NOT PRESENT
MISERICORDIOSAMENTE	I	6	9	NOT PRESENT
BANDIERA	I	6	10	NOT PRESENT
CALDAIA	**I**	**6**	**19**	**1.21.56**
CONVENTO	I	6	19	2.21.62; 3.22.90; 3.29.109; 3.30.129

RIDEVOLE	I	6	20	NOT PRESENT
BIZZARRIA	I	6	20	NOT PRESENT
CROCIATO	I	7	2	NOT PRESENT
VIZIOSO	I	7	4	NOT PRESENT
IPOCRITA	**I**	**7**	**4**	**1.23.92**
DISUSARE	**I**	**7**	**4**	**2.10.2**
PARTENERE	I	7	8	NOT PRESENT
ISTRAZIARE	I	7	10	NOT PRESENT
GRAMATICA	I	7	11	NOT PRESENT
VERSIFICATORE	I	7	11	NOT PRESENT
SUFFICIENZA	I	7	26	NOT PRESENT
NOBILISSIMAMENTE	I	7	28	NOT PRESENT
SOPRANOME	I	8	6	2.16.139; 3.15.138
ZIZZANIA	I	8	9	NOT PRESENT
FAVILLUZZA	I	8	12	NOT PRESENT
VILLANAMENTE	I	9	4	NOT PRESENT
PERSECUTORE	**I**	**9**	**7**	**2.15.113**
FREGIO	I	10	5	1.14.72; 3.16.132
FREGIATO	**I**	**10**	**6**	**3.31.50**
INSENSIBILE	I	10	6	NOT PRESENT
MILENSAGGINE	I	10	6	NOT PRESENT
LAVANDAIA	I	10	6	NOT PRESENT
MERENDARSI	I	10	17	NOT PRESENT
LUPINO	I	10	17	NOT PRESENT
SAPORE	I	10	17	2.16.91; 2.20.117; 2.28.133; 2.30.81; 3.17.117
RICONFERMARE	I	11	5	NOT PRESENT
CONTINUANZA	I	11	7	NOT PRESENT
RIVO	I	11	15	#SIX
OMBROSO	I	11	15	NOT PRESENT
LEUTO	**I**	**11**	**16**	**1.30.49**
OBGETTO	I	11	19	NOT PRESENT
RIMIRARE	I	11	20	#SEVENTEEN
GUSTARE	I	11	21	#TEN
CAROLETTA	I	11	22	NOT PRESENT
FORMOSO	2	0	4	NOT PRESENT
ZOPPO	2	1	5	NOT PRESENT
DISCORRIMENTO	2	1	6	NOT PRESENT

VEDITORE	2	1	6	NOT PRESENT
STORCERE	2	1	11	1.19.64; 1.34.66
RATRATTO	2	1	11	NOT PRESENT
TRAVOLGERE	2	1	14	1.20.11; 1.20.17; 2.33.66
RIDIRIZZATO	2	1	14	NOT PRESENT
BEFFATORE	2	1	17	NOT PRESENT
ISCHERNIRE	2	1	17	NOT PRESENT
CARMINARE	2	1	22	NOT PRESENT
TAGLIABORSE	2	1	22	NOT PRESENT
RUVIDO	**2**	**1**	**23**	**2.9.98**
COLLA [n.]	2	1	24	NOT PRESENT
PRESENTAGIONE	2	1	27	NOT PRESENT
INCAUTAMENTE	2	2	4	NOT PRESENT
AVOLA	2	2	12	NOT PRESENT
FREDDURA	2	2	15	1.31.123; 1.32.53; 1.33.101
SPORTATO	2	2	17	NOT PRESENT
PAGLIERICCIO	2	2	17	NOT PRESENT
DELIBERARE	**2**	**2**	**21**	**3.2.94**
TRIEMITO	2	2	22	NOT PRESENT
CHIARITÀ	**2**	**2**	**23**	**3.21.90**
CALDEZZA	2	2	27	NOT PRESENT
ADEMPIERE	2	2	39	2.12.131; 3.15.66; 3.22.62; 3.22.63
ROVAIO	2	2	42	NOT PRESENT
IMPOVERIRE	2	3	1	NOT PRESENT
POSA	2	3	4	1.3.54; 1.5.45; 2.6.150; 3.14.132; 3.16.93
RICCAMENTE	2	3	24	NOT PRESENT
PRATICO	2	3	24	NOT PRESENT
COLTRICETTA	2	3	27	NOT PRESENT
DISDETTA	**2**	**3**	**29**	**2.3.109**
DUBITAZIONE	**2**	**3**	**31**	**3.4.64**
POPPELLINA	2	3	32	NOT PRESENT
TAVOLETTA	2	3	35	NOT PRESENT
EFFIGIARE	**2**	**3**	**35**	**2.10.67**
REALMENTE	2	3	44	NOT PRESENT
SOLENNEMENTE	2	3	44	NOT PRESENT
CONTEA	2	3	46	NOT PRESENT
CONQUISTARE	2	3	48	NOT PRESENT

ELEVARE	2	4	3	NOT PRESENT
RIUSCITA	2	4	4	NOT PRESENT
GAETA	2	4	5	1.26.92; 3.8.62
CITTADETTA	2	4	5	NOT PRESENT
COMPERATORE	2	4	9	NOT PRESENT
GUERNIRE	2	4	9	NOT PRESENT
SCILOCCO	2	4	13	NOT PRESENT
PECUNIA	2	4	14	NOT PRESENT
CIURMA	2	4	15	NOT PRESENT
SFONDOLARE	2	4	15	NOT PRESENT
FARSETTINO	2	4	15	NOT PRESENT
PROSPERAMENTE	2	4	16	NOT PRESENT
STRITOLARE	2	4	17	NOT PRESENT
LONTANARE	**2**	**4**	**19**	**2.33.117**
GROPPO	2	4	20	1.11.96; 1.13.123; 1.33.97
RIVERSARE	2	4	20	1.6.11; 1.7.101; 1.33.93
SPUGNA	**2**	**4**	**22**	**2.20.3**
STOVIGLI	2	4	22	NOT PRESENT
SALSO	2	4	22	NOT PRESENT
RAVVISARE	**2**	**4**	**23**	**2.23.48**
TRANQUILLO	2	4	24	2.33.19; 3.5.100; 3.15.13
CALORE	2	4	25	2.19.1; 2.25.77; 2.28.99; 3.19.19; 3.31.140
SCONFICCARE	2	4	26	NOT PRESENT
BALESTRARE	2	4	27	1.13.98; 2.25.112
DRAPPIERE	2	4	28	NOT PRESENT
SACCHETTO	**2**	**4**	**29**	**1.17.65**
COZZONE	2	5	3	NOT PRESENT
CONTEZZA	2	5	7	2.20.29; 2.24.36
FONDARE	2	5	9	3.24.74; 3.24.90; 3.26.36; 3.28.109
AVVINGHIARE	2	5	15	1.5.6; 1.34.70
INCORTINATO	2	5	17	NOT PRESENT
INGRATITUDINE	2	5	20	NOT PRESENT
GUELFO	**2**	**5**	**22**	**3.6.107**
CAVALLERESSA	2	5	23	NOT PRESENT
PALAZZO	2	5	23	2.10.68; 3.21.8
COMPOSTAMENTE	2	5	25	NOT PRESENT
BALBETTARE	2	5	25	NOT PRESENT

NOMINATAMENTE	2	5	29	NOT PRESENT
DIPORRE	2	5	37	1.19.44; 2.11.135; 2.18.84
CONTRAPORRE	2	5	38	NOT PRESENT
CAPOLEVARE	2	5	38	NOT PRESENT
CONFIGGERE	**2**	**5**	**39**	**1.23.115**
MURETTO	2	5	41	NOT PRESENT
CHIASSOLINO	2	5	41	NOT PRESENT
PROVERBIOSAMENTE	2	5	43	NOT PRESENT
FIORDALISO	2	5	44	2.20.86; 2.29.84
FINGERE	**2**	**5**	**49**	**2.32.69**
ABBAIARE	2	5	49	1.6.28; 1.7.43
BACALARE	2	5	52	NOT PRESENT
SBADIGLIARE	**2**	**5**	**52**	**1.25.89**
BASTONATA	2	5	53	NOT PRESENT
FERRAMENTO	2	5	57	NOT PRESENT
SCARABONE	2	5	59	NOT PRESENT
CARRUCOLA	2	5	65	NOT PRESENT
SPONDA	2	5	68	#NINE
PASTURALE	**2**	**5**	**77**	**2.16.110**
MITRA	2	5	77	NOT PRESENT
PUNTELLO	2	5	78	NOT PRESENT
DIROTTISSIMAMENTE	2	5	80	NOT PRESENT
MANUCARE	2	5	82	NOT PRESENT
PERSEGUITARE	2	5	83	NOT PRESENT
RADDOLCIRE	2	6	4	NOT PRESENT
DIURNO	**2**	**6**	**11**	**2.19.1**
ALLUNGARE	2	6	11	1.25.114; 2.7.64; 2.13.32; 2.15.140; 3.7.32
LATTE	2	6	15	3.5.82; 3.11.129; 3.23.57; 3.23.122; 3.30.83
POPPARE	2	6	16	NOT PRESENT
DINOMINARE	2	6	25	NOT PRESENT
FOCE	2	6	25	#TWELVE
VEDOVILE	2	6	26	NOT PRESENT
SERVA	**2**	**6**	**28**	**3.21.70**
VAGABUNDO	**2**	**6**	**33**	**3.11.128**
FERVENTISSIMAMENTE	2	6	35	NOT PRESENT
FREMERE	2	6	38	NOT PRESENT

STENTARE	2	6	39	1.23.121
SCHIANTARE	2	6	44	1.9.70; 1.13.33; 2.20.45; 2.28.120; 2.33.58
GENEROSO	2	6	52	NOT PRESENT
ORIGINE	2	6	52	NOT PRESENT
CUPIDITÀ	**2**	**6**	**53**	**3.15.3**
INSIDIA	**2**	**6**	**53**	**3.17.95**
MECCANICO	2	6	54	NOT PRESENT
SPIRAZIONE	2	6	65	NOT PRESENT
PUERILE	2	6	66	3.3.26; 3.32.47
LINEAMENTO	2	6	66	NOT PRESENT
SENSITIVO	2	6	66	NOT PRESENT
TRASCUTAGGINE	2	6	67	NOT PRESENT
ITERARE	**2**	**6**	**69**	**2.7.2**
REBELLIONE	2	6	73	NOT PRESENT
INQUISIZIONE	2	6	74	NOT PRESENT
TRATTAMENTO	2	6	74	NOT PRESENT
INTRODURRE	2	6	79	NOT PRESENT
LIETISSIMAMENTE	2	6	81	NOT PRESENT
SCONFITTA	2	7	9	NOT PRESENT
CORREDARE	**2**	**7**	**9**	**3.6.112**
CONTRARIETÀ	2	7	12	NOT PRESENT
FOGA	2	7	13	2.5.18; 2.12.103; 2.31.18
ACCHETARE	2	7	14	NOT PRESENT
FATTEZZA	2	7	21	NOT PRESENT
CONTENZIONE	2	7	22	NOT PRESENT
CALCARE	2	7	23	NOT PRESENT
VENERE	2	7	26	2.25.132; 2.28.65
COZZARE	**2**	**7**	**30**	**1.32.51**
ASSENTIRE	2	7	30	1.18.45; 2.19.86; 2.21.101; 2.22.126
CASTELLANO	2	7	31	NOT PRESENT
SCONOSCIUTAMENTE	2	7	34	NOT PRESENT
ISPAZIO	2	7	40	NOT PRESENT
CORDOGLIO	2	7	40	NOT PRESENT
RIOTTA	2	7	42	NOT PRESENT
COSTUMATAMENTE	2	7	50	NOT PRESENT
CAMERIERE	2	7	52	NOT PRESENT
FISAMENTE	2	7	56	1.21.22; 2.13.13; 3.20.33

RICENTE	2	7	57	**1.16.11**
SANGUINOSO	2	7	57	1.27.44; 1.34.54; 2.14.64
RUVINA	2	7	61	#ELEVEN
COMMETTITORE	2	7	61	NOT PRESENT
ECCESSO	2	7	**61**	**3.19.45**
CONGREGARE	2	7	62	NOT PRESENT
FRONTIERA	2	7	69	NOT PRESENT
PODESTÀ	2	7	**70**	**1.6.96**
VO[G]ARE	2	7	74	NOT PRESENT
EGINA	2	7	**74**	**1.29.59**
PROVEDIMENTO	2	7	**76**	**2.6.143**
AFFRONTARE	2	7	**79**	**3.25.40**
DISPERDERE	2	7	79	NOT PRESENT
FAMIGLIARITÀ	2	7	80	NOT PRESENT
STUZZICARE	2	7	89	NOT PRESENT
PRISTINO	2	7	100	NOT PRESENT
AUTOREVOLE	2	7	109	NOT PRESENT
MONASTERO	2	7	**109**	**2.18.122**
VENERANDO	2	7	114	NOT PRESENT
CONFERIRE	2	8	**5**	**3.4.74**
CUSTODIA	2	8	5	NOT PRESENT
PALTONE	2	8	28	NOT PRESENT
MISFATTO	2	8	30	NOT PRESENT
LIMOSINARE	2	8	32	NOT PRESENT
RIGUARDATORE	2	8	39	NOT PRESENT
BASSAMENTE	2	8	41	NOT PRESENT
GIULIVO	2	8	61	NOT PRESENT
TORNEO	2	8	69	NOT PRESENT
SCADERE	2	8	72	NOT PRESENT
CANUTO	2	8	81	NOT PRESENT
BARBUTO	2	8	**81**	**2.7.102**
SCHIFO	2	8	**83**	**1.31.122**
RITRATTO	2	8	83	NOT PRESENT
INGIURIOSO	2	8	94	NOT PRESENT
SUOCERA	2	8	100	NOT PRESENT
COMPASSIONEVOLE	2	9	2	NOT PRESENT
TRAVALICARE	2	9	4	NOT PRESENT
SCUDIERE	2	9	9	NOT PRESENT
ACCORTAMENTE	2	9	9	NOT PRESENT

GABBARE	2	9	11	NOT PRESENT
ACERBAMENTE	2	9	17	NOT PRESENT
GUASTAMENTO	2	9	19	NOT PRESENT
STURBARE	2	9	23	NOT PRESENT
OBLIGAGIONE	2	9	24	NOT PRESENT
ARTIFICIATO	2	9	25	NOT PRESENT
SITO	2	9	26	#SEVEN
ALPESTRO	2	9	28	1.12.2; 2.14.32; 3.6.51
FARSETTACCIO	2	9	41	NOT PRESENT
RAGUNANZA	2	9	45	NOT PRESENT
DISDICEVOLE	2	9	52	NOT PRESENT
RESTITUZIONE	2	9	60	NOT PRESENT
FALSITÀ	**2**	**9**	**64**	**1.11.59**
MASCHILE	**2**	**9**	**67**	**1.20.45**
REAMENTE	2	9	68	NOT PRESENT
VESPA	2	9	75	1.3.66; 2.32.133
FAVOLOSO	2	10	4	NOT PRESENT
LUCERTOLA	2	10	6	NOT PRESENT
VERMINARO	2	10	6	NOT PRESENT
RISTORATIVO	2	10	7	NOT PRESENT
STIMATORE	2	10	8	NOT PRESENT
APOSTOLO	2	10	9	NOT PRESENT
ECCEZIONE	2	10	9	NOT PRESENT
SALVATICAMENTE	2	10	24	NOT PRESENT
POCOLINO	2	10	25	NOT PRESENT
SMIMORATO	2	10	31	NOT PRESENT
BANDITORE	2	10	32	NOT PRESENT
SAGRA [n.]	2	10	32	NOT PRESENT
DIGIUNE [n.]	2	10	32	NOT PRESENT
RAGUARDATORE	2	10	33	NOT PRESENT
INCOMPORTABILE	2	10	35	NOT PRESENT
MORTAIO	2	10	37	NOT PRESENT
ISQUADRO	2	10	38	NOT PRESENT
GEOMETRIA	2	10	38	NOT PRESENT
PIANETA	2	10	38	#SIX
RIZZARE	2	10	39	NOT PRESENT
MAZZATA	2	10	39	NOT PRESENT
TISICUZZO	2	10	39	NOT PRESENT
SCODELLINO	2	10	40	NOT PRESENT

INTERESSE	2	10	40	NOT PRESENT
CIVANZA	2	10	40	NOT PRESENT
FRULLO	2	10	42	NOT PRESENT
FURO	2	10	42	1.21.45; 1.27.127
CHINO	2	10	43	#SEVEN
APRILE	2	11	3	NOT PRESENT
SINTILLANTE	2	11	3	NOT PRESENT
TEDIOSO	2	11	5	NOT PRESENT
STATUIRE	2	11	10	NOT PRESENT
GIARDINETTO	2	11	11	NOT PRESENT
EQUALE	2	11	14	NOT PRESENT
AGUALE	2	11	14	NOT PRESENT
PIO	2	11	15	#SEVENTEEN
RANCIO	3	0	2	1.23.100; 2.2.9
POGGETTO	3	0	3	NOT PRESENT
SIGNOREGGIARE	**3**	**0**	**4**	**3.9.50**
PERGOLATO	3	0	6	NOT PRESENT
VITE	3	0	6	2.25.78; 3.24.111
UVA	**3**	**0**	**6**	**2.4.21**
ROSAIO	3	0	6	NOT PRESENT
CEDRO	3	0	8	NOT PRESENT
ODORATO	3	0	8	NOT PRESENT
PIENO [n.]	3	0	10	NOT PRESENT
LEPRE	3	0	13	NOT PRESENT
CERBIATTO	3	0	13	NOT PRESENT
ROMANZO	**3**	**0**	**15**	**2.26.118**
COCOLLA	3	1	2	3.9.78; 3.22.77
OMICCIUOLO	3	1	6	NOT PRESENT
ATTIGNERE	3	1	8	NOT PRESENT
SERVIGETTO	3	1	8	NOT PRESENT
CALZARE	3	1	8	NOT PRESENT
CEPPO	**3**	**1**	**14**	**3.16.106**
GIOVANACCIO	3	1	24	NOT PRESENT
SUORA	3	1	30	2.22.114; 2.23.120; 2.27.104; 3.23.56; 3.24.28
COMUNQUE	3	1	30	NOT PRESENT
MONACELLA	3	1	35	NOT PRESENT

RESULTARE	3	I	36	NOT PRESENT
SCILINGUAGNOLO	3	I	36	NOT PRESENT
INTITOLARE	3	I	41	NOT PRESENT
MONACHINO	3	I	42	NOT PRESENT
DISAVEDUTO	3	2	3	NOT PRESENT
SOLIO	3	2	4	NOT PRESENT
CONVENIENZA	**3**	**2**	**6**	**3.5.45**
MAZZUOLA	3	2	13	NOT PRESENT
ACCIAIO	3	2	14	NOT PRESENT
SIMILITUDINE	**3**	**2**	**18**	**3.14.7**
LANTERNETTA	3	2	24	NOT PRESENT
MESCOLATO	3	3	6	NOT PRESENT
FILATRICE	3	3	6	NOT PRESENT
FILATO	3	3	6	NOT PRESENT
SODISFAZIONE	3	3	6	NOT PRESENT
ASSEDIO	3	3	11	NOT PRESENT
SFACCIATO	**3**	**3**	**26**	**2.23.101**
STIZZA	3	3	27	NOT PRESENT
RIPETERE	3	3	34	NOT PRESENT
TIEPIDAMENTE	3	3	34	NOT PRESENT
IER MATTINA	**3**	**3**	**40**	**1.15.52**
DISUBIDIRE	3	3	46	NOT PRESENT
SPERGIURO	**3**	**3**	**47**	**1.30.118**
MORDIMENTO	3	3	47	NOT PRESENT
PERPLESSO	3	3	47	NOT PRESENT
SVERGOGNATO	**3**	**3**	**48**	**2.23.106**
MECCERE	3	3	50	NOT PRESENT
ANDATORE	3	3	50	NOT PRESENT
APRITORE	3	3	50	NOT PRESENT
SALITORE	**3**	**3**	**50**	**2.25.9**
IMPRONTITUDINE	3	3	51	NOT PRESENT
LUCIGNOLO	3	3	54	NOT PRESENT
SCARDASSO	3	3	54	NOT PRESENT
PREGHIERA	3	4	2	1.26.70; 2.11.22
BIZZOCO	3	4	4	NOT PRESENT
SCOPATORE	3	4	5	NOT PRESENT
CASOLANO	3	4	6	NOT PRESENT
CONVENTUALE	3	4	7	NOT PRESENT
APPALESARE	3	4	13	NOT PRESENT

DANNAZIONE	3	4	15	NOT PRESENT
VENIALE	3	4	15	NOT PRESENT
CAVIGLIUOLO	3	4	17	NOT PRESENT
TRINITÀ	3	4	18	NOT PRESENT
PROFITTEVOLE	3	4	22	NOT PRESENT
DIMENAMENTO	3	4	24	NOT PRESENT
MOTTEGGEVOLE	3	4	25	NOT PRESENT
AVEZZARSI	3	4	32	NOT PRESENT
ACERBETTO	3	5	2	NOT PRESENT
INFELICEMENTE	3	5	5	NOT PRESENT
RIFERMARE	3	5	10	NOT PRESENT
CONTO	3	5	11	#EIGHT
IMMERITAMENTE	3	5	13	NOT PRESENT
AMMOLLIRE	3	5	13	NOT PRESENT
MATTINATA	3	5	17	NOT PRESENT
AFFETTUOSO	**3**	**5**	**17**	**1.5.87**
PODESTERIA	3	5	29	NOT PRESENT
SANTESE	3	6	3	NOT PRESENT
SALVATICHEZZA	3	6	8	NOT PRESENT
ATTARE	3	6	21	NOT PRESENT
SVERGOGNARE	3	6	34	NOT PRESENT
RINNEGATO	3	6	36	NOT PRESENT
BRACCO	3	6	38	NOT PRESENT
VENDICO	3	6	48	NOT PRESENT
TENERISSIMAMENTE	3	6	50	NOT PRESENT
SAVISSIMAMENTE	3	6	50	NOT PRESENT
PROFETA	3	7	21	3.12.60; 3.12.136; 3.24.136
RIVELARE	3	7	22	3.21.120; 3.29.133
PROFONDO [n.]	3	7	28	NOT PRESENT
PONTIFICALE	3	7	34	NOT PRESENT
PAONEGGIARE	3	7	34	NOT PRESENT
GIACCHIO	3	7	35	NOT PRESENT
FIMBRIA	3	7	35	NOT PRESENT
ELEMOSINA	3	7	37	NOT PRESENT
ISPAVENTAMENTO	3	7	37	NOT PRESENT
SGRIDATORE	3	7	38	NOT PRESENT
RESTITUTORE	3	7	38	NOT PRESENT
VESCOVADO	3	7	38	NOT PRESENT

SCARICAMENTO	3	7	39	NOT PRESENT
ODIERNO	**3**	**7**	**40**	**3.20.54**
POLTRONERIA	3	7	41	NOT PRESENT
PERDONATORE	3	7	41	NOT PRESENT
POLTRONEGGIARE	3	7	41	NOT PRESENT
ASTINENTE	3	7	42	NOT PRESENT
EVANGELIO	3	7	42	#FIVE
VISITATORE	3	7	43	NOT PRESENT
MATRIMONIALE	3	7	44	NOT PRESENT
SPONTANEO	3	7	45	NOT PRESENT
TAPINO	3	7	46	1.24.11; 1.30.91
MAGNIFICARE	3	7	48	NOT PRESENT
FRATICELLO	3	7	50	NOT PRESENT
MANICATORE	3	7	52	NOT PRESENT
BILANCIA	3	7	53	1.23.102; 2.2.5; 3.5.62; 3.13.42
SBANDEGGIAMENTO	3	7	54	NOT PRESENT
PUNTA	3	7	58	#TWELVE
REMOTO	3	7	62	#SIX
UCCIDITORE	3	7	76	NOT PRESENT
INTRODUZIONE	3	7	77	NOT PRESENT
MAFATTORE	3	7	81	NOT PRESENT
INREPUGNABILE	3	7	84	NOT PRESENT
TACITURNITÀ	3	7	87	NOT PRESENT
ABBAIATORE	3	7	93	NOT PRESENT
RUGGINUZZA	3	7	94	NOT PRESENT
SONORO	3	7	95	NOT PRESENT
FREQUENTATO	**3**	**8**	**4**	**3.22.38**
RECREAZIONE	3	8	5	NOT PRESENT
MODESTISSIMAMENT	3	8	6	NOT PRESENT
LESIONE	3	8	31	NOT PRESENT
CHIOSTRO	3	8	31	2.15.57; 2.26.128; 3.21.118; 3.22.50; 3.25.127
SCIGNERE	3	8	33	NOT PRESENT
FUMOSITÀ	3	8	33	NOT PRESENT
TOMBA	3	8	35	#SIX
FASCIO	**3**	**8**	**35**	**1.31.135**
VISITAZIONE	3	8	36	NOT PRESENT

TRAVESTITO	3	8	37	NOT PRESENT
CACARE	3	8	62	NOT PRESENT
CASCIATO	3	8	66	NOT PRESENT
PONTARE	3	8	68	1.32.3; 2.20.74; 3.4.26
ISMOVERE	3	8	68	NOT PRESENT
ISMOVITURA	3	8	68	NOT PRESENT
REVELARE	**3**	**8**	**70**	**2.3.143**
REVELAZIONE	**3**	**8**	**74**	**3.25.96**
GUERREGGIARE	3	9	28	NOT PRESENT
VACUO	3	9	33	NOT PRESENT
ALBERGATRICE	3	9	36	NOT PRESENT
TRITAMENTE	3	9	37	NOT PRESENT
AFFETTUOSISSIMAMENTE	3	9	49	NOT PRESENT
MISVENIRE	3	9	59	NOT PRESENT
ALPI	3	10	3	1.14.30; 2.17.1
SPELUNCA	3	10	3	1.20.49; 3.22.77
DATTERO	**3**	**10**	**8**	**1.33.120**
ROMITO	**3**	**10**	**9**	**2.6.72**
TENTAZIONE	3	10	10	NOT PRESENT
DISCIPLINA	**3**	**10**	**10**	**2.23.105**
RESURREZIONE	**3**	**10**	**13**	**3.7.146**
MOLESTIA	3	10	14	NOT PRESENT
ATTUTARE [2]	**3**	**10**	**29**	**2.26.72**
FACULTÀ	3	10	32	NOT PRESENT
FALCE	3	11	4	NOT PRESENT
SECONDA [n.]	**3**	**11**	**5**	**2.4.93**
TIEPIDO	3	11	7	NOT PRESENT
DISPREGIARE	3	11	13	1.11.111; 2.8.132; 2.22.87; 2.22.147
TUTUTTO	3	11	14	NOT PRESENT
VESTA	3	11	16	2.1.75; 2.8.29; 3.14.39; 3.25.92; 3.27.55
OBLIARE	3	11	17	1.11.61; 1.28.54; 2.2.75
TOSA	3	11	18	NOT PRESENT
SUBLIME	**3**	**11**	**18**	**3.28.102**
PROSA	**4**	**0**	**3**	**2.26.118**
ISTILO	4	0	3	NOT PRESENT
SCROLLARE	4	0	4	NOT PRESENT

DIRADICARE	4	0	4	NOT PRESENT
MATURAMENTE	4	0	6	NOT PRESENT
DISPETTOSAMENTE	4	0	7	NOT PRESENT
DETRIMENTO	4	0	7	NOT PRESENT
SOFFIAMENTO	4	0	8	NOT PRESENT
ATROCE	4	0	8	NOT PRESENT
MILITARE	4	0	8	3.12.35; 3.25.52; 3.25.57
REPULSA [n.]	4	0	10	NOT PRESENT
CELLETTA	4	0	15	NOT PRESENT
ABITUARE	**4**	**0**	**18**	**2.29.146**
IMBECCARE	4	0	29	NOT PRESENT
RIPRENSORE	4	0	30	NOT PRESENT
BASCIARI	4	0	31	NOT PRESENT
MELLIFLUO	4	0	32	NOT PRESENT
ROMITELLO	4	0	32	NOT PRESENT
DANTE	**4**	**0**	**33**	**2.30.55**
TESSERE	4	0	36	NOT PRESENT
POETA	4	0	38	#THIRTY
ORIGINALE	4	0	39	NOT PRESENT
TURBO	4	0	40	1.3.30; 1.26.137; 3.22.99
ECCELSO	4	0	40	2.33.65; 3.26.110; 3.27.100;3.29.142
VALLETTO	4	1	6	NOT PRESENT
SOFFIONE	4	1	7	NOT PRESENT
FESSO	4	1	8	1.20.24; 2.9.75
RITURARE	4	1	9	NOT PRESENT
NODO	4	1	12	#ELEVEN
CAPPIO	4	1	12	NOT PRESENT
BRONCO	**4**	**1**	**12**	**1.13.26**
CARELLO	4	1	17	NOT PRESENT
DECEVOLE	4	1	27	NOT PRESENT
FORTISSIMAMENTE	4	1	31	NOT PRESENT
DILIBERATO	4	1	37	NOT PRESENT
ABBASSO	4	1	38	NOT PRESENT
MASSA	4	1	39	NOT PRESENT
ANIMOSITÀ	4	1	41	NOT PRESENT
MIRABILMENTE	4	1	42	1.20.11; 1.21.6; 2.25.86

ZAPPARE	4	I	43	NOT PRESENT
SPANDERE	4	I	45	#NINE
SMUOVERE	4	I	48	NOT PRESENT
DISPIETATO	**4**	**I**	**53**	**I.30.9**
CHINARE	4	I	55	#TWENTY
VELARE	4	I	61	#NINE
SEPOLCRO	**4**	**I**	**62**	**I.10.7**
RECREARE	4	2	4	NOT PRESENT
PROPOSTO	4	2	4	I.2.138; I.22.123
ARTIFICIALMENTE	4	2	5	NOT PRESENT
RUBESTO	4	2	5	I.31.106; 2.5.125
SALVAZIONE	**4**	**2**	**5**	**I.2.30**
ECCELLENTE	4	2	6	3.9.41; 3.32.60
GHERMINELLA	4	2	8	NOT PRESENT
FALSARIO	4	2	10	NOT PRESENT
OMICIDA	**4**	**2**	**10**	**I.11.37**
PREDICATORE	4	2	10	NOT PRESENT
COMMESSARIO	4	2	11	NOT PRESENT
DIPOSITARIO	4	2	11	NOT PRESENT
CONFESSORO	4	2	11	NOT PRESENT
CONSIGLIATORE	4	2	11	NOT PRESENT
ASCESI [2]	**4**	**2**	**11**	**3.11.53**
BAMBO	4	2	12	NOT PRESENT
CA'	**4**	**2**	**12**	**I.15.54**
COMMODO	4	2	14	NOT PRESENT
MESTOLO	4	2	16	NOT PRESENT
BADERLA	4	2	24	NOT PRESENT
MATTAPAN	4	2	24	NOT PRESENT
POCOFILA	4	2	27	NOT PRESENT
GALLORIA	4	2	29	NOT PRESENT
MOSSA [n.]	**4**	**2**	**30**	**I.33.126**
GIUMENTA	4	2	30	NOT PRESENT
GIACITURA	4	2	32	NOT PRESENT
MANCO	4	2	36	#EIGHT
MARIDO	4	2	43	NOT PRESENT
MO	4	2	43	#ELEVEN
VU	4	2	43	NOT PRESENT
NOVELLUZZA	4	2	45	NOT PRESENT
DUCATO	4	2	48	NOT PRESENT

MACELLO	4	2	52	NOT PRESENT
LORDURA	**4**	**2**	**56**	**1.11.60**
INCOLPARE	4	3	1	NOT PRESENT
SOVRA	4	3	2	#MANY
REDINA	4	3	4	NOT PRESENT
INCONSIDERATO	4	3	4	NOT PRESENT
RATTENIMENTO	4	3	5	NOT PRESENT
POSSEDITORE	**4**	**3**	**14**	**2.15.62**
CASSONE	4	3	18	NOT PRESENT
MAESTRA	4	3	23	NOT PRESENT
PRESTISSIMAMENTE	4	3	24	NOT PRESENT
SOTTRARRE	**4**	**3**	**26**	**1.26.91**
INFINTAMENTE	4	3	30	NOT PRESENT
UDITA [n.]	4	4	3	NOT PRESENT
SAGACISSIMAMENTE	4	4	8	NOT PRESENT
FAMELICO	4	4	24	NOT PRESENT
ARMENTO	**4**	**4**	**24**	**1.25.30**
GIOVENCO	4	4	24	NOT PRESENT
APPAGAMENTO	4	4	24	NOT PRESENT
DISOTTERRARE	4	5	1	NOT PRESENT
SCONCIO [n.]	4	5	7	NOT PRESENT
INSTANTEMENTE	4	5	10	NOT PRESENT
DISPARIRE	4	5	13	1.22.136; 2.15.95; 2.26.134; 3.30.93
IMBUSTO	4	5	16	NOT PRESENT
PERSA [n.]	4	5	17	NOT PRESENT
ROSATO	4	5	17	NOT PRESENT
INAFFIARE	4	5	17	NOT PRESENT
GRASSEZZA	4	5	19	NOT PRESENT
CAPELLATURA	4	5	21	NOT PRESENT
DISAVENTURATO	4	5	23	NOT PRESENT
GRASTA	4	5	24	NOT PRESENT
MENZIONE	4	6	3	NOT PRESENT
VERISIMILE	4	6	4	NOT PRESENT
PREMOSTRATO	4	6	5	NOT PRESENT
SECONDO [adj.]	4	6	7	#THIRTY-TWO
SOTTERRA	4	6	10	NOT PRESENT
SOSPECCIARE	4	6	11	1.10.57; 2.12.129
MANCAMENTO	4	6	13	NOT PRESENT

COLLARE	4	6	15	NOT PRESENT
VELTRA	4	6	16	NOT PRESENT
RESISTENZA	4	6	16	2.31.70; 3.12.102
SCONFORTO	4	6	18	NOT PRESENT
GREMBIO	4	6	20	NOT PRESENT
RITIRARE	**4**	**6**	**20**	**1.25.131**
CONSAPEVOLE	4	6	22	NOT PRESENT
LAGRIMOSO	**4**	**6**	**22**	**1.3.133**
FRANCAMENTE	4	6	32	NOT PRESENT
PUBLICAMENTE	4	6	40	NOT PRESENT
GENGIA	4	7	12	NOT PRESENT
CAMBIAMENTO	4	7	13	NOT PRESENT
PRONTARE	**4**	**7**	**16**	**2.13.20**
FRIVOLO	4	7	18	NOT PRESENT
PUNITORE	4	7	18	NOT PRESENT
SCARDASSIERE	4	7	20	NOT PRESENT
RIVENIRE	4	7	21	3.7.82; 3.10.70
VENENIFERO	4	7	23	NOT PRESENT
FIATO	4	7	23	#SIX
LEALMENTE	4	8	5	NOT PRESENT
TRAFFICARE	4	8	11	NOT PRESENT
TELO	**4**	**8**	**17**	**2.12.28**
TRANQUILLITÀ	4	8	20	NOT PRESENT
RITOCCARE	4	8	25	NOT PRESENT
PRESENZIALMENTE	4	8	26	NOT PRESENT
MALAVOGLIENZA	4	8	27	NOT PRESENT
CORROTTO	4	8	30	NOT PRESENT
DIFFICILE	4	8	32	NOT PRESENT
IMMOBILE	4	8	33	2.19.126; 2.20.139; 3.33.98
INSEPARABILE	4	8	35	NOT PRESENT
ASSISA [n.]	4	9	5	NOT PRESENT
DISARMATO	4	9	11	NOT PRESENT
PENNONCELLO	4	9	13	NOT PRESENT
VIVANDETTA	4	9	16	NOT PRESENT
MINUZZARE	4	9	16	NOT PRESENT
SELLARE	4	9	24	NOT PRESENT
CIRUGIA	4	10	4	NOT PRESENT
INFREDDATO	4	10	4	NOT PRESENT

LADRONECCIO	4	10	7	**1.11.59**
INFAMARE	4	10	7	NOT PRESENT
COMPOSIZIONE	4	10	10	NOT PRESENT
FEDITA	4	10	20	NOT PRESENT
MASSERIZIE	4	10	21	NOT PRESENT
DIGERIRE	4	10	23	2.25.43; 3.10.55;
				3.17.132;3.25.94
STUPEFAZIONE	4	10	23	NOT PRESENT
SMEMORARE	4	10	23	NOT PRESENT
BRANCOLARE [2]	4	10	26	**1.33.73**
GUASTADA	4	10	44	NOT PRESENT
CRISTIANELLA	4	10	48	NOT PRESENT
MACINIO	4	10	48	NOT PRESENT
STORIA	4	10	49	2.10.52; 2.10.71; 3.19.18
ONCIA	4	10	53	1.30.83; 3.9.57
INFELICITÀ	4	11	2	NOT PRESENT
BOCCUCCIA	4	11	4	NOT PRESENT
RUBINETTO	4	11	4	**3.19.4**
PROPOSIZIONE	4	11	6	**3.24.98**
TRADIRE	4	11	11	1.11.66; 1.33.86;
				1.33.129
BILTATE	4	11	14	NOT PRESENT
EMISPERIO	5	0	2	#TEN
DANZETTA	5	0	4	NOT PRESENT
DEFORME	5	1	4	NOT PRESENT
ISCHERNO	5	1	4	NOT PRESENT
BESTIONE	5	1	4	NOT PRESENT
IMPRESSIONE	5	1	8	NOT PRESENT
CITTADINESCO	5	1	8	NOT PRESENT
DEA	5	1	10	2.32.8; 3.28.121
ROZZEZZA	5	1	12	NOT PRESENT
RUSTICITÀ	5	1	13	NOT PRESENT
RUSTICO	5	1	19	NOT PRESENT
BELLICO	5	1	19	NOT PRESENT
FEROCE	5	1	19	#EIGHT
INFONDERE	5	1	21	3.1.52; 3.8.86; 3.13.44
ECCITATORE	5	1	22	NOT PRESENT
OBUMBRAZIONE	5	1	22	NOT PRESENT

TRASANDARE	5	1	23	NOT PRESENT
NAVALE	5	1	26	NOT PRESENT
SOMMERGERE	5	1	27	#SIX
RAMPICONE	5	1	28	NOT PRESENT
SEGUITO	5	1	28	NOT PRESENT
POGGIARE	5	1	43	#SIX
MAESTRATO	5	1	45	NOT PRESENT
SENATO	5	1	45	NOT PRESENT
APPRESTAMENTO	5	1	48	NOT PRESENT
PROVATORE	5	1	55	NOT PRESENT
INSENSATO	**5**	**1**	**56**	**3.11.1**
ANIMOSO	**5**	**1**	**57**	**1.10.37**
RISPITTO	**5**	**1**	**60**	**2.30.43**
CONTASTO	**5**	**1**	**67**	**1.7.85**
RICIDERE	5	1	67	1.7.100; 1.18.17; 2.5.66; 3.23.63
RISCOSSA [n.]	5	1	69	NOT PRESENT
TURBAMENTO	5	1	70	NOT PRESENT
TRASRICCHIRE	5	2	7	NOT PRESENT
ISFONDOLATO	5	2	7	NOT PRESENT
NAVICELLA	5	2	10	1.17.100; 2.1.2; 2.32.129
TIMONE	5	2	11	NOT PRESENT
LINGUAGGIO	5	2	26	1.27.14; 1.31.78; 1.31.80
BARBARESCO	5	2	28	NOT PRESENT
COMUNALMENTE	5	2	32	NOT PRESENT
SUSCITARE	**5**	**2**	**36**	**3.20.110**
ARCIONE	**5**	**3**	**11**	**2.6.99**
SENTIERUOLO	5	3	21	NOT PRESENT
ABITANZA	5	3	24	NOT PRESENT
CALPESTIO	5	3	31	NOT PRESENT
CAVRETTO	5	3	36	NOT PRESENT
CAVEZZINA	5	3	44	NOT PRESENT
ATTERRARE	5	3	44	#SIX
STROZZARE	5	3	44	NOT PRESENT
SVENTRARE	5	3	44	NOT PRESENT
DOLCISSIMAMENTE	5	3	53	NOT PRESENT
SFUGGITA [n.]	5	4	14	NOT PRESENT
RITROSETTO	5	4	23	NOT PRESENT
RUSIGNUOLO	5	4	23	NOT PRESENT

MORSA [n.]	5	4	29	NOT PRESENT
GABBIA	5	4	38	NOT PRESENT
AZZUFFARSI	5	5	1	NOT PRESENT
DILETICARE	5	5	2	NOT PRESENT
GIOVENTUDINE	5	5	4	NOT PRESENT
SOLDATO	5	5	4	NOT PRESENT
TENUTA	5	5	15	NOT PRESENT
SIGNORTO	5	5	17	NOT PRESENT
CONTESA	5	5	21	NOT PRESENT
RUBA [n.]	5	5	27	NOT PRESENT
RIMESCOLAMENTO	5	5	31	NOT PRESENT
MARGINE	5	5	33	1.14.83; 1.14.141; 1.15.1
CROCETTA	5	5	33	NOT PRESENT
DRITTO	5	5	35	#FORTY-FOUR
CONTENDERE	5	5	35	2.17.129; 2.23.49
INTROMETTERSI	5	5	39	NOT PRESENT
ISTRABOCCHEVOLE	5	6	3	NOT PRESENT
CONCA	**5**	**6**	**6**	**1.9.16**
CAGIONEVOLE	5	6	9	NOT PRESENT
DAPPRESSO	5	6	14	NOT PRESENT
AGGRAPPARE	5	6	15	1.16.134; 1.24.29; 1.34.80
PICCHIO	5	6	15	NOT PRESENT
ANTENNETTA	5	6	15	NOT PRESENT
REITERARE	**5**	**6**	**19**	**2.13.30**
TOSTAMENTE	**5**	**6**	**34**	**1.23.22**
COMPENSARE	**5**	**6**	**42**	**3.26.6**
PROSCIOGLIERE	5	7	1	NOT PRESENT
INCARICO	5	7	2	NOT PRESENT
FRANCO	5	7	5	1.2.132; 1.27.54
SOPRATENERE	5	7	6	NOT PRESENT
TEMOROSO	5	7	9	NOT PRESENT
GRAGNUOLA	5	7	12	NOT PRESENT
GRANDINE	**5**	**7**	**14**	**1.6.10**
GRADINARE	5	7	16	NOT PRESENT
ENTRARE [n.]	5	7	17	NOT PRESENT
DISGRAVIDARE	5	7	17	NOT PRESENT
LUNGHESSO	5	7	24	2.2.10; 2.19.27
INFIGGERE	5	7	34	NOT PRESENT

CORSIERE	**5**	**8**	**16**	**2.32.57**
ETERNALE	5	8	21	1.14.37; 3.5.116
ISCHIENA	5	8	24	NOT PRESENT
INTERIORA	5	8	24	NOT PRESENT
FUGGA	5	8	25	NOT PRESENT
GUIDATRICE	5	9	3	NOT PRESENT
SMODERATAMENTE	5	9	3	NOT PRESENT
PREGIATO	5	9	5	NOT PRESENT
STRETTISSIMAMENTE	5	9	7	NOT PRESENT
GUATATURA	5	9	14	NOT PRESENT
LAVORIETTO	5	9	19	NOT PRESENT
RISTORO	5	9	20	2.14.34; 3.5.31
SCHEDONE	5	9	26	NOT PRESENT
TAGLIERE	5	9	86	NOT PRESENT
ACCIDENTALE	5	10	3	NOT PRESENT
COMPRESSO	**5**	**10**	**7**	**1.21.21**
AMMENDAMENTO	5	10	8	NOT PRESENT
PIOVOSO	5	10	9	NOT PRESENT
INDARNO	5	10	12	#NINE
FOCOLARE	5	10	16	NOT PRESENT
PENTOLA	5	10	20	NOT PRESENT
STRANGUGLIONE	5	10	21	NOT PRESENT
FORBITO	5	10	22	1.15.69; 1.33.2
ZOTICO	5	10	22	NOT PRESENT
AMMORBIDIRE	5	10	22	NOT PRESENT
PANNACCIO	5	10	28	NOT PRESENT
SACCONE	5	10	28	NOT PRESENT
CHIUSO [n.]	**5**	**10**	**34**	**2.3.79**
IMBIANCARE	5	10	36	1.2.128; 2.9.2; 3.7.81; 3.8.112; 3.12.87
TEGGHIUZZA	5	10	36	NOT PRESENT
FUMMO	5	10	36	#EIGHTEEN
PERFIDISSIMO	5	10	44	NOT PRESENT
FIUTARE	5	10	48	NOT PRESENT
GONGOLARE	5	10	55	NOT PRESENT
PICCHIAPETTO	5	10	56	NOT PRESENT
TIGNOSO	5	10	58	NOT PRESENT
ULIVELLO	5	11	9	NOT PRESENT
IMBOTTARE	5	11	11	NOT PRESENT

OTTOBRE	**5**	**II**	**II**	**2.6.144**
NICCHIO	5	II	13	NOT PRESENT
GIRE	5	II	17	#THIRTY-EIGHT
SFARE	5	II	19	NOT PRESENT
ODOROSO	6	0	3	NOT PRESENT
CONCISTORO	6	0	4	2.9.24; 3.16.114
ATTEMPATETTO	6	0	7	NOT PRESENT
SUPERBO	6	0	7	#SEVENTEEN
ISPARGIMENTO	6	0	8	NOT PRESENT
BADA	**6**	**0**	**9**	**1.31.139**
PECORONE	6	0	10	NOT PRESENT
FINALE	6	0	12	NOT PRESENT
SCOPARE	6	0	15	NOT PRESENT
LUNGHETTO	6	I	6	NOT PRESENT
REPLICARE	6	I	9	NOT PRESENT
PECORECCIO	6	I	10	NOT PRESENT
INTENDITORE	6	I	12	NOT PRESENT
NOVELLATORE	6	I	12	NOT PRESENT
GABBO	**6**	**I**	**12**	**1.32.7**
FINITA	6	I	12	NOT PRESENT
MALADICERE	6	2	4	NOT PRESENT
INCERTO	**6**	**2**	**5**	**2.10.19**
MINISTRA	6	2	6	1.7.78; 1.29.55
ESSERCERE	6	2	8	NOT PRESENT
SPLENDIDISSIMAMENTE	6	2	9	NOT PRESENT
GREMBIULE	6	2	11	NOT PRESENT
MUGNAIO	6	2	11	NOT PRESENT
STAGNATO	6	2	11	NOT PRESENT
SPURGARE	6	2	12	NOT PRESENT
SAPORITAMENTE	6	2	12	NOT PRESENT
MESCERE	**6**	**2**	**16**	**3.17.12**
INFORNARE	6	2	16	NOT PRESENT
BOTTICELLO	6	2	28	NOT PRESENT
RACCORDARE	6	2	28	NOT PRESENT
RISPONDITORE	6	3	4	NOT PRESENT
POPOLINO	6	3	7	NOT PRESENT
PALIO	6	3	8	NOT PRESENT
CONTAMINAZIONE	6	3	10	NOT PRESENT

AIUTATRICE	6	4	3	NOT PRESENT
CAVALLERESCO	6	4	4	NOT PRESENT
FIUMANA	6	4	14	1.2.108; 2.19.101; 3.30.64
SPARUTO	6	5	1	NOT PRESENT
TURPISSIMO	6	5	3	NOT PRESENT
SFORMATO	6	5	4	NOT PRESENT
PIATTO [adj.]	**6**	**5**	**4**	**1.19.75**
RICAGNATO	6	5	4	NOT PRESENT
ARMARIO	6	5	4	NOT PRESENT
OPERATRICE	6	5	5	NOT PRESENT
STILE	**6**	**5**	**5**	**2.12.64**
VISIVO	6	5	5	3.26.71; 3.30.47
IGNORANTE	6	5	6	NOT PRESENT
USURPARE	6	5	7	3.15.143; 3.27.22
PIOVA [n.]	6	5	10	1.6.7; 1.14.132; 2.30.113
MANTELLACCIO	6	5	11	NOT PRESENT
MOLLE	6	5	12	#EIGHT
SCHIZZO	6	5	12	NOT PRESENT
ZACCHEROSO	6	5	12	NOT PRESENT
RISCHIARARE	6	5	12	3.14.69; 3.23.18
DISORREVOLE	6	5	13	NOT PRESENT
DISPARUTO	6	5	13	NOT PRESENT
GHIGNARE	6	6	6	NOT PRESEN
GOCCIOLONE	6	6	6	NOT PRESENT
PROPORZIONATO	6	6	14	NOT PRESENT
MASCELLONA	6	6	14	NOT PRESENT
TURPITUDINE	6	6	17	NOT PRESENT
NOBILITARE	**6**	**7**	**2**	**3.33.5**
INGIUNGERE	6	7	2	NOT PRESENT
SCONSIGLIATO	6	7	9	NOT PRESENT
CONTUMACIA	**6**	**7**	**9**	**2.3.136**
TAPINELLO	6	7	14	NOT PRESENT
ANGELICO	6	8	5	#THIRTEEN
STIZZOSO	6	8	5	NOT PRESENT
SMANCERIA	6	8	7	NOT PRESENT
FECCIOSO	6	8	9	NOT PRESENT
LOICO	**6**	**9**	**8**	**1.27.123**
SPECULARE	6	9	9	NOT PRESENT
ABSTRATTO	6	9	9	NOT PRESENT

EPICURO [adj.]	6	9	9	NOT PRESENT
SPECULAZIONE	6	9	9	NOT PRESENT
PORFIDO	**6**	**9**	**10**	**2.9.101**
SALTO [n.]	6	9	12	3.11.126;3.18.135
CERTALDO	**6**	**10**	**5**	**3.16.50**
BRIGANTE	6	10	7	NOT PRESENT
RETTORICO	6	10	7	NOT PRESENT
TULIO	**6**	**10**	**7**	**1.4.141**
QUINTILIANO	6	10	7	NOT PRESENT
BENVOGLIENTE	6	10	7	NOT PRESENT
CALONICA	6	10	8	NOT PRESENT
DEBITO [n.]	**6**	**10**	**10**	**2.10.108**
PREDICAZIONE	6	10	10	NOT PRESENT
ANNUNZIARE	**6**	**10**	**11**	**1.33.41**
NAZARETTE	**6**	**10**	**11**	**3.9.137**
ARISTOTILE	**6**	**10**	**16**	**2.3.43**
SENECA	**6**	**10**	**16**	**1.4.141**
SUGLIARDO	6	10	17	NOT PRESENT
NEGLIGENTE [2]	**6**	**10**	**17**	**2.4.110**
MALDICENTE	6	10	17	NOT PRESENT
TECCHERELLA	6	10	17	NOT PRESENT
CESTONE	6	10	21	NOT PRESENT
AVOLTOIO	6	10	21	NOT PRESENT
CAROGNA	6	10	21	NOT PRESENT
UNQUANCHE	**6**	**10**	**22**	**1.33.140**
UNTUME	6	10	23	NOT PRESENT
CALDERONE	6	10	23	NOT PRESENT
RIPEZZATO	6	10	23	NOT PRESENT
SMALTATO	6	10	23	NOT PRESENT
TARTARESCO	6	10	23	NOT PRESENT
INDIANO	6	10	23	NOT PRESENT
VILUPPO	6	10	26	NOT PRESENT
CASSETTINA	6	10	26	NOT PRESENT
MORBIDEZZA	6	10	27	NOT PRESENT
DISFACIMENTO	6	10	27	NOT PRESENT
ESPRESSO	6	10	37	NOT PRESENT
BOLLARE	6	10	37	NOT PRESENT
CONIO	6	10	39	1.18.66; 1.30.115; 3.19.141; 3.24.87; 3.29.126

BUSECCHIA	6	10	40	NOT PRESENT
SACCA	6	10	41	NOT PRESENT
ADENTRO	6	10	42	NOT PRESENT
PENNATO	6	10	42	NOT PRESENT
INCREDIBILE	6	10	42	1.13.50; 3.16.124; 3.17.93
NOCE	**6**	**10**	**42**	**3.2.24**
GUSCIO	6	10	42	NOT PRESENT
RITAGLIO	6	10	42	NOT PRESENT
PATRIARCA	6	10	44	1.4.58; 3.11.121; 3.22.70
CIUFFETTO	**6**	**10**	**45**	**1.28.33**
SERAFINO	6	10	45	3.4.28; 3.8.27; 3.21.92
AMPOLETTA	6	10	47	NOT PRESENT
OMORE	6	10	51	1.30.53; 1.30.126; 2.25.78
CAMISCIONE	6	10	54	NOT PRESENT
CROCIARE	6	10	55	NOT PRESENT
SMASCELLARE	6	10	55	NOT PRESENT
VULGO	6	10	56	3.9.36; 3.29.119
ISTORRE	6	11	8	NOT PRESENT
TRIBUNALE	6	11	9	NOT PRESENT
MACULARE	**6**	**11**	**11**	**1.1.33**
TERRORE	6	11	12	NOT PRESENT
SMAGARE	6	11	12	1.25.146; 2.10.106; 2.27.104;3.3.36
RITONDO	**6**	**11**	**20**	**3.14.2**
SESTA [n.]	6	11	20	NOT PRESENT
MANUALE	6	11	20	NOT PRESENT
GIRO	6	11	20	#TWENTY-EIGHT
DIGRADARE	6	11	21	1.6.114; 2.22.133; 3.32.14
TEATRO	6	11	21	NOT PRESENT
CIRIEGIO	6	11	22	NOT PRESENT
SPANNA	6	11	22	1.6.25; 3.19.81
CARRO	6	11	23	#SEVENTEEN
FRASSINO	6	11	23	NOT PRESENT
ABETE	**6**	**11**	**24**	**2.22.133**
CIPRESSO	6	11	24	NOT PRESENT

BALZO	6	II	25	#SIX
VELOCISSIMO	6	II	26	3.7.8; 3.27.99
MISTURA	6	II	27	1.6.100; 2.28.29; 3.7.125
GHIAIA	6	II	27	NOT PRESENT
RIPA	6	II	28	#THIRTY-TWO
CAPACITÀ	6	II	28	NOT PRESENT
VALLONCELLO	6	II	28	NOT PRESENT
DISTANTE	6	II	35	#SEVEN
MERIGGIANA	6	II	38	NOT PRESENT
BALIA	6	II	44	1.19.92; 2.1.66
VINCIGLIO	6	II	45	NOT PRESENT
TEMPERA	6	II	48	NOT PRESENT
LUCERE	7	0	2	#FOURTEEN
LUCIFERO	7	0	2	1.31.143; 1.34.89
BIANCHEGGIANTE	7	0	2	1.24.9; 2.10.72; 2.16.143; 3.14.98
STREPITO	7	0	3	NOT PRESENT
SPUNTARE	7	0	4	NOT PRESENT
GAIAMENTE	7	0	4	NOT PRESENT
RIPROVEGGERE	7	0	5	NOT PRESENT
NOTA [n.]	7	0	6	#TWENTY-TWO
VIVACE	7	0	7	#EIGHT
SCHIERA	7	0	7	#NINETEEN
TAPPETTO	7	0	10	NOT PRESENT
VALEVOLE	7	I	3	NOT PRESENT
STAMAIUOLO	7	I	4	NOT PRESENT
UFICETTO	7	I	4	NOT PRESENT
BERNARDO	7	I	5	3.31.102; 3.31.139; 3.33.49
MATELDA	7	**I**	**5**	**2.33.119**
CIANCIONE	7	I	5	NOT PRESENT
SEMPLICITÀ	7	I	6	NOT PRESENT
OGNINDÌ	7	I	10	NOT PRESENT
LESSARE	7	I	12	NOT PRESENT
LESSO	7	**I**	**13**	**1.21.135**
PUNZECHIARE	7	I	16	NOT PRESENT

BISUNTO	7	1	27	NOT PRESENT
CACHERELLO	7	1	27	NOT PRESENT
INCANTAZIONE	7	1	30	NOT PRESENT
RAFFRENAMENTO	7	2	5	NOT PRESENT
MOMENTO	7	2	6	NOT PRESENT
MURATORE	7	2	7	NOT PRESENT
GONNELLUCCIA	7	2	14	NOT PRESENT
SPENZOLARE	7	2	15	NOT PRESENT
IMPASTRICCIATO	7	2	29	NOT PRESENT
ISPOGLIARE	7	2	31	NOT PRESENT
CAMISCIONE	7	2	31	NOT PRESENT
RADIMADIA	7	2	31	NOT PRESENT
MICOLINO	7	2	32	NOT PRESENT
SFRENATO	7	2	34	NOT PRESENT
LEGGIADRETTO	7	3	7	NOT PRESENT
TRONFIO	7	3	9	NOT PRESENT
COLORITO	7	3	9	NOT PRESENT
CRESTA	**7**	**3**	**9**	**1.34.42**
PETTORUTO	7	3	9	NOT PRESENT
ALBERELLO	7	3	10	NOT PRESENT
LATTOVARO	7	3	10	NOT PRESENT
UNGUENTO	7	3	10	NOT PRESENT
COLMO [adj.]	7	3	10	NOT PRESENT
MALVAGIA [n.]	7	3	10	NOT PRESENT
TRABOCCANTE	7	3	10	NOT PRESENT
UNGUENTARIO	7	3	10	NOT PRESENT
GOTTOSO	7	3	10	NOT PRESENT
SOBRIAMENTE	7	3	10	NOT PRESENT
GOTTA	7	3	11	NOT PRESENT
ORARE [n.]	7	3	12	#SIX
DOMENICO [san]	7	3	12	3.10.95; 3.12.70
TINTILLANO	7	3	12	NOT PRESENT
LOICA	7	3	22	NOT PRESENT
PIACEVOLETTO	7	3	23	NOT PRESENT
TONICELLA	7	3	26	NOT PRESENT
BESCIO	7	3	29	NOT PRESENT
SANCTIO	7	3	29	NOT PRESENT
SVENIRE	7	3	29	NOT PRESENT
BORSETTA	7	3	39	NOT PRESENT

REFE	7	3	39	NOT PRESENT
LENA	7	3	40	#SIX
ARTISTA	7	4	3	3.13.77; 3.16.51; 3.18.51;3.30.33
SEMPLICETTO	**7**	**4**	**4**	**2.16.88**
INACQUARE	7	4	27	NOT PRESENT
COMPONITORE	7	5	3	NOT PRESENT
INSIDIATORE	7	5	3	NOT PRESENT
DILIGENTISSIMO	7	5	3	NOT PRESENT
CERCATORE	7	5	3	NOT PRESENT
REGGITORE	7	5	4	NOT PRESENT
PREGIONIERO	7	5	8	NOT PRESENT
IMPAZIENTEMENTE	7	5	9	NOT PRESENT
PIETRUZZA	7	5	14	NOT PRESENT
FUSCELLINO	7	5	14	NOT PRESENT
CAPPELLANO	7	5	19	NOT PRESENT
CORO	7	5	20	#SEVEN
CONTEGNOSO	7	5	22	NOT PRESENT
PETRUZZA	7	5	23	NOT PRESENT
CHERICHETTO	7	5	33	NOT PRESENT
GARZONETTO	7	5	44	NOT PRESENT
BECCHERIA	7	5	52	NOT PRESENT
MALIGNO	7	5	52	#SIX
ARPIONE	7	6	11	NOT PRESENT
RIPREGARE	**7**	**7**	**18**	**1.26.66**
ARRA	7	7	25	1.15.94; 2.28.93; 3.19.145
FEDELTÀ	7	7	35	NOT PRESENT
SALIGASTRO	7	7	40	NOT PRESENT
FESTANTE	**7**	**7**	**43**	**3.31.131**
INGENTILIRE	7	8	4	NOT PRESENT
SPAGHETTO	7	8	8	NOT PRESENT
ADIRATAMENTE	7	8	18	NOT PRESENT
AMACCARE	7	8	19	NOT PRESENT
LAMPANA	7	8	23	NOT PRESENT
INNANIMATO	7	8	26	NOT PRESENT
ISCUSA	7	8	27	NOT PRESENT
RIFRENARE	7	8	31	NOT PRESENT
DIMOLTO	7	8	35	NOT PRESENT

DONZELLA	7	8	42	NOT PRESENT
RIMESCOLARE	7	8	42	NOT PRESENT
GAGLIARDIA	7	8	43	NOT PRESENT
FRACIDUME	7	8	46	NOT PRESENT
MERCATANTUZZO	7	8	46	NOT PRESENT
TROIATA	7	8	46	NOT PRESENT
PUTTANA	7	8	47	1.18.133; 2.32.149; 2.32.160
GASTIGATOIA	7	8	47	NOT PRESENT
MERCATANTUOLO	7	8	48	NOT PRESENT
RUVIDAMENTE	**7**	**9**	**13**	**1.33.92**
RIPARLARE	7	9	16	NOT PRESENT
INTRALASCIARE	7	9	17	NOT PRESENT
OSTINAZIONE	7	9	18	NOT PRESENT
SCIAMITO	7	9	32	NOT PRESENT
GETO	7	9	32	NOT PRESENT
MALCONTENTO	7	9	34	NOT PRESENT
LUCIGNOLETTO	7	9	38	NOT PRESENT
TANAGLIA	**7**	**9**	**53**	**1.29.87**
MAGAGNA	7	9	73	1.33.152; 2.6.110; 2.15.46
TRASVEDERE	7	9	73	NOT PRESENT
DISCREDERE	7	9	73	NOT PRESENT
SERVATORE	7	10	3	NOT PRESENT
RAMMENTARE	7	10	5	2.33.95; 3.10.31; 3.18.110
APPAREGGIARE	7	10	5	NOT PRESENT
BESSAGGINE	7	10	7	NOT PRESENT
POPOLARE	7	10	8	NOT PRESENT
VANGARE	7	10	15	NOT PRESENT
SILOGIZZARE	7	10	30	3.10.138; 3.24.77
ZEFIRO	**7**	**11**	**1**	**3.12.47**
BOTOLO	**7**	**11**	**3**	**2.14.46**
AURA	7	11	6	#TWELVE
RIPOSAMENTE	7	11	6	NOT PRESENT
DISTRINGERE	7	11	11	1.19.127; 2.6.104
SUBSEGUIRE	7	11	16	NOT PRESENT
CHIESETTA	8	0	2	NOT PRESENT

RENDITORE	8	I	5	NOT PRESENT
INGORDIGIA	8	I	8	NOT PRESENT
FORESOZZA	8	2	9	NOT PRESENT
TARCHIATO	8	2	9	NOT PRESENT
BORRANA	8	2	9	NOT PRESENT
RIDDA	8	2	9	NOT PRESENT
BALLONCHIO	8	2	9	NOT PRESENT
MOCCICHINO	8	2	9	NOT PRESENT
SMANIA	8	2	10	NOT PRESENT
AIATO	8	2	10	NOT PRESENT
RAGGHIARE	8	2	10	NOT PRESENT
AGLIO	8	2	11	NOT PRESENT
CANESTRUCCIO	8	2	11	NOT PRESENT
BACCELLO	8	2	11	NOT PRESENT
MALIGIO	8	2	11	NOT PRESENT
SCALOGNO	8	2	11	NOT PRESENT
CAGNESCO	8	2	12	NOT PRESENT
RIMORCHIARE	8	2	12	NOT PRESENT
CONTEGNO	8	2	12	1.17.60; 1.22.17
ZAZEATO	8	2	13	NOT PRESENT
COMPARIGIONE	8	2	14	NOT PRESENT
PARENTORIO	8	2	14	NOT PRESENT
PERICOLATORE	8	2	14	NOT PRESENT
DIFICIO	8	2	14	1.34.7; 2.32.142
COMBINA	8	2	15	NOT PRESENT
COREGGIATO	8	2	15	NOT PRESENT
BALCO	**8**	**2**	**17**	**2.9.2**
ZACONATO	8	2	17	NOT PRESENT
SEMENTA	8	2	19	#SIX
CAVOLINO	8	2	19	NOT PRESENT
TREBBIARE	8	2	19	NOT PRESENT
SCARSO	8	2	24	#SEVEN
FRENELLO	8	2	25	NOT PRESENT
STAME	8	2	25	NOT PRESENT
FILATOIO	8	2	28	NOT PRESENT
PERSO [adj.]	8	2	28	1.5.89; 1.7.103; 2.9.97
SCAGGIALE	8	2	28	NOT PRESENT
PROMETTITORE	8	2	30	NOT PRESENT
CETERATOIO	8	2	30	NOT PRESENT

DUAGIO	8	2	35	NOT PRESENT
TREAGIO	8	2	35	NOT PRESENT
QUATTRAGIO	8	2	35	NOT PRESENT
RIGATTIERE	8	2	35	NOT PRESENT
BASCIOZZO	8	2	38	NOT PRESENT
SERGOZZONE	8	2	43	NOT PRESENT
SOPPIDIANO	8	2	44	NOT PRESENT
PREGO [n.]	8	2	44	#SEVEN
ISCREZIO	8	2	46	NOT PRESENT
VENDEMMIA	8	2	46	NOT PRESENT
MOSTO	8	2	46	NOT PRESENT
CASTAGNA	8	2	46	NOT PRESENT
RAPPATUMARE	8	2	46	NOT PRESENT
GOZZOVIGLIA	8	2	46	NOT PRESENT
RINCARTARE	8	2	47	NOT PRESENT
SONAGLIUZZO	8	2	47	NOT PRESENT
TABERNACULO	8	3	6	NOT PRESENT
EFFICACEMENTE	8	3	7	NOT PRESENT
OCA	**8**	**3**	**9**	**1.17.63**
RAVIUOLO	8	3	9	NOT PRESENT
GRATTUGIATO	8	3	9	NOT PRESENT
TOMO	8	3	18	NOT PRESENT
SATOLLA	8	3	18	NOT PRESENT
MACIGNO	8	3	19	1.15.63; 2.19.48
FARINA	**8**	**3**	**19**	**3.22.78**
SMERALDO	8	3	19	2.7.75; 2.29.125; 2.31.116
RILUCERE	8	3	19	2.18.110; 2.27.133
FORARE	8	3	19	#EIGHT
SCARSELLA	8	3	29	NOT PRESENT
CAMBIATORE	8	3	29	NOT PRESENT
SCHICCHERARE	8	3	29	NOT PRESENT
LUMACA	**8**	**3**	**29**	**1.25.132**
FATTA [n.]	8	3	33	NOT PRESENT
AMBIADURA	8	3	35	NOT PRESENT
GHERONE	8	3	40	NOT PRESENT
ANALDA	8	3	40	NOT PRESENT
CODOLO	8	3	48	NOT PRESENT
LAPIDANDO	8	3	48	NOT PRESENT

GABELLIERE	8	3	49	NOT PRESENT
NIQUITOSO	8	3	52	NOT PRESENT
MACERO	8	3	52	NOT PRESENT
SCINTO	8	3	54	NOT PRESENT
SODURRE	8	3	57	NOT PRESENT
SEZZAIO	**8**	**3**	**57**	**3.18.93**
SOLLECITATORE	8	4	3	NOT PRESENT
POGGIO	8	4	4	#SIX
SPIACEVOLEZZA	8	4	7	NOT PRESENT
PRONTEZZA	8	4	9	NOT PRESENT
MARTELLO	**8**	**4**	**13**	**3.2.128**
ZITTO	8	4	16	NOT PRESENT
GUERCIO	8	4	21	1.7.40; 2.19.8
SCIANCATO	**8**	**4**	**21**	**1.25.148**
MONCO	8	4	21	1.13.30; 2.19.9
CAGNAZZO	**8**	**4**	**22**	**1.32.70**
CORTICELLA	8	4	30	NOT PRESENT
ISTANCHETTO	8	4	32	NOT PRESENT
IMPRONTO	8	4	37	NOT PRESENT
PIDOCCHIERIA	8	5	4	NOT PRESENT
INNATO	**8**	**5**	**4**	**2.18.62 [2]**
ARATRO	8	5	4	NOT PRESENT
CALZOLERIA	8	5	4	NOT PRESENT
MAGNANO	8	5	5	NOT PRESENT
CRIMINALE	8	5	5	NOT PRESENT
PENNAIUOLO	8	5	7	NOT PRESENT
CERCA [n.]	**8**	**5**	**8**	**3.16.63**
SQUASIMODEO	8	5	8	NOT PRESENT
LEMBO	8	5	12	1.15.24; 2.7.72; 2.27.30
LADRONCELLO	8	5	12	NOT PRESENT
RISOLARE	8	5	12	NOT PRESENT
GHIOTTONCELLO	8	5	13	NOT PRESENT
TRECCA	8	5	13	NOT PRESENT
SPAZZATURA	8	5	13	NOT PRESENT
VENTRAIUOLO	8	5	13	NOT PRESENT
SGROPPATO	8	5	14	NOT PRESENT
LIBELLO	**8**	**5**	**15**	**3.12.135**
SINDACATO	8	5	17	NOT PRESENT
SPERIENZA	8	6	1	NOT PRESENT

DICEMBRE	8	6	4	NOT PRESENT
CIURMARE	8	6	13	NOT PRESENT
ISPICCARE	8	6	15	NOT PRESENT
MOGLIEMA	8	6	27	NOT PRESENT
GENTILOTTO	8	6	33	NOT PRESENT
CASCIO	8	6	35	NOT PRESENT
LIBRA	8	6	39	NOT PRESENT
PATICO	8	6	39	NOT PRESENT
ISMARRIRE	8	6	39	NOT PRESENT
ZUCCHERO	8	6	39	NOT PRESENT
SEGNALUZZO	8	6	39	NOT PRESENT
CANINO	8	6	44	NOT PRESENT
NOCCIUOLA	8	6	48	NOT PRESENT
RIMEDIRE	8	6	53	NOT PRESENT
BEFFARDO	8	6	53	NOT PRESENT
BISCOTTO	8	6	54	NOT PRESENT
RISCALDAMENTO	8	6	56	NOT PRESENT
VERNO	8	7	1	1.27.51; 1.30.92; 1.32.26; 2.4.81; 3.13.133
RETRIBUZIONE	8	7	3	NOT PRESENT
SCELTA	8	7	4	NOT PRESENT
CITTADINESCAMENT	8	7	5	NOT PRESENT
INCAPESTRARE	8	7	6	NOT PRESENT
PAOLINO [n.]	8	7	8	NOT PRESENT
FILOSOFICO	8	7	10	1.4.132; 3.26.25
VANAMENTE	8	7	11	NOT PRESENT
AIA	8	7	13	NOT PRESENT
TRITO	**8**	**7**	**29**	**3.13.34**
PERTUGETTO	8	7	31	NOT PRESENT
SCANTONARE	8	7	33	NOT PRESENT
ALBA	8	7	41	2.1.115; 2.9.52; 2.19.5; 3.23.9
BISTENTO	8	7	41	NOT PRESENT
RATTRAPPATO	8	7	44	NOT PRESENT
TACCARE	8	7	56	NOT PRESENT
STAGNO	8	7	56	1.14.119; 1.22.141
CASTAGNUOLO	8	7	61	NOT PRESENT
CESPUGLIO [2]	8	7	65	1.13.123; 1.13.131
SALCE	8	7	66	NOT PRESENT

PERIGLIO	8	7	82	1.8.99; 1.26.113; 2.14.69; 3.4.101
MAGNANIMITÀ	8	7	86	NOT PRESENT
CRESPA	8	7	89	NOT PRESENT
DOLOROSETTO	8	7	89	NOT PRESENT
PIETATE	8	7	93	1.2.5; 2.5.87; 2.33.19
SEVERO	8	7	93	1.24.119; 3.4.84
RIGIDEZZA	8	7	93	NOT PRESENT
AGEVOLARE	**8**	**7**	**98**	**2.9.57**
IMPARARE	**8**	**7**	**102**	**2.6.3**
PULCE	**8**	**7**	**103**	**1.17.51**
INSIPIDO	8	7	103	NOT PRESENT
SCALDARE	8	7	108	#TEN
SCOPERTA	8	7	113	NOT PRESENT
COTTURA	8	7	113	NOT PRESENT
PROFONDAMENTE	8	7	113	NOT PRESENT
ISCHIANTARE	8	7	114	NOT PRESENT
ABBRUSCIARE	8	7	114	1.15.27; 2.25.137
SPUNTONE	8	7	116	NOT PRESENT
AGGIUNTA	8	7	117	NOT PRESENT
ANGOSCIATO	**8**	**7**	**117**	**2.11.28**
ISCEMARE	8	7	119	NOT PRESENT
TRAFITTURA	8	7	120	NOT PRESENT
CHIAZZATO	8	7	120	NOT PRESENT
ASCIUGAGGINE	8	7	123	NOT PRESENT
ARSURA	8	7	123	1.14.142; 1.30.127; 2.26.81
RIARSO	**8**	**7**	**124**	**2.14.82**
SOLLENAMENTO	8	7	125	NOT PRESENT
UCCISIONE	8	7	128	NOT PRESENT
SPASIMARE	8	7	130	NOT PRESENT
SCAPPARE	8	7	133	NOT PRESENT
MISERABILE	8	7	135	NOT PRESENT
RITORTA	8	7	138	1.19.27; 1.31.111
TRAVERSO	8	7	138	1.30.87; 2.5.22; 2.9.99
SPUNTO	8	7	140	NOT PRESENT
INARSICCIATO	8	7	140	NOT PRESENT
CEPPERELLO	8	7	140	NOT PRESENT
SALVAMENTE	8	7	142	NOT PRESENT

SMUCCIARE	8	7	142	NOT PRESENT
MUGGHIARE	8	7	142	1.5.29; 1.27.7; 1.27.10
ERBAIO [2]	8	7	143	NOT PRESENT
INDOZZAMENTO	8	7	146	NOT PRESENT
FRASCHEGGIARE	8	7	149	NOT PRESENT
RAMORBIDIRE	8	8	3	NOT PRESENT
INNACERBITO	8	8	3	NOT PRESENT
DOTTANZA	8	8	14	NOT PRESENT
RICONFERMAZIONE	8	8	26	NOT PRESENT
UMANAMENTE	8	8	29	NOT PRESENT
ACCOMUNARE	8	9	2	NOT PRESENT
BATALO	8	9	5	NOT PRESENT
NOVELLAMENTE	8	9	6	2.2.51; 3.1.74
PECORAGGINE	8	9	12	NOT PRESENT
QUALITATIVO	8	9	15	NOT PRESENT
MELLONAGGINE	8	9	15	NOT PRESENT
BACINO	8	9	20	NOT PRESENT
ORCIUOLO	8	9	20	NOT PRESENT
MELODIA	8	9	21	2.29.22; 3.14.32; 3.23.97; 3.23.109
BARBANICCHI	8	9	23	NOT PRESENT
CIANCIANFERA	8	9	23	NOT PRESENT
SEMISTANTE	8	9	23	NOT PRESENT
SCALPEDRA	8	9	23	NOT PRESENT
SCHINCHIMURRA	8	9	24	NOT PRESENT
BOSSOLO	8	9	25	NOT PRESENT
COMINO	8	9	25	NOT PRESENT
DOGE	8	9	25	NOT PRESENT
CALCOLA	8	9	26	NOT PRESENT
TESSITRICE	8	9	26	NOT PRESENT
VOLGARMENTE	8	9	29	NOT PRESENT
LATTIME	8	9	31	NOT PRESENT
DISIDERABILE	8	9	31	NOT PRESENT
ORINALE	8	9	34	NOT PRESENT
AVICENA	**8**	**9**	**38**	**1.4.143**
FEMINACCIA	8	9	39	NOT PRESENT
IMPIASTRO	**8**	**9**	**39**	**1.24.18**
CETERA	**8**	**9**	**47**	**3.20.22**
SAGGINALE	8	9	47	NOT PRESENT

ARTAGOTICAMENTE	8	9	47	NOT PRESENT
STRACANTATO	8	9	47	NOT PRESENT
BAGATTINO	8	9	51	NOT PRESENT
PETIZIONE	8	9	53	NOT PRESENT
CERVELLO	8	9	53	1.32.129; 2.33.81
USATTO	8	9	53	NOT PRESENT
CALTERITO	8	9	55	NOT PRESENT
SEGRETARO	8	9	56	NOT PRESENT
PRIMAIO	8	9	56	#TEN
ISPOSARE	8	9	56	NOT PRESENT
MOLLARE	8	9	61	NOT PRESENT
CARAPIGNARE	8	9	61	NOT PRESENT
ORINA	8	9	70	NOT PRESENT
FRASTAGLIATAMENTE	8	9	72	NOT PRESENT
IMPROMETTERE	**8**	**9**	**73**	**1.2.126**
CULATTARIO	8	9	73	NOT PRESENT
SEME	8	9	74	#TWENTY-THREE
NACCHERA	8	9	74	NOT PRESENT
TRIBUTO	8	9	74	NOT PRESENT
PIOMBINO	8	9	76	NOT PRESENT
SOMMESSO [n.]	8	9	85	NOT PRESENT
SFIDARE	8	9	86	NOT PRESENT
CONVENTARE	8	9	87	NOT PRESENT
SOPPANO	8	9	104	NOT PRESENT
AZZURRINO	9	0	2	NOT PRESENT
CILESTRO	**9**	**0**	**2**	**2.26.6**
FIORETTO	9	0	2	1.2.127; 2.28.56; 2.32.73; 3.30.111
AVVIARSI	9	0	2	NOT PRESENT
CERVO	9	0	2	NOT PRESENT
CACCIATORE	**9**	**0**	**2**	**2.14.59**
INALZARE	9	0	3	NOT PRESENT
INGHIRLANDATO	9	0	4	NOT PRESENT
FESTEGGIANTE	9	0	5	NOT PRESENT
DISERVIRE	9	1	21	NOT PRESENT
MOZZARE	9	1	22	NOT PRESENT
SCANNARE	9	1	25	NOT PRESENT
MALIOSO	9	1	27	NOT PRESENT

SBANDITO	**9**	**1**	**30**	**3.7.37**
SCALPICCIO	9	1	30	NOT PRESENT
PAVESE	9	1	30	NOT PRESENT
BRANCOLONE	9	1	34	NOT PRESENT
RECISO	9	1	36	NOT PRESENT
PAZZIA	9	2	2	NOT PRESENT
LEGGIADRAMENTE	9	2	3	NOT PRESENT
GASTIGATORE	9	2	4	NOT PRESENT
OCCULTISSIMAMENTE	9	2	6	NOT PRESENT
NEGAZIONE	9	2	7	NOT PRESENT
INCOGLIERE	9	2	7	NOT PRESENT
BADARE	9	2	8	2.4.75; 3.7.88
SOPRAPENDIMENTO	9	2	11	NOT PRESENT
USULIERE	9	2	14	NOT PRESENT
PALLOTTOLA	9	3	5	NOT PRESENT
INSEGNA	9	3	17	#SIX
SQUACCHERATAMENTE	9	3	25	NOT PRESENT
BEVANDA	9	3	28	NOT PRESENT
RISOLVERE	9	3	28	3.2.135; 3.28.82
OVUNQUE	**9**	**3**	**33**	**2.25.98**
SPREGNARE	9	3	33	NOT PRESENT
STOLTIZIA	9	4	3	NOT PRESENT
LEGATO [n.]	9	4	6	NOT PRESENT
CAVALCATURA	9	4	6	NOT PRESENT
PIGGIORRARE	9	4	18	NOT PRESENT
MARRA	**9**	**4**	**21**	**1.15.96**
GUARNELLO	9	5	9	NOT PRESENT
IMBARDARSI	9	5	11	NOT PRESENT
LAMMIA	9	5	15	NOT PRESENT
ACCOZZARE	9	5	35	NOT PRESENT
BRANCA	9	5	36	1.7.69; 1.17.13; 1.17.105; 1.27.45
GRIFARE	9	5	37	NOT PRESENT
BISCHERI	9	5	37	NOT PRESENT
VERMIGLIUZZO	9	5	37	NOT PRESENT
SOSTA	**9**	**5**	**39**	**2.29.72**
ANELLETTO	9	5	41	NOT PRESENT
ONORETTO	9	5	41	NOT PRESENT
INCENSO	9	5	47	1.24.110; 2.10.61

BAZZICARE	9	5	49	NOT PRESENT
PIUVICO	9	5	53	NOT PRESENT
CAVALCIONE	9	5	57	NOT PRESENT
AGRATIGLIARE	9	5	58	NOT PRESENT
ARRABBIARE	**9**	**5**	**62**	**1.30.79**
SUGO	9	5	64	NOT PRESENT
RIMBROTTO	9	5	67	NOT PRESENT
VIANDANTE	9	6	4	NOT PRESENT
ALLATTARE	9	6	5	NOT PRESENT
RINCONTRO	9	6	11	NOT PRESENT
PAUROSAMENTE	9	6	13	NOT PRESENT
TENTONE	9	6	16	NOT PRESENT
RADORMENTARE	9	6	17	NOT PRESENT
ORZA	**9**	**6**	**17**	**2.32.117**
TIGNA	9	7	9	1.15.III; 1.22.93
MALIZIOSAMENTE	9	7	10	NOT PRESENT
AGNELLETTO	9	7	12	NOT PRESENT
GHIOTTISSIMO	9	8	4	NOT PRESENT
GHIOTTORNIA	9	8	4	NOT PRESENT
PICCOLETTO	9	8	5	NOT PRESENT
ZAZZERINA	9	8	5	NOT PRESENT
STORIONE	9	8	7	NOT PRESENT
CECE	9	8	11	NOT PRESENT
SORRA	9	8	11	NOT PRESENT
FRITTO	9	8	11	NOT PRESENT
NERBORUTO	9	8	13	NOT PRESENT
CONVOLGERE	**9**	**8**	**26**	**1.21.46**
MALCONCIO	9	8	28	NOT PRESENT
SOTTOMETTERE	9	9	3	NOT PRESENT
SUBGETTO	**9**	**9**	**5**	**2.17.107**
RICONDURRE	9	9	6	NOT PRESENT
SOLLAZZEVOLEMENTE	9	9	8	NOT PRESENT
INTERPRETARE	**9**	**9**	**8**	**3.12.81**
MORALMENTE	**9**	**9**	**8**	**2.33.72**
LABILE	**9**	**9**	**9**	**3.20.12**
UNIVERSO	9	9	10	#THIRTEEN
MOSTRATORE	9	9	10	NOT PRESENT
ARDUO	9	9	10	3.30.36; 3.31.34
DISGRAZIA	9	9	13	NOT PRESENT

INTRODOTTO	9	9	14	NOT PRESENT
CAROVANA	9	9	16	NOT PRESENT
ATTRAVERSARE	9	9	18	1.23.118; 1.25.81; 1.31.9; 2.31.25; 3.4.91
FERIALMENTE	9	9	23	NOT PRESENT
ORGOGLIO	9	9	25	1.16.74; 1.21.85; 2.2.126; 2.28.72; 3.6.49
ISTIZZA	9	9	28	NOT PRESENT
COSTATO	9	9	30	NOT PRESENT
ANCA	9	9	30	1.19.43; 1.21.35; 1.23.72; 1.24.9; 1.34.77
COSTURA	**9**	**9**	**30**	**2.13.83**
CORVO	9	10	3	NOT PRESENT
MATURITÀ	9	10	3	NOT PRESENT
INCANTATORE	9	10	5	NOT PRESENT
BASTEVOLE	9	10	8	NOT PRESENT
RICONOSCIMENTO	9	10	8	NOT PRESENT
ZITELLA	9	10	11	NOT PRESENT
GROSSETTO	9	10	13	NOT PRESENT
SCHIENA	9	10	18	1.18.19; 1.22.20; 1.34.59
PIVUOLO	9	10	18	NOT PRESENT
SOLCO	**9**	**10**	**18**	**3.2.14**
RADICALE	9	10	20	NOT PRESENT
PERPETUARE	9	11	5	NOT PRESENT
MAESTREVOLE	9	11	7	NOT PRESENT
MERZÉ	**9**	**11**	**8**	**3.32.73**
GHIRLANDELLA	9	11	10	NOT PRESENT
NUVOLETTO	10	0	2	NOT PRESENT
RISCIACQUARE	10	0	4	NOT PRESENT
ONORABILE	10	1	2	NOT PRESENT
BARONIA	10	1	6	NOT PRESENT
ABEVERARE	10	1	11	NOT PRESENT
FRIERE	10	2	1	NOT PRESENT
INIMICARE	10	2	3	NOT PRESENT
APPETIRE	10	2	4	NOT PRESENT
REMESSIONE	10	2	4	NOT PRESENT
RAGAZZETTO	10	2	7	NOT PRESENT
SCOMUNICAZIONE	10	2	9	NOT PRESENT

INTERDETTO	10	2	9	**2.33.71**
SCOMUNICARE	10	2	9	NOT PRESENT
ALTIEREZZA	10	2	12	NOT PRESENT
CORNIGLIA	10	2	12	1.4.128; 3.15.129
ISPEZIELTÀ	10	2	14	NOT PRESENT
DANNEVOLE	10	2	25	NOT PRESENT
PRIORIA	10	2	31	NOT PRESENT
SPEDALE	10	2	31	**1.29.46**
CORTESEGGIARE	10	3	7	NOT PRESENT
ANNULLARE	10	3	7	NOT PRESENT
VECCHIERELLA	10	3	10	NOT PRESENT
POMPOSO	10	3	12	NOT PRESENT
DIPUTARE	10	3	16	NOT PRESENT
CIRCUIZIONE	10	3	19	NOT PRESENT
DEGENERARE	10	3	20	NOT PRESENT
PASSEGGIARE	10	3	25	#SEVEN
VEGLIARDO	10	3	25	NOT PRESENT
FEDELMENTE	10	3	27	NOT PRESENT
DISMONTARE	10	3	27	1.11.115; 1.14.118; 1.24.73
AMASSARE	10	3	31	NOT PRESENT
SGUARDO	10	4	8	#TWELVE
INCOMPARABILE	10	4	23	NOT PRESENT
ISPESA	10	4	26	NOT PRESENT
EQUITÀ	10	4	27	NOT PRESENT
EGREGIAMENTE	10	4	30	NOT PRESENT
FIGLIOLINO	10	4	31	NOT PRESENT
SCETTRO	10	4	47	NOT PRESENT
MALFATTORE	10	4	47	NOT PRESENT
SOLLICITAZIONE	10	5	5	NOT PRESENT
PENTIMENTO	10	5	12	**2.30.145**
GUASTATORE	10	5	22	**1.11.38**
RATTIEPIDITO	10	5	26	NOT PRESENT
COMPARARE	10	5	26	**3.23.100**
STRETTEZZA	10	6	3	NOT PRESENT
CAVALLERESCAMENTE	10	6	4	NOT PRESENT
GHIBELLINI	10	6	5	**3.6.103**
CASTAGNO	10	6	6	NOT PRESENT
AVVERSO	10	6	7	1.9.68; 1.10.46; 3.2.63; 3.27.28

SENTORE	10	6	10	NOT PRESENT
INANELLATO	10	6	11	NOT PRESENT
GHIRLANDETTA	10	6	11	NOT PRESENT
PROVINCA	10	6	11	NOT PRESENT
LINO	**10**	**6**	**11**	**2.25.79**
FASCETTO	10	6	12	NOT PRESENT
UTELLO	10	6	12	NOT PRESENT
FACCELLINA	10	6	12	NOT PRESENT
FRUGARE	10	6	15	1.30.70; 2.3.3; 2.14.39; 2.15.137; 2.18.4
GUIZZARE	10	6	16	#SIX
SIMIGLIEVOLE	10	6	19	NOT PRESENT
PIATTELLO	10	6	21	NOT PRESENT
GERARCHIA	**10**	**6**	**22**	**3.28.121**
ANGELO	10	6	22	#THIRTY-ONE
OSTIERE	10	6	23	NOT PRESENT
PANIA	10	6	24	NOT PRESENT
SUPPLICIO	10	6	30	NOT PRESENT
GUERRIERE	10	6	33	NOT PRESENT
LAUDEVOLMENTE	10	6	36	NOT PRESENT
VIRILE	10	7	2	NOT PRESENT
COMMENDEVOLE	10	7	3	NOT PRESENT
CANTATORE	10	7	11	NOT PRESENT
SONATORE	10	7	11	NOT PRESENT
ESSALTAZIONE	10	7	13	NOT PRESENT
PARVENZA	10	7	21	#SEVEN
GRAVENZA	10	7	21	NOT PRESENT
SPIACENZA	10	7	21	NOT PRESENT
ARDIMENTO	**10**	**7**	**21**	**2.29.24**
SICURANZA	10	7	22	NOT PRESENT
CHERERE	10	7	22	NOT PRESENT
MEMBRANZA	10	7	22	NOT PRESENT
SCUDO	10	7	22	1.22.116; 2.32.19; 2.32.159; 3.12.53; 3.29.114
LANZA	10	7	22	NOT PRESENT
INTONARE	10	7	23	NOT PRESENT
SCOVRIRE	10	7	26	1.16.123; 2.33.102; 3.3.2; 3.5.36; 3.22.60

SOPRANSEGNA	10	7	48	NOT PRESENT
ISCAMPARE	10	8	1	NOT PRESENT
TRIUMVIRATO	10	8	5	NOT PRESENT
FRATELLANZA	10	8	7	NOT PRESENT
CONSIDERATORE	10	8	11	NOT PRESENT
INGANNEVOLE	10	8	13	NOT PRESENT
LIBIDINE	10	8	14	NOT PRESENT
MATRIGNA	10	8	16	NOT PRESENT
FIGLIASTRO	**10**	**8**	**16**	**1.12.112**
MOSTRUOSO	10	8	16	NOT PRESENT
SCONVENIRE	10	8	23	NOT PRESENT
VIOLARE	10	8	25	NOT PRESENT
INGIUSTAMENTE	**10**	**8**	**27**	**3.4.15**
SCONVENEVOLEZZA	10	8	32	NOT PRESENT
INDEGNO	10	8	34	1.2.19; 1.3.54
LEGGERISSIMAMENT	10	8	38	NOT PRESENT
SDEGNOSETTO	10	8	52	NOT PRESENT
IMMORTALE	**10**	**8**	**56**	**1.2.14**
AVVILIRE	10	8	59	NOT PRESENT
PROVIDENZIA	10	8	64	NOT PRESENT
FIORENTISSIMO	10	8	67	NOT PRESENT
MARCIRE	**10**	**8**	**68**	**1.29.51**
ANNALE	10	8	68	NOT PRESENT
LAMENTANZA	10	8	74	NOT PRESENT
MACULA	10	8	77	NOT PRESENT
RATTORE	10	8	78	NOT PRESENT
INSIDIARE	10	8	81	NOT PRESENT
BESTIALMENTE	10	8	84	NOT PRESENT
FATO	10	8	105	1.9.97; 1.21.82; 2.30.132
TIEPIDEZZA	10	8	108	NOT PRESENT
DIFFIDENZA	10	8	108	NOT PRESENT
SACRATISSIMO	10	8	112	NOT PRESENT
RILEGARE	10	8	112	NOT PRESENT
INVITATRICE	10	8	114	NOT PRESENT
SCHERNO	10	8	115	NOT PRESENT
DILAZIONE	10	8	117	NOT PRESENT
TURBA	10	8	119	#TWELVE
CONSORTE	10	8	119	#NINE

MAGICO	10	9	1	**1.20.117**
DERETANO	10	9	2	NOT PRESENT
DIFFUSO	10	9	4	NOT PRESENT
PROVINCIA	**10**	**9**	**7**	**2.6.78**
SALUTO [n.]	10	9	12	NOT PRESENT
SCALZARE	10	9	15	3.11.80; 3.11.83
SPROVEDERE	10	9	19	NOT PRESENT
GUAZZO	10	9	21	1.12.139; 1.32.72
GRADO [vb.]	10	9	24	NOT PRESENT
STAMATTINA	10	9	24	NOT PRESENT
RICCHISSIMAMENTE	10	9	25	NOT PRESENT
FODERARE	10	9	31	NOT PRESENT
MERCATANTESCO	10	9	32	NOT PRESENT
RINUNZIARE	10	9	35	NOT PRESENT
ADIO	**10**	**9**	**48**	**2.8.3**
FALCONIERE	**10**	**9**	**50**	**1.17.129**
RICOMPERA [n.]	10	9	52	NOT PRESENT
CADUCO	**10**	**9**	**72**	**3.20.12**
SUPPREMO	10	9	75	2.4.34; 2.15.52; 3.13.74; 3.23.108; 3.27.36
VELLUTO	**10**	**9**	**76**	**1.34.73**
COMPASSO	10	9	76	NOT PRESENT
GUANCIALE	10	9	76	NOT PRESENT
FORTIFICAMENTO	10	9	84	NOT PRESENT
CARBUNCULO	10	9	86	NOT PRESENT
GUERNIMENTO	10	9	86	NOT PRESENT
APPREZZARE	**10**	**9**	**86**	**3.5.21**
SPEDIRE	10	9	87	1.26.18; 2.20.5; 3.17.100; 3.30.37
SAGRESTANO	10	9	88	NOT PRESENT
BACO	10	9	89	NOT PRESENT
DUBITOSO	10	9	90	NOT PRESENT
ARABESCO	10	9	96	NOT PRESENT
BARBASSORO	10	9	105	NOT PRESENT
RACQUISTO	10	9	109	NOT PRESENT
RITOGLIERE	10	9	109	NOT PRESENT
REPATRIAZIONE	10	9	112	NOT PRESENT
DISSIMILE	**10**	**10**	**7**	**3.7.80**
TROVATORE	10	10	8	NOT PRESENT

SCARMIGLIATO	10	10	19	NOT PRESENT
ESSALTAMENTO	10	10	25	NOT PRESENT
VILLESCO	10	10	25	NOT PRESENT
MARCHESATO	10	10	26	NOT PRESENT
DOTTARE	10	10	35	NOT PRESENT
SOFFERENZA	10	10	40	NOT PRESENT
GIOVENILMENTE	10	10	40	NOT PRESENT
SOMIERE	10	10	45	NOT PRESENT
VERGINITÀ	10	10	45	NOT PRESENT
PANCALE	10	10	52	NOT PRESENT
FRATELLINO	10	10	57	NOT PRESENT
MENTECATTAGGINE	10	10	58	NOT PRESENT
VANTO	10	10	63	1.2.25; 1.2.108; 1.31.64
PIOVERE	10	10	68	#ELEVEN
ATTRATTIVO	10	11	4	NOT PRESENT
FRATERNALE	10	11	5	NOT PRESENT
GAVILLARE	10	11	6	NOT PRESENT
GAIO	10	11	11	3.15.60; 3.26.102
ACUORARE	10	11	13	NOT PRESENT
BLANDIMENTO	**10**	**11**	**14**	**3.16.30**
DANNAGGIO	**10**	**11**	**14**	**1.30.136**
RAGIONEVOLE	11	11	4	NOT PRESENT
FORO	11	11	5	1.19.14; 1.34.85; 2.5.73; 2.21.83
MORTADELLO	11	11	5	NOT PRESENT
SERPENTE	11	11	6	#TWELVE
DRAGONE	11	11	6	NOT PRESENT
EVA	11	11	6	2.8.99; 2.12.71; 2.24.116; 2.29.24
CHIOVO	**11**	**11**	**6**	**2.8.138**
CONFICCARE	11	11	6	NOT PRESENT
ASCOLTATORE	11	11	8	NOT PRESENT
FEBRICITANTE	11	11	9	NOT PRESENT
LOTO	**11**	**11**	**11**	**1.8.21**
RIVERENDO	11	11	12	NOT PRESENT
SCRITTURA	11	11	12	3.4.43; 3.13.128; 3.19.83; 3.32.68
PERVERSAMENTE	11	11	12	NOT PRESENT

MIGLIACCIO	II	II	15	NOT PRESENT
SCRITTORE	**II**	**II**	**17**	**3.29.41**
COLTIVARE	II	II	18	NOT PRESENT
ORTICA	**II**	**II**	**18**	**2.31.85**
TRIBOLO	II	II	18	NOT PRESENT
ESQUISITO	II	II	18	NOT PRESENT
MISURATAMENTE	**II**	**II**	**18**	**2.8.84**
UTILMENTE	**II**	**II**	**21**	**2.23.6**
ZELO	II	II	22	NOT PRESENT
OPPOSIZIONE	**II**	**II**	**23**	**2.22.50**
CAPRINO	II	II	26	NOT PRESENT
PIATO [n.]	**II**	**II**	**26**	**1.30.147**
STABILITÀ	II	II	27	NOT PRESENT
SOPRASCRITTO	II	II	27	NOT PRESENT

Index